COMMUNION WITH GOD
IN THE NEW TESTAMENT

The Fernley-Hartley Lecture 1953

COMMUNION WITH GOD

IN THE NEW TESTAMENT

BY

A. RAYMOND GEORGE, M.A.
Lamplough Tutor in Systematic and Pastoral Theology
and Philosophy of Religion
Wesley College, Headingley, Leeds

WIPF & STOCK · Eugene, Oregon

Wipf and Stock Publishers
199 W 8th Ave, Suite 3
Eugene, OR 97401

Communion with God in the New Testament
By George, Raymond

ISBN 13: 978-1-60608-733-6
Publication date 4/30/2009
Previously published by Epworth Press, 1953

First English edition 1953 by Epworth Press
This edition published by arrangement with Epworth Press

TO

MY MOTHER AND FATHER

In affection and gratitude

PREFACE

THE INVITATION of the Fernley-Hartley Trustees to deliver the lecture of 1953 has given me the opportunity of writing on a subject which has engaged my interest, amid many other occupations, for several years. My chief difficulty has been to keep the subject within bounds. I had originally hoped to continue the study into the Fathers, but the New Testament has proved a large enough task, and even here the connexions of my chosen theme with others have been so great that I cannot hope to have touched on everything that is relevant. I have tried to satisfy two requirements and perhaps to cater for two classes of reader. For the more general reader of theological books I have tried to provide a summary, a bird's-eye view, of much that has been going on in this field. There are many who have not the opportunity of studying the great Word Book of Kittel or such important monographs as that by Seesemann, who may be glad to have some of the fruits of these researches combined together in their relation to this theme. If such readers want the conclusion set out as simply as possible, they will find it in the first part of the last chapter, without the distracting footnotes and the use of Greek which I have found impossible to avoid in the body of the work: the only Greek word in that section is κοινωνία, usually translated 'fellowship'. I hope, however, that anyone who begins there will wish to find the detailed evidence for the statements there made, and will also read the earlier chapters, which cannot be understood unless he works with a Bible in his hand: a knowledge of Greek is essential for some parts, but not for all.

I have tried, secondly, to satisfy the requirements of the technical scholar by making some modest contribution to the technical study of these questions. In a field so large and broad I have naturally made considerable use of work already done, but there are certain particular features which, in addition to the perspective of the whole work, I hope may be regarded as original contributions to the discussion.

First, in the hope of obtaining a convenient set of categories for the discussion of New Testament piety, I have set Professor

Heiler's famous distinction between 'mystical' and 'prophetic' piety in relation to certain other classifications.

Second, unlike Professor Heiler, I have discarded the term 'mysticism' altogether in connexion with the New Testament, and have given reasons for this.

Third, I have revived Deissmann's distinction between 'union' and 'communion', and have protested against the widespread use of 'union' and certain similar words in connexion with the New Testament.

Fourth, I have found that a study of piety supports the conclusions reached by many scholars on more general grounds that the thought of most New Testament writings, and notably the Pauline and Johannine, is fundamentally Jewish rather than Greek.

Fifth, I have studied the prayers of Jesus more closely than is fashionable now that interest in His 'personality' is decried, and have indicated the solution they afford to the theoretical difficulties about petition and intercession.

Sixth, I have given reasons for the view that the Bishop of Oxford (Dr Kirk) lays excessive stress on the phrase 'vision of God'; and after some linguistic examination, while approving the phrase 'knowledge of God', have concluded that 'communion with God' is the most convenient generic phrase.

Seventh, I have examined the considerable literature that has grown up about the word κοινωνία. Anderson Scott's view that 'the fellowship' was an alternative name for the Church, though widely followed by general writers, has been attacked by almost all who have studied the linguistic usage in detail. Several Pauline instances are also in various other ways disputed. Seesemann's able book superseded all previous writing on this; it has been used by Professor Hauck in Kittel's Word Book, but it is essential to go back to Seesemann himself. I am in general agreement with his conclusions, some of which have been recently attacked by Professor G. V. Jourdan. In the course of this book I have re-examined all the New Testament occurrences of the word.

Eighth, in my last chapter I have tentatively considered the relation of this theme to certain other great doctrines. I have made a comment on the Catholic-Protestant controversy, and raised various questions which still await full discussion.

My interest in this subject was first aroused by the late Rev.

Dr H. Maldwyn Hughes, then Principal of Wesley House, Cambridge, whose memory I treasure, and by the Rev. Dr R. Newton Flew, then Tutor and now Principal of Wesley House, whom I thank most warmly for his interest and encouragement. I thank also the Professors of Marburg, and particularly Professor Friedrich Heiler, for the help which they gave to me in the early stages of this study.

My warm thanks are due to the Fernley-Hartley Trustees for the honour which they have done me in inviting me to give this lecture.

Many friends have given me most generous help in the preparation of this book, and it is a pleasure to record my deep gratitude to them. In particular, the Rev. Dr Vincent Taylor, Principal of this College, has read the greater part of the typescript with meticulous care, and made many valuable criticisms; the Rev. Wesley F. Swift has given a great deal of his time and skill to preparing the typescript for the press and to reading the proofs, though the responsibility for such errors as remain is not his; my colleague the Rev. Dr John H. S. Kent has kindly prepared the Index of Proper Names; and Mr Jack Mole, B.A., B.D., of this College has read a large part of the typescript, making a number of helpful suggestions, and has also prepared the Index of Scripture Passages. To them all I am greatly indebted.

A. Raymond George.

Wesley College
Headingley
Leeds
2nd June 1953

CONTENTS

BIBLIOGRAPHY

(A) GENERAL

AULÉN, G., in *The Universal Church in God's Design* (London 1948).

BAILLIE, D. M., *God was in Christ* (London 1948).

BAILLIE, J., *Our Knowledge of God* (London 1939).

BARRETT, C. K., *The Holy Spirit and the Gospel Tradition* (London 1947).

BARNES, E. W., *The Rise of Christianity* (London 1947).

BARTH, K., *Die Kirkliche Dogmatik*, I.2 (1938). Cited as Barth.
The Teaching of the Church regarding Baptism (E.T., London 1948).

BAUER, W., *Wörterbuch zum N.T.* (4th edn, Berlin 1949-52).

BELL, G. K. A., and DEISSMANN, A. (ed.), *Mysterium Christi* (London 1930).

BOOBYER, G. H., *St Mark and the Transfiguration Story* (Edinburgh 1942).

BOUSSET, W., *Kyrios Christos* (2nd edn, Göttingen 1921).

BRIGHTMAN, F. E., *Liturgies Eastern and Western*, I (Oxford 1896).

BRUNNER, E., *Die Mystik und das Wort* (2nd edn, Tübingen 1928).
The Mediator (E.T., London 1934).
Revelation and Reason (E.T., London 1947).

BULTMANN, R., *Jesus and the Word* (London 1935; E.T. of *Jesus*. 2nd edn, Berlin 1934). References are to the E.T., cited as Bultmann, except when marked *Jesus*, cited from 1st edn, 1929.
Die Geschichte der synoptischen Tradition (2nd edn, Göttingen 1931).
Theology of the New Testament, I (E.T., London 1952). Cited as *Theology*.

BURKITT, F. C., *Christian Beginnings* (London 1924).

BUTLER, C., *Western Mysticism* (London 1922).

CADBURY, H. J., *The Peril of Modernizing Jesus* (New York 1937).

CADOUX, C. J., *The Historic Mission of Jesus* (London 1941).

Catholicity (London 1947).

CHASE, F. H., *The Lord's Prayer in the Early Church* (Cambridge 1891). In J. A. Robinson (ed.), *Texts and Studies*, I.

CHAVASSE, C., *The Bride of Christ* (London 1940).

Church Relations in England (London 1950).

CULLMANN, O., *Baptism in the New Testament* (E.T., London 1950).
Christ and Time (E.T., London 1951). Cited as Cullmann.

DALMAN, G., *The Words of Jesus*, I (E.T., Edinburgh 1902).

DAVIES, W. D., *Paul and Rabbinic Judaism* (London 1948).

DEISSMANN, A., *Paul* (E.T., 2nd edn, London 1926).

The Religion of Jesus and the Faith of Paul (London 1923; 2nd edn, 1926). Cited as *Religion.*

DIBELIUS, M., *From Tradition to Gospel* (E.T., London 1934).

Gospel Criticism and Christology (London 1935). Cited as Dibelius.

DIX, G., *The Question of Anglican Orders* (London 1944).

The Shape of the Liturgy (London 1945). Cited as Dix.

DODD, C. H., *The Parables of the Kingdom* (London 1935; 2nd edn, 1936). Cited as *Parables.*

The Apostolic Preaching and its Developments (London 1936; new edn, 1944). Cited as *Preaching.*

History and the Gospel (London 1938). Cited as *History.*

FARMER, H. H., *The World and God* (London 1935; 2nd edn, 1936).

FLEMINGTON, W. F., *The New Testament Doctrine of Baptism* (London 1948).

FLEW, R. N., *The Idea of Perfection in Christian Theology* (London 1934). Cited as *Perfection.*

Jesus and His Church (London 1938). Cited as *Church.*

FLEW, R. N., and DAVIES, R. E. (ed.), *The Catholicity of Protestantism* (London 1950).

Foundations (London 1912).

GLASSON, T. F., *The Second Advent* (London 1945).

GORE, C., *Dissertations on Subjects connected with the Incarnation* (2nd edn, London 1896).

HAHN, W. T., *Das Mitsterben und Mitauferstehen mit Christus bei Paulus* (Gütersloh, 1937).

HARRISON, P. N., *The Problem of the Pastoral Epistles* (London 1921).

HASTINGS, J. (ed.), *A Dictionary of the Bible*, I (Edinburgh 1898). Cited as *HDB.*

Encyclopaedia of Religion and Ethics (Edinburgh 1908-26). Cited as *ERE.*

HEILER, F., *Prayer* (London 1932; E.T. of *Das Gebet*; 5th edn, München 1923). References are to the E.T., cited as Heiler, except for passages omitted therein, which are cited from the German and marked *Das Gebet.*

Urkirche und Ostkirche (München 1937). Cited as *Urkirche.*

HERRMANN, W., *The Communion of the Christian with God* (2nd edn, London 1906). E.T. of *Der Verkehr des Christen mit Gott.*

HIGGINS, A. J. B., *The Lord's Supper in the New Testament* (London 1952).

HODGES, H. A., *Objectivity and Impartiality* (London 1946).

HODGSON, L., *The Doctrine of the Trinity* (London 1943; 2nd edn, 1944).

HOPWOOD, P. G. S., *The Religious Experience of the Primitive Church* (Edinburgh 1936).

HORT, F. J. A., *The Christian Ecclesia* (London 1897).

HORTON, W. M., *Contemporary Continental Theology* (London 1938).

HOWARD, W. F., *The Fourth Gospel in Recent Criticism and Interpretation* (London 1931).

Christianity according to St John (London 1943). Cited as Howard.

INGE, W. R., *Christian Mysticism* (London 1899).

JAMES, W., *The Varieties of Religious Experience* (London 1902; 13th imp., 1907).

JEREMIAS, J., *Hat die Urkirche die Kindertaufe geübt?* (2nd edn, Göttingen 1949).

JOHNSTON, G., *The Doctrine of the Church in the New Testament* (Cambridge 1943).

KENNEDY, H. A. A., *St Paul and the Mystery Religions* (London 1913).

KIRK, K. E., *The Vision of God* (London, 1931; 2nd edn, 1932).

(ed.) *The Apostolic Ministry* (London 1946).

KITTEL, G., and FRIEDRICH, G., *Theologisches Wörterbuch zum Neuen Testament* (Stuttgart 1933-). Cited as *KTW*. (*KTW*, I.688-719, which is cited in this book, has also an E.T.: R. Bultmann, *Gnosis* (London 1952).)

KNOX, W. L., *St Paul and the Church of the Gentiles* (Cambridge 1939).

KRÜGER, H., *Verständnis und Wertung der Mystik im neueren Protestantismus* (München 1938).

LACEY, T. A., *The One Body and the One Spirit* (London 1925).

LAMPE, G. W. H., *The Seal of the Spirit* (London 1951).

LEWIS, C. S., *Beyond Personality* (London 1944).

Miracles (London 1947).

LINDSTRÖM, H., *Wesley and Sanctification* (Stockholm 1946).

LOHMEYER, E., ΣΥΝ ΧΡΙΣΤΩΙ in *Festgabe für Adolf Deissmann*, pp. 218-57 (Tübingen 1927).

LOOFS, F., *Leitfaden zum Studium der Dogmengeschichte* (4th edn, Halle 1906).

MACKINTOSH, H. R., *Types of Modern Theology* (London 1937).

MANSON, T. W., *The Teaching of Jesus* (Cambridge 1931; 2nd edn, 1935). Cited as *Teaching*.

The Church's Ministry (London 1948).

The Sayings of Jesus (London 1949). Originally part of *The Mission and Message of Jesus*. Cited as *Sayings*.

MANSON, W., *Jesus the Messiah* (London 1943).

MARSH, J., *The Fulness of Time* (London 1952).

MCFADYEN, J. E., *The Prayers of the Bible* (London 1906).

MERSCH, E., *The Whole Christ* (E.T., London 1938).

MICKLEM, N. (ed.), *Christian Worship* (London 1936).

MOFFATT, J., *The New Testament: a New Translation* (London, edn of 1933).

MOULTON, J. H., and HOWARD, W. F., *A Grammar of New Testament Greek* (Edinburgh: I, *Prolegomena*, 3rd edn, 1908; II, 1929). Cited as Moulton-Howard.

MOULTON, J. H., and MILLIGAN, G., *The Vocabulary of the Greek Testament* (London 1914-29).

NELSON, J. R., *The Realm of Redemption* (London 1951).

NICHOLLS, W., *Ecumenism and Catholicity* (London 1952).

NIEBUHR, REINHOLD, *The Nature and Destiny of Man*, II (London 1943).

NYGREN, A., *Agape and Eros*, Part I (E.T., London 1932).

OTTO, R., *The Kingdom of God and the Son of Man* (E.T., London 1938).

OULTON, J. E. L., *Holy Communion and Holy Spirit* (London 1951).

PHYTHIAN-ADAMS, W. J., *The People and The Presence* (London 1942).

PRATT, J. B., *The Religious Consciousness* (New York 1920; edn of 1945).

QUICK, O. C., *Doctrines of the Creed* (London 1938).

RAMSEY, A. M., *The Glory of God and the Transfiguration of Christ* (London 1949).

RAWLINSON, A. E. J., *The New Testament Doctrine of the Christ* (London 1926; 3rd imp., 1949).
(ed.), *Essays on the Trinity and the Incarnation* (London 1928).

RICHARDSON, A., *Christian Apologetics* (London 1947).
(ed.), *A Theological Word Book of the Bible* (London 1950). Cited as *RTW*.

ROBINSON, H. W., *The Christian Experience of the Holy Spirit* (London 1928; 8th imp., 1944).

ROBINSON, J. A. T., *In the End, God . . .* (London 1950).
The Body (London 1952).

SCHMAUCH, W., 'ΕΝ ΧΡΙΣΤΩΙ 'ΙΗΣΟΥ, 'ΕΝ ΧΡΙΣΤΩΙ, 'ΕΝ ΚΥΡΙΩΙ (Gütersloh 1935). Also published under the title *In Christus*.

SCHMITZ, O., *Die Christus-Gemeinschaft des Paulus im Lichte seines Genetivgebrauchs* (Gütersloh 1924).

SCHNEIDER, J., *Die Passionsmystik des Paulus* (Leipzig 1929).

SCHWEITZER, A., *The Quest of the Historical Jesus* (E.T., London 1910). Cited as *Quest*.

The Mysticism of Paul the Apostle (E.T., London 1931). Cited as *Mysticism*.

SCOTT, C. A. ANDERSON, *Christianity according to St Paul* (Cambridge 1927).

The Fellowship of the Spirit (London 1921).

SEESEMANN, H., *Der Begriff* ΚΟΙΝΩΝΙΑ *im Neuen Testament* (Giessen 1933).

SMITH, C. RYDER, *The Bible Doctrine of Salvation* (London 1941).

SNAITH, N. H., *The Distinctive Ideas of the Old Testament* (London 1944; 4th edn, 1950).

STREETER, B. H., *The Four Gospels* (London 1924; 5th imp., 1936).

(ed.) *The Spirit* (London 1919).

SWETE, H. B., *The Holy Spirit in the New Testament* (2nd edn, London 1910).

TAYLOR, V., *Jesus and His Sacrifice* (London 1937). Cited as *JS*.

The Atonement in New Testament Teaching (London 1940). Cited as *ANTT*.

Forgiveness and Reconciliation (London 1941; 2nd edn, 1946). Cited as *FR*.

in The Headingley Lectures: *The Doctrine of the Holy Spirit* (London 1937; 2nd imp., 1941). Cited as *HS*.

TEMPLE, W., *Christus Veritas* (London 1924).

Christian Faith and Life (London 1931).

The Fulness of Christ (London 1950).

THORNTON, L. S., *The Common Life in the Body of Christ* (London 1942).

UNDERHILL, E., *The Mystic Way* (London 1913; edn of 1929).

WEISS, J., *The History of Primitive Christianity* (E.T., London 1937). Cited as Weiss.

WREDE, W., *Paul* (E.T., London 1907).

(B) COMMENTARIES

BACON, B. W., *The Gospel of Mark* (New Haven 1925).

BERNARD, J. H., *The Gospel according to St John* (*The International Critical Commentary*, abbreviated as *ICC*; Edinburgh 1928).

BRIGGS, C. A., and BRIGGS, E. G., *The Book of Psalms* (*ICC*; Edinburgh 1906-7).

CHARLES, R. H., *The Revelation of St John* (*ICC*; Edinburgh 1920).

CRANFIELD, C. E. B., *The First Epistle of Peter* (London 1950).

CREED, J. M., *The Gospel according to St Luke* (London 1930).

DIBELIUS, M., *An die Thessalonicher I, II; An die Philipper* (*Handbuch zum Neuen Testament*, 3rd edn, Tübingen 1937). Cited as *Philippians*.

DODD, C. H., *The Epistle of Paul the Apostle to the Romans* (*The Moffatt New Testament Commentary*; London 1932).

The Johannine Epistles (*The Moffatt New Testament Commentary*; London 1946).

HOSKYNS, E. C., and DAVEY, F. N., *The Fourth Gospel* (London 1940). Cited as Hoskyns.

JACKSON, F. J. FOAKES, and LAKE, K., *The Beginnings of Christianity* (London 1920-33).

LIETZMANN, H., *An die Korinther*, I, II (*Handbuch zum Neuen Testament*; 3rd edn, Tübingen 1931).

LIGHTFOOT, J. B., *St Paul's Epistle to the Philippians* (2nd edn, London 1869).

St Paul's Epistles to the Colossians and to Philemon (London 1875). Cited as Lightfoot.

LOCK, W., *The Pastoral Epistles* (*ICC*; Edinburgh 1924).

MAYOR, J. B., *The Epistle of St Jude and the Second Epistle of St Peter* (London 1907).

MCNEILE, A. H., *The Gospel according to St Matthew* (London 1915; 2nd edn, 1928).

NICOLL, W. R. (ed.), *The Expositor's Greek Testament*, II (4th edn, London 1912). Cited as *EGT*.

PEAKE, A. S., *Hebrews* (*The Century Bible*, Edinburgh n.d.).

(ed.) *A Commentary on the Bible* (London 1931).

PLUMMER, A., *The Second Epistle of St Paul to the Corinthians* (*ICC*; Edinburgh 1915; edn of 1948).

RAWLINSON, A. E. J., *The Gospel according to St Mark* (*Westminster Commentaries*; London 1925; 3rd edn, 1931).

ROBERTSON, A., and PLUMMER, A., *The First Epistle of St Paul to the Corinthians* (*ICC*; Edinburgh 1911; 2nd edn, 1914).

ROBINSON, J. A., *St Paul's Epistle to the Ephesians* (London 1903).

SELWYN, E. G., *The First Epistle of St Peter* (London 1946).

TAYLOR, V., *The Gospel according to St Mark* (London 1952).

TEMPLE, W., *Readings in St John's Gospel*, complete edn (London 1945). Cited as Temple.

WEISS, J., *Das Markusevangelium* (in *Die Schriften des Neuen Testaments*, I) (3rd edn, revised by W. Bousset, Göttingen 1917). Cited as *Mark*.

WESTCOTT, B. F., *The Gospel according to St John* (reprinted from *The Speaker's Commentary*; London 1882; 17th imp., 1924).

(C) JOURNALS

Bulletin of the John Rylands Library.

Journal of Biblical Literature. Cited as *JBL.*

Journal of Theological Studies.

London Quarterly and Holborn Review. Cited as *LQR.*

Scottish Journal of Theology. Cited as *SJT.*

The Expositor.

The Expository Times.

Theology.

The Student World.

(D) LITERATURE SPECIFICALLY ON THE WORD KOINΩNIA

This list of books on one specific theme can be understood by reference to the preceding lists. It contains some additional information, and is in chronological order.

ROBINSON, J. A., *HDB*, I.460-2 (1898).

CARR, A., 'The Fellowship (Κοινωνία) of Acts 2_{42} and Cognate Words', in *The Expositor*, 8th Series, V.458-64 (1913).

SCOTT, C. A. ANDERSON, 'The Communion of the Body', in *The Expositor*, 8th Series, XVIII.121-30 (1919).

'What happened at Pentecost', in (ed.) Streeter, *The Spirit*, pp. 117-58 (1919).

The Fellowship of the Spirit, pp. 69-71 (1921).

WOOD, W. S., 'Fellowship', in *The Expositor*, 8th Series, XXI.31-40 (1921).

SCOTT, C. A. ANDERSON, 'The "Fellowship" or Κοινωνία', in *The Expository Times*, XXXV.567 (1923-4).

LACEY, T. A., p. 247 (1925).

SCOTT, C. A. ANDERSON, *Christianity according to St Paul*, pp. 159-61, 186ff. (1927).

MOULTON, J. H., and MILLIGAN, G., pp. 350-1 (1914-29).

CAMPBELL, J. Y., 'KOINΩNIA and its cognates in the New Testament', in *JBL*, LI.352-80 (1932).

JACKSON, F. J. FOAKES, and LAKE, K., III.22-3; IV.27-8; V.389-90 (1926-33).

SEESEMANN, H. (1933).

FLEW, R. N., *Jesus and His Church*, pp. 151-3 (1938).

HAUCK, F., *KTW*, III.789-810 (1938).

Taylor, V., pp. 109-13 (1941; 2nd edn, 1946).

Thornton, L. S., pp. 5-33, 66-78, 156-64, 322-37, 448-51 (1942).

Dodd, C. H., *The Johannine Epistles*, pp. 6-9 (1946).

Jourdan, G. V., 'KOINΩNIA in 1 Corinthians 10_{16}', in *JBL*, LXVII.111-24 (1948).

Cranfield, C. E. B., *RTW*, pp. 81-3 (1950).

Nelson, J. R., pp. 53-66 (1951).

Oulton, J. E. L., pp. 60-4 (1951).

Bauer, W., columns 795-6 (1952).

COMMUNION WITH GOD
IN THE NEW TESTAMENT

CHAPTER ONE

INTRODUCTION

DEFINITION OF THE THEME

COMMUNION with God might well be called the main theme of Christianity. But the word κοινωνία occurs only nineteen times in the New Testament, and the books which include 'communion' in their titles are not as common as those on many other subjects. On the whole, the theme has been handled under other categories, and thus we shall have to consider a large number of related ideas. Indeed, the word could be used as a peg on which to hang an account of the God with whom we have communion, the Christ through whom we have it, the men who have it, and so on. Thus Herrmann set out his whole position in a book on this theme.[1] Christian theology is an organic whole, and this theme is linked with every other. Thus before we define our theme more positively, we must provisionally indicate its relations to some themes which we propose to omit. We shall return to these relations in the last chapter.

We omit the doctrine of God. Our theme implies that God is and that He reveals Himself, primarily, at least, in Christ. We omit the light which our communion with God throws on the doctrine of Christ's Deity. Nor can we consider the doctrine of the Holy Spirit, for, though He is in the most intimate relations with the spirit of man, He is on the Godward side of the gulf between God and man. We omit, as far as possible, the doctrine of the Trinity, on the ground that, when our communion is 'through Christ' or 'in the Spirit', it is nevertheless communion with the Triune God. Indeed the doctrine of περιχώρησις would further assert that the Persons interpenetrate each other in the performance of these functions. We omit also the question whether God reveals Himself otherwise than to the Christian. He did indeed reveal Himself to the fathers by the prophets,[2] but we shall not be dealing with the Old Testament save as a background to the New. He does not leave men without some witness

[1] Herrmann, *The Communion of the Christian with God.* [2] cf. He 1_1.

to Himself[3] even in non-Christian religions. But we are to ask simply what kind of communion with God the Christian enjoys: that is what communion with God is in its best and highest form. This book is not a work of apologetics, and the Christian standpoint is assumed. The communion of the Christian is practically the only kind of communion in which the New Testament takes any interest. It is indeed a relevant question whether there is for the Christian any communion with God in nature, though a question in which the New Testament takes little interest,[4] but we are not concerned either to affirm or deny this possibility for the non-Christian.

Our theme is thus religious experience, a term which calls for some comment at this point in the history of theology. The substitution of revelation for experience as the dominant category of theology has brought great comfort to many in our century, as it did to Hoskyns. Though revelation and religious experience are to some extent correlative, they conjure up very different associations, and it makes a great deal of difference which term is more used. An excessive stress on revelation leads to authoritarianism as in Romanism, Fundamentalism, or Barthianism; an excessive stress on experience leads in the most diverse ways to Protestant Modernism, Quakerism, and Pietism. Some would add to this latter list Methodism, and even assert that Schleiermacher simply formulated intellectually what was already implicit in Wesley. But Wesley laid an equal stress on the revelation in scripture, and used the soteriological and Biblical terms more frequently than 'experience', which (ἐμπειρία) does not occur in the New Testament. Possibly the term came into nineteenth-century Methodism largely through external pietist influences and helped to lend colour to the unjustified charges about 'justification by feeling': but it served in its time a most valuable purpose in safeguarding religion against the academic, impersonal, and merely institutional. At its best, Methodism has preserved the balance between revelation and experience. But revelation is not really the characteristic word of this century; it was found, though in a weakened sense, in Ritschl. The more common terms now are the I-thou relationship, confrontation, and encounter.[5] These terms are probably preferred because they definitely

[3] cf. Ro 2_{15}. [4] But see Ro 1_{20}.

[5] On the relation of 'experience' to this, cf. J. Baillie, pp. 222-4.

suggest the meeting of persons, whereas 'experience', with its somewhat anthropocentric flavour, rather suggests, though it does not definitely imply, the handling of things. We do not want the slightest risk of that ignoring of personal relationships which has been termed the Cartesian Faux-Pas. It is possible to study 'experience' in a way which ignores the God who reveals Himself therein. 'Experience', like 'idea' in a representationalist or three-term theory of perception, may come between us and (in this case) God. Into this trap the so-called Psychology of Religion often falls.

But the word 'experience' need not be so misunderstood. Unless religious experience be an illusion, it implies the existence of the divine. Similarly, a religion which stresses revelation must also give some account of experience, even though it does not use the term. Therefore the use of the term in this work does not imply either the acceptance or the rejection of that brand of theology which uses the term most. An interesting example of the middle position in this matter is to be found in Friedrich Heiler, a master in the investigation of the history of piety. The divine, he says, is not the creation of human experiences (*Erlebnisse*), but the highest Reality. Nevertheless (he goes on), this realistic conception is radically different from the exaggerated *Objektivismus* of a Barth, a Gogarten, and a Brunner. He who condemns religious experience robs the human soul of that which is most precious and most holy. Taking as our motto Augustine's *Deum et animam scire cupio* (I desire to know God and the soul), we must steer between the Scylla of modern *Objektivismus* and the Charybdis of liberal *Subjektivismus*.[6]

Religious experience is, however, a wider term than communion with God. The sinner's sense of guilt is religious,[7] but it is not communion with God. Our theme is thus not religious experience in general, but communion with God. Nor is it a study of the initial stage of the Christian life, regeneration, conversion, or justification, but of life from that stage to death. Nor yet is it a study of that state in all its aspects; for this state has a soteriological aspect which dominates evangelical theology. The description of this state as salvation stresses that *from* which we are saved, whether wholly in justification or gradually in sanctification. From this standpoint the believer is continually

[6] Heiler, *Das Gebet*, p. xi. [7] cf. Temple, *Christus Veritas*, p. 37.

receiving that blessing the first reception of which constituted his conversion. He never ceases to need and to receive the forgiveness of sins and all other benefits of Christ's Passion; he is continually being cleansed from the guilt and power of sin, and being reconciled to God. Even the perfect man described in Wesley's theology still needs the Atonement.[8] Yet these processes are means to a greater end, which is, in one aspect, holiness; in another, communion with God. Reconciliation is reconciliation *to* communion; and communion is the means, but also the end, of the process of sanctification. There is no mysterious paradox here; as often, the analogy of human relationships will make it clear. A friendship may be very much coloured by the fact that it began in the forgiveness of a great injury, but the enjoyment of the friendship is something more than the acceptance of the forgiveness; and though friendship often strengthens the character, it is not, at its best, undertaken simply with that end. Nevertheless, we must remember the truth suggested by the illustration; our communion with God is all coloured and indeed deepened by its association with forgiveness. It is thus deeper than the fellowship which sinless beings, such as angels, could enjoy. 'They know not Christ as Saviour.' *O felix culpa!*

We assume the Pauline view that man is not saved by the works of the law, but by faith, with which the author of the General Epistle of James would not have been likely to disagree, had he understood Paul's meaning. As faith is the ground or condition of communion, it is not communion. To describe it as a ground need not imperil the complementary truth 'by grace alone'; faith is a necessary condition for the appropriation both of salvation in its initial stage and of the Christian's communion with God in general, and thus describes rather the attitude of one of the participants than the nature of the relationship. The term does however strongly suggest that the relationship is itself to be described in personal terms. Moreover, it is sometimes used to describe a particular type of piety. Thus Heiler, who lets the distinction of mystical and prophetic piety stand in the text of the fifth edition of *Das Gebet*, yet says in the Preface to that edition that he would now rather say, following Otto, mysticism and faith-piety (*Glaubensfrömmigkeit*).[9] In such contexts,

[8] cf. Lindström, pp. 149-52. [9] Heiler, *Das Gebet*, p. x.

the use of the term will be very relevant to us. Moreover, faith is an attitude determined by its Object, and this implies a relationship. The term 'faith' does not itself determine the issue whether 'union', 'communion', 'knowledge', 'vision', 'faith-union', or the like, is the most suitable way of describing this relationship; this issue indeed is our theme, and the term 'faith' views the matter from a different aspect, and is no substitute for these terms. Thus we shall not be studying faith as such, though it can never be far from our thoughts.

A somewhat similar concept is love. Catholicism has always stressed our love of God, and Protestantism has not been at its best when it has stressed faith to the exclusion of love. Methodist perfectionism has preserved the balance. Nygren indeed has thrown a new light on the matter by showing in a most illuminating book that a history of the Christian idea of love is virtually a history of Christian doctrine. We cordially accept the broad outline of his distinction; but it is not easy to accept his account of our love for God; indeed, we might almost say that his book is of more value as a general history of doctrine than as an account of love. He rightly points out that Paul rarely speaks of man's love to God or Christ. This is in harmony, he says, with the correct view of Agape as spontaneous and uncaused. Man's response to God, not being uncaused, requires a different name, faith. This is plausible until we recall that Christ Himself spoke of our Agape toward God; we are not entirely reassured by being told that Paul in this is clearer than the synoptics, or by reading that there is a 'weakening' of the idea of love in the Johannine writings. We may, however, accept the conclusion that 'faith is a love to God that is receptive, not spontaneous'.[10] If, however, we assume that love is to supplement or even replace faith as the chief word used to describe man's attitude to God, we may still say of it, as we have just said of faith, that it 'describes rather the attitude of one of the participants than the nature of the relationship' (in this case, of course, of both of the participants). It reminds us to speak in personal terms of the relationship, but does not describe the nature of the communion, which is our theme.

Two more groups of terms connected with communion in its soteriological aspect call for comment. The first group concerns the goal of salvation; entire sanctification, the second blessing,

[10] Nygren, p. 93; cf. 91-2, 111-17.

Christian perfection, scriptural holiness, perfect love. It is much discussed whether, and, if so, in what sense, this goal is attainable in this life. If it is conceived as a violent crisis, a kind of second sudden conversion (as the phrase 'second blessing' is often used to suggest), then we might have to give two separate accounts of communion with God, one before, the other after, this crisis. But though it is at least arguable that it is attainable in this life, yet there is no sign in the New Testament of any change in the *mode* of our communion with God. Communion with God is simply realized in the perfect man less imperfectly. We say 'less imperfectly' rather than 'perfectly', for it is doubtful whether perfect communion is enjoyed in this life even by the man who from the soteriological aspect has attained perfection, a status itself not free from many qualifications in Methodist doctrine. The New Testament rather suggests that within communion with God the real dichotomy lies between imperfect communion in this life and perfect communion in the life to come.

The other important soteriological term is grace. Grace is an admirable term to emphasize the Pauline truths that we deserve nothing in ourselves, but that God is gracious; He acts *ex gratia*. 'Catholics', however (to use the word 'Catholic' as opposed to 'Protestant' and not in the credal sense), often give the impression of a mechanical rather than a personal view of grace; and Protestants similarly often give the impression that we receive something other than Christ Himself. Grace is in danger of being conceived as some third thing, neither God nor man, neither matter nor spirit. Other words which at first sight represent things have been personified, but attached to particular Persons of the Godhead, as, for instance, Word or Spirit; but they serve as titles of those Persons; whereas grace is in danger of being considered in too great separation from the God who is gracious. The division into preventing, sustaining, saving, grace and so on, conceals the truth that it is always the same gracious God.

But the word 'grace' has given us the phrase 'means of grace'. Our theme is the whole nature of communion, and not only its 'means'; yet the phrase indicates one aspect of our theme. Nevertheless, the phrase has four objections from our point of view. First, by including the word 'grace', we run the risk, to which we have just referred, of thinking too impersonally, as though grace itself were a means or medium between God and man. Second, it is often, though not always, confined to soteriological contexts, as though grace were only concerned with the forgiveness of sins, which is not the sole content of communion with God. Third, it stresses the Godward side rather than the manward, and the external rather than the psychological, whereas we must consider both. Thus, for instance, when we speak of the Lord's Supper as a means of grace, we think of its institution and transmission down the centuries, its traditional rituals, and the relation of Christ to the elements; all this depicts it as a way in which grace is offered to the soul; but we have still to ask what is to be the attitude of the recipient, how precisely he is to receive the grace thus offered, and with what results. Fourth, it refers in practice to ecclesiastical activities, which are surely not the only field of God's operation. The phrase 'means (or media) of communion with God' has substantially the same meaning, but avoids these associations.

The use of the term 'communion' is at this stage provisional. Other terms have been suggested for our relationship with God, apart from those soteriological and other terms from which we have already distinguished our theme. Deissmann's[11] distinction between *unio* and *communio* must be considered. Kirk, writing on a very similar theme, prefers the word 'vision'. Herrmann uses *Verkehr* rather than *Gemeinschaft*. Thus we shall at first use κοινωνία, *communio*, *Gemeinschaft*, 'communion', generically as a rough description of this whole field of concepts; but as we proceed, we shall try, by examining the occurrences of κοινωνία, to see whether this really is the best word to use in this connexion.

Moreover, when we speak of 'means', we should say 'means (if any)'—for it has been disputed whether there are any such means. The Roman notions of mediation through the saints, the priesthood, and the sacraments, are opposed to the Protestant doctrines of the sole mediatorship of Christ, the priesthood of all believers, and salvation by faith alone. Again, the idea that communion (or, as they would say, union) with God is mediated would be denied by many mystics, mostly but not exclusively 'Catholic', who claim immediate access to God, sometimes with little regard even to the mediatorship of Christ. The fact that many non-Christian mystics make the same claim in such similar language is one of the most striking and, some would say, suspicious features of mysticism.[12] A similar claim to dispense,

[11] Deissmann, *Paul*, esp. pp. 150-4. [12] cf. Herrmann, p. 23.

not indeed with the mediatorship of Christ, but with the means of grace, troubled the early Methodist societies. The advocates of 'stillness' were chiefly concerned to discourage the use of the means of grace before conversion lest they should replace faith; but they also sometimes referred to the use of the means of grace by believers as merely optional. This was met by the sturdy common sense of John Wesley, and is only a curiosity of Christian history, though in all the Churches disparagement of particular means is common enough. But the claim of the mystics is more serious. The word 'mystical' is so commonly used in this whole field of study that we must attempt a provisional definition of it; this will introduce the more positive definition of our theme.

DEFINITION OF MYSTICISM

What is mysticism? What constitutes a mystic? The common discussions whether Christ or Paul or John or anyone else who is being considered was or was not a mystic are largely due to the fact that the term is used in various senses. To consider its meaning may indeed involve us in judging later types of piety when our avowed aim was to examine the source of Christian piety in the New Testament. But to start there without some definition would only lead to confusion; and in general, we must have some categories in which to conduct the discussion. We must not of course force the evidence to fit a ready-made scheme, but we can hardly start at all without the use of some provisional hypotheses and definitions, which we must allow to be progressively modified in the course of the discussion. Thus the use of terms in handling the material and the modification of those terms in the light of the material must proceed *pari passu*.

The careful definition of mysticism will not alter the fact that some theologians are favourable to it and some not. Nevertheless their differences have been accentuated by the fact that those who are most hostile to mysticism usually define it rather narrowly and those most favourable to it rather widely. A survey of the attitudes taken to it in modern Protestantism will illustrate this point and lead to another.[13] There is first a class which rejects

[13] The threefold division which follows is based on the useful collection of views in Krüger. He confines himself to German writers, but a few British and American additions readily suggest themselves.

mysticism entirely. Here we may place first Ritschl and his school. As Flew says: 'Ritschl denies that in this life any communion between God and the soul can take place, except in the form of what he calls Faith.'[14] He was even shocked by the title (*Verkehr*) of the work of his greatest disciple, Herrmann. As Mackintosh says: 'Ritschl failed to distinguish fitly between different types of mysticism, less and more evangelical in character.' 'He has certainly not proved his case against that personalistic type of mystical thought which is to be found at its profoundest in the pages of St Paul and the Fourth Evangelist, and is indeed very much equivalent to the deepest and most intimate kind of personal religion.' But Ritschl would answer that no New Testament writer was a mystic in the proper sense of the word 'for the sufficient reason that no New Testament writer ever employs or recommends a mystical technique, or is tempted to rise superior to historical revelation or to the distinction between good and evil'.[15] This shows clearly how a narrow conception of what mysticism is goes hand in hand with its rejection. Moreover, though Ritschl's followers may have 'atoned' (to use Flew's word)[16] for his failure to give an adequate account of communion with God, they were no more favourably disposed to mysticism; thus Herrmann was clearly against it.[17] This school on the whole lays its stress rather on faith.

With the opponents of mysticism we must include also the 'dialectical' theologians, who separate the Gospel from 'Religion', of which mysticism is the most dangerous product. Thus Barth relates mysticism more closely to atheism than to religion. He speaks of God's revelation as the abolition (*Aufhebung*) of religion. Religion is lack of faith (*Unglaube*), the concern of the godless man. But the weakness and inadequacy of Religion have now induced men to take a critical attitude to the attempt to depict God. This criticism takes two forms, mysticism and atheism. Of these, mysticism makes only an indirect attack. It respects religious observance, but treats its external features as merely a picture of the ineffable; it lives on its opponent, religious dogmatics and ethics.[18] Brunner is equally opposed to it. Indeed, in his

[14] Flew, *Perfection*, p. 391; cf. 392.

[15] Mackintosh, pp. 146-7.

[16] Flew, *Perfection*, p. 393.

[17] Herrmann, pp. 19-56, 195-201. For another view, typical of this school, cf. Loofs, pp. 179-81.

[18] Barth, pp. 304, 327, 348-9.

book *Die Mystik und das Wort*, he uses the word as a short description of the whole system which he abhors, though he admits that it is used only in a weakened sense when applied to Schleiermacher. His conclusion is clear: 'Either mysticism or the Word.'[19] A like opposition is almost taken for granted by Reinhold Niebuhr.[20] Writers of this school use 'mysticism' to cover so many tendencies which they regard as incompatible with the Gospel that they might seem to disprove the assertion that the opponents of mysticism usually define it rather narrowly; but it is clear that they do not include within it such characteristically Christian types of piety as the Pauline and Johannine.

Krüger adds to the Ritschlians and the 'dialectical' theologians a third group, the school of Erich Seeberg. We might add also Nygren, who regards it as belonging to the Eros-tradition.[21]

From these sub-divisions among the opponents of mysticism we turn to the second main group, those who seek to distinguish between true and false mysticism, usually giving to the former some such name as faith-mysticism. On this view, mysticism is not a separate type of piety from Christianity: there may indeed be non-Christian mystics, but that is false mysticism. True mysticism is one element in the best Christian piety, to which it gives a certain warmth and intimacy. Deissmann, whom we shall consider later in connexion with Paul, is a good example of this view.

The third group consists of those who strongly support mysticism. Often they are those who have given much attention to the comparative study of religion or to the 'Catholic' revival in Protestantism or both. Sometimes they belong to the Society of Friends. Among this group we may reckon Troeltsch, Söderblom, Otto, and Heiler.[22] Heiler is in Germany regarded as a strong supporter of mysticism; in England he is often regarded, quite erroneously, as opposed to it. It is true that his attitude changed somewhat between the second and the fifth editions of *Das Gebet*, but he is certainly not to be regarded as being as hostile to mysticism as Kirk's isolated quotations would suggest.[23]

[19] Brunner, *Die Mystik und das Wort*, p. 399; cf. p. v; many passages in, and the title of *The Mediator*; and *Revelation and Reason*, p. 224.

[20] e.g. Niebuhr, p. 117 n.2, with its phrase from Denney: 'I would rather be saved in Christ than lost in God.'

[21] Nygren, p. 172.

[22] Otto's liturgical reforms had a strong Quaker element.

[23] It is astonishing that so careful a writer as Kirk should have treated Heiler in so misleading a way. He must have thought, quite wrongly, that Heiler's admiration for Luther makes him a typical Protestant. cf. Kirk, pp. 429-31; Heiler, *Das Gebet*, p. x; Taylor, *FR*, p. 169 n.3.

We must add Schweitzer to the supporters of mysticism, but he views it in a way all his own. Of those who write in English, we may mention W. R. Inge, Evelyn Underhill, and Rufus Jones. The support of Orthodox and Roman writers may be taken for granted, though we may refer to the immense influence of von Hügel. As we should expect, those who prize it most highly usually find traces of it most widely, especially in the New Testament: to this Heiler is an exception. Evelyn Underhill is a conspicuous example of the claim to find it in Christ Himself.

CLASSIFICATION OF TYPES OF PIETY

The further point (which we said would emerge) is that the classification of varying attitudes to mysticism suggests a classification of types of piety in general. Of the opponents of mysticism, Ritschl thought that the proper word to describe the relation of the soul to God was faith; and, of its keenest supporters, Heiler uses 'faith-piety' (*Glaubensfrömmigkeit*) to describe piety of a non-mystical type. We might then try to classify types of piety according to the proportions in which they contain mysticism and faith.

The first type will be that which all writers include in mysticism, whatever else they include or exclude. To a Ritschl, a Niebuhr, or a Bultmann, this is mysticism *par excellence*. To Heiler it would be a part only of mysticism, the purest example, but not the best type of piety; for the best type lies in a fruitful synthesis. To Otto it would be *Unendlichkeitsmystik*; to Deissmann, *unio-Mystik*. Those who deny that Jesus was a mystic may only mean that He was not of this type. It is characterized by absorption in, or union with, the Transcendent Being, who is often not personally conceived. It is common outside Christianity, into which it came through Neoplatonism and pseudo-Dionysius. In its Christian form it is still Deissmann's *unio-Mystik*, but in Otto's categories we should call this a part of *Gottesmystik*. It is a controversial question how far the combination of this with Christianity is satisfactory, but it is hard to maintain that it is to be found in the New Testament. Those who claim to find mysticism there do not usually claim to find it in its extremest form, though Evelyn Underhill is perhaps an exception. Such phrases as 'I am thou' are characteristic of this type. Thus a mystic may say:

'I am at once I and thou, thou art at once thou and I. I am confused as to whether thou art I or I thou.'[24] In such a sentence, though indeed 'I' and 'thou' occur frequently enough, we clearly do not find I-thou religion. The mystic supposes, whether or not erroneously, that that relationship has been transcended. And though there are many instances in which mystics of the extremest type address God as 'thou' without any such qualifications, yet the goal of this type of piety seems always to be union, *unio*, ἕνωσις. We may therefore call it the *first* type, not merely in an arbitrary classification, but in the sense that the mystic *tends*, at least, to speak of God in the *first* person.

Our second type, similarly, speaks of God in the second person. It speaks not of absorption, but of an I-thou relationship. It often has a stronger sense than the first type of God as a Person, active in history. It speaks of κοινωνία, *Verkehr*, *Gemeinschaft*, *communio*, communion. This is at the least a real conversation with God, not a mere belief that He is. But within this second type there are two sub-divisions. Though it is a genuine type and not a mere compromise between types one and three, yet its nature varies according to whether it approaches more nearly to the first type or to the third. When piety of this second type approaches the frontier with type one, then its language becomes warm and intimate. Though there is no talk of union, yet it speaks of mutual indwelling and the like. But when it approaches the frontier of type three, then it keeps, as it were, a certain distance from the holiness, purity, and 'otherness' of God. There is still intercourse with Him, and He is really present, but the language of this type uses the metaphors of hearing and speaking (usually with the phrase 'Word of God') rather than those of seeing or others even more intimate. Whereas piety of our first main type will universally be called mysticism, opinion varies whether piety of this second type can rightly be so called. A Bultmann would hardly call any of it mysticism; Deissmann, on the other hand, would call it all mysticism, distinguishing it as *communio-Mystik* from piety of the first type. Others would draw the line between mystical and non-mystical piety somewhere in the middle of this second type. Thus that part of the second type which is nearer to the first type would probably be included within Otto's *Gottesmystik*

[24] This is taken from the numerous examples in Heiler, *Das Gebet*, p. 306 (shortened in E.T., p. 190). It is not Christian.

and Heiler's 'mystical piety', whereas that part which borders more closely on type three would be part of *Glaubensfrömmigkeit* (faith-piety) to Otto, and of 'prophetic piety' to Heiler.[25]

The third type of piety lays stress on man's separation from God. It speaks of sin and salvation rather than communion; the second type also uses soteriological categories, but not to the exclusion of those of communion. We may perhaps compare the third type with the tendency of some anti-perfectionist Protestants to stress justification at the expense of sanctification, seeing justification as a goal, an end in itself, rather than as a means to holiness of life and communion with God. The doctrine of justification by faith may be corrupted into antinomianism and quietism. A theology which stresses faith is not indeed in this peril if by faith is meant *fiducia*, a living trust, a personal relationship, as in most of the New Testament and the Reformers; but it may degenerate into mere *assensus*, intellectual belief—and to stress belief in God in that sense may preclude a strong sense of communion. The metaphor of hearing the Word of God may also come to suggest a message conveyed by various channels rather than personal contact. It is not easy to find a great name to illustrate this type of piety; it is rather a theoretically possible extreme, a tendency; anyone who professes to be a Christian must surely sometimes address God as 'Thou'. But such features as the disapproval of *Verkehr* show how near piety may come to this extreme.

To return to the question of mysticism, where usage is so varied, we must either define it arbitrarily or avoid the word altogether. We shall seek not to use it save where the context makes it clear in which of these senses it is being used. But clarity of definition does not alter the fact that different types of piety are variously assessed by different writers.[26]

[25] These identifications are, of course, only approximate. The authors have not committed themselves to these precise descriptions. But such an approximate method is the only possible procedure if these various schemes are to be related to each other.

[26] Heiler, *Das Gebet*, pp. 248-9, claims that derivation and ancient usage alike support a narrow use of the word; and indeed he is something of an exception to the generalization that those who take a favourable view use the word in a broad sense. Nevertheless he uses the word in a broader sense than many; and these pages may be a relic of that Ritschlianism which he had largely abandoned in his fifth edition. The wider use is defended by Deissmann, *Paul*, pp. 148-9. For a list of definitions, see Inge, pp. 335-48, to which many might now be added. cf. Barth, p. 348.

MEDIATION IN MYSTICISM

We return to the question whether mysticism (leaving out the question of mediation through Christ) is justified in its claim to be immediate. Immediacy, directness, and the like, have usually been held to be its differentiae.[27] But there is another stream within mysticism itself. We pass over sacramental mysticism or cult-mysticism, in which, in its Christian form, the Eucharist plays a prominent part,[28] and turn to the conception that God is to be worshipped in and through His creatures. To this in its extreme form the name 'nature-mysticism' has been given.[29] Heiler treats of a type that resembles this, his contemplative-aesthetic type.[30] He assigns this to poets and artists, but it is found also in 'religious' personalities. The most austerely ascetic of those who are mystics in the narrowest sense of the word occasionally allow the possibility, or even desirability, of mediate experiences of God. Thus Thomas à Kempis writes: 'If thy heart were right, then every creature would be to thee a mirror of life, and a book of holy doctrine.'[31] That, of course, is very far from pantheism, but it goes much beyond, say, Paul.[32] Other mystics are almost exclusively of this type. They are not the majority of mystics, but they constitute an important class, to which the name of mystic is not usually denied. Thus, for instance, Inge, a leading writer who has allowed their claims, can make no use in his definition of any word such as 'direct' or 'immediate'.[33]

This introduces a cross-division into our types of piety. It is true that our first type, *unio*-mysticism, cannot very well be other than immediate. We can conceive of mediated communion, but

[27] cf. Butler, p. 3; Deissmann, *Paul*, p. 149.

[28] Heiler, *Das Gebet*, pp. 322-31.

[29] As God is found in nature, so theoretically He might be found in human nature. There is, of course, nuptial or erotic mysticism. (Heiler, *Das Gebet*, pp. 331-41. cf. Chavasse, who indeed goes beyond mysticism in many senses of that word.) But this merely means that imagery connected with human relations is used to describe our confrontation with God; God is not actually seen or met in another person, apart from the claim made by ritual-prostitution. But in nature-mysticism it is not merely said that we know God as we know nature, but that we know God *in* nature. In the Incarnation God is known in a Person, and this may well account for the reluctance to use this line of approach elsewhere.

[30] Heiler, *Das Gebet*, pp. 410-14.

[31] *Imitatio Christi*, II.4.i.

[32] We omit the delight in nature in the Psalms and in Christ Himself, which may be 'prophetic piety', and is very far from the pantheism to which nature-mysticism is prone.

[33] Inge, p. 5.

hardly of mediated union. Within the piety of the second type, we must distinguish not only that which tends toward the first type from that which tends toward the third, but that which claims to be immediate from that which admits the use of media; and the two divisions will not necessarily correspond.

QUESTIONS TO BE ASKED

We have thus reached a provisional account of the main types of Christian piety. The division into two types, mystical and prophetic, has suggested a more complex scheme, but the main principles stand. We thus have a vocabulary with which to discuss the New Testament. We must not assume that its piety will fit neatly into these categories. It may be that the normative documents of the faith, and above all the piety of Christ Himself, will contain elements which transcend these divisions. Nevertheless, they are a necessary starting-point.

We can now define our theme thus: What account do we find in the New Testament of what we may provisionally call communion with God? We shall proceed by taking each of the main strands of the New Testament separately. After preliminary observations about the nature of the source, we shall briefly survey the general character of its teaching as a background to our special investigations. We shall then examine its specific teaching on communion with God. In some cases, particularly when we deal with Christ Himself, we shall have to consider practice as well as teaching: and thus we shall consider the prayers of Jesus in some detail. We shall consider the actual linguistic use of certain important words, notably κοινωνία: we shall then relate our theme to the conclusions reached in numerous existing works about Church, ministry, and sacraments, in order to determine how far this communion is corporate. We shall then be in a position to ask under which of our three types of piety the piety of this strand or writer falls: combining this result with our linguistic investigations, we shall seek the right word to describe it, thus either confirming or upsetting our provisional use of 'communion': finally, omitting the question of mediation through Christ, we shall ask whether this communion (or whatever we may decide to call it) is mediated, and, if so, by what media.

CHAPTER TWO

THE SYNOPTIC GOSPELS

THE QUEST OF THE HISTORICAL JESUS

THE investigation of communion with God in the New Testament must naturally begin, if it can, with Christ Himself. But can it? Have we any reliable information? The investigation of the life of Jesus (*Leben-Jesu-Forschung*) has ceased to be popular. When once the old belief in the literal and verbal inerrancy of the Bible was abandoned, a process of dissolution was natural, in which doubt was thrown, now on this group of sayings and now on that. The investigation of the synoptic problem proceeded on the assumption that it was in the synoptic Gospels rather than in the Fourth Gospel that the true record was to be found. The actual source-criticism of the synoptic Gospels did not greatly affect the problem, though there was a tendency to prefer the contents of Mark and Q to those of M and L, as the special sources of Matthew and Luke[1] were called:[2] but the detailed scientific examination of the Gospels led to an unexpected result. At first it led to what is now rather ambiguously called a liberal portrait of Jesus, but by an irony of history the continued use of the method led to the re-discovery of those elements in the records which are most shattering to theological liberalism, for Schweitzer's portrait of Jesus so stressed the futurist eschatology in His teaching that it was scarcely possible any longer to treat Christ as the basis of a left-wing or humanist theology: or at least anyone who sought 'the Spirit of Jesus', as Schweitzer himself did, seemed compelled to accept also the view that He was a kind of deluded fanatic. So Cadoux asked: 'If it is hard to see the Christ of tradition in the Jesus of liberalism, how much harder is it to see him in the deluded visionary whom Schweitzer puts in his place?'[3] In fact, Schweitzer probably went too far, and tended to

[1] The first and third Gospels will be called Matthew and Luke respectively: the question of their authorship is not raised.

[2] Deissmann, *Religion*, pp. 27-39, esp. 35, defended a use of the sources (in connexion with the study of piety) which Weiss called 'synoptic eclecticism'.

[3] Cadoux, p. 6; cf. the whole passage.

overlook the non-eschatological sayings which would have corrected the picture. But the result of these developments was to throw doubt on the possibility of writing a life of Jesus.

But it did not end there. The *formgeschichtliche Methode* provided a technique of investigation which seemed to throw as much doubt on the genuineness of many sayings in Mark and Q as had been thrown formerly, first on the Fourth Gospel, and then on M and L. The form-critics themselves are curiously unperturbed by the destructive effect of their investigations, for a widespread continental theological movement, to which many of them in varying degrees belong, enables them to base their theology on the Word of God, which even in its aspect as the written Word, that is, Holy Scripture, is said to be unaffected by the historicity of the sayings contained in it. Bultmann, a leading exponent of this, has written, in a series of biographies of 'the immortals' (*Die Unsterblichen*), what at first sight appears to be a biography of Jesus; but he tells us that he is not concerned with the personality of Jesus, but with the teaching contained in the oldest layer of the synoptic tradition. Jesus was probably, he thinks, the bearer of these ideas; but anyone who wishes to read 'Jesus' in inverted commas may do so.[4] Yet the dialectical and anti-liberal character of his theology comes out clearly in his collected essays and other writings. There is indeed, (and increasingly since he popularized the word *Entmythologisierung*) a tendency on the part of the dialectical theologians themselves to disown him, probably just because his frankness reveals too clearly the essential difficulty of this position.[5] So Barth combines a conservative theology with the belief that there is nothing remarkable in the life, teaching, and character of Jesus.[6]

There is of course some truth in this effort to free theology from subservience to history. Certainly religion must be freed from the presuppositions of the liberal-rationalist approach to history. History cannot be treated 'objectively' like a natural science. What is now called the sociology of knowledge has taught us to be careful about 'objectivity'. This view, in its proper form, has a reputable ancestry in Augustine's *crede ut intelligas* and Anselm's

[4] Bultmann, pp. 13-14; see Cadoux, pp. 7-8.

[5] Thus Brunner, *The Mediator*, p. 157n., says that his *Jesus* 'suffers from a remarkable discord'. cf. pp. 187, 190n. But see Cadoux, p. 8 n.2, on Brunner.

[6] cf. D. M. Baillie, pp. 9-58, esp. 36.

credo ut intelligam.[7] But this valuable insight may easily lead to a sheer subjectivism or a crude existentialism. Moreover, a religion that includes the Incarnation can never be free from the facts of history: this point, despite much talk about the 'scandal of particularity', is often forgotten today. We must then find a basis for our theology in the life and teaching of Jesus: and we must either claim that in all honesty we do in fact find there, *a posteriori*, the basis for an orthodox theology, or, following the argument whithersoever it leads or appears to lead, we must follow it into the realms of Protestant modernism:[8] Catholic modernism does not claim such a basis in the life of Christ.

In recent years there has been a reaction in favour of the former view that we do in fact find a sufficient basis in the life and teaching of Jesus for traditional theology. No first-class life of Jesus has been written, but the writings of such men as Dodd, Vincent Taylor, T. W. Manson, and W. Manson (to mention only a few leading names) show that men thoroughly conversant with the methods of form-criticism can believe that we know a good deal about Jesus, and that what we thus know is not utterly unlike the traditional picture. But the following testimony is the more striking in so far as it comes from an unexpected quarter and to some extent constitutes a recantation. Brunner says: 'Even the most intensive historical criticism leaves "more than enough" of the Gospel story and its picture of the central Person to enkindle and to support faith'; and again: 'The picture of the life and the person of the Lord remains in essentials the same as it was in the days of our fathers.'[9] His point is not the old point that history hardly matters for theology, but that *even if* we go to the farthest lengths of criticism, enough history remains. (He does not discuss the further point whether it is necessary to go so far, which is what the British writers mentioned would ask.) Thus we may proceed with confidence in the assumption that the main outlines of the life and teaching of Jesus, as they are depicted by the best modern scholarship, may be taken as the background for any particular aspect which we may wish to investigate.

[7] For a sober statement of it, see Quick, pp. 146-61; cf. Richardson, pp. 89-109; and Hodges.

[8] An extreme example is Barnes, pp. vi, 267; his use of 'independent scholar' is most questionable.

[9] Brunner, *Revelation and Reason*, pp. 284-5, and see p. 284 n.21.

THE PROCLAMATION OF THE KINGDOM

We are not concerned simply with the teaching of Jesus,[10] but with the whole mystery of His Person: but if we begin, not indeed with His teaching in the sense in which that word is now used but with His proclamation, we shall in fact be considering His Person also. The dominant theme of that proclamation is the kingdom. Eschatology, which was once thought of as the theme of the last chapter of a work of dogmatics, has now, by a paradox which is no mere device of exposition but the paradox of the Gospel itself, became a part of the prolegomena, the setting in which all else is proclaimed. This makes a fundamental difference to the doctrine of communion with God. For if the Good News (only partly good, in that case) is that at some future date the kingdom will come, then clearly whatever communion is now enjoyed is likely to be inferior to the communion which will be possible when the kingdom has come. But if the kingdom is in some sense already here, then the communion at present enjoyed is likely to be correspondingly rich and full. Thus we must refer to recent discussions of the kingdom, which, as they are well-known, can be treated briefly.[11]

The older ideas, still often held, were that the kingdom was to be identified with the Church, or that it was a Utopia to be realized by human effort. It was Schweitzer, as already mentioned in another connexion, who, following Johannes Weiss, took the view that the kingdom lay wholly in the future and was wholly the work of God: the Parousia of Jesus in glory, which would end this world and inaugurate the kingdom, was imminent. This involves us in various difficulties, some of which have already been mentioned. In particular, it raises the same difficulty about communion with God that it does about ethics. When the imminent kingdom dominates everything, there is no real interest in ethics, and men live by an 'interim-ethic'; similarly there can be no real interest in communion with God, and we may perhaps coin a term and say that men enjoy an 'interim-communion'.

Before we come to the modern view, we may pause at Deissmann, not because he makes a major contribution to the subject

[10] Deissmann, *Religion*, p. 24.

[11] An admirable summary of them is in Flew, *Perfection*, pp. 8-40; and *Church*, pp. 27-40; cf. Nelson, pp. 211-34.

of the kingdom, but because he studied it, as we are doing, for the sake of the light it throws on communion with God. Writing after Schweitzer, he thought it was 'a great service rendered by the newer study of the Bible that it strongly emphasised the coming character of the kingdom according to Jesus'. Passages which seem to indicate that it is already present are cases of 'prophetic anticipation'. Moreover, he prefers the dynamic rendering 'sovereignty' to the local rendering 'kingdom' as a translation of βασιλεία. In view of this it is strange that he does not regard the kingdom as imminent or as otherworldly, but makes the coming kingdom the theological basis for what we should now call 'the social Gospel' in a way quite alien to the thought of the eschatological school. Similarly his account of communion with God is not affected as we might have expected it to be. The message of the kingdom 'vitalises for us, in the strongest form, the consciousness which Jesus Himself had of God, and reveals to us what God really is, combining kindness and holiness'.[12] These somewhat vague phrases do not suggest that the warmth of our communion with God suffers in any way, on Deissmann's view, from the stress on the future kingdom.

There were, however, other signs of a fresh emphasis. In the very year, 1910, in which the English translation of Schweitzer's *Von Reimarus zu Wrede* appeared, with the title *The Quest of the Historical Jesus*, there appeared also *The Eschatology of the Gospels* by Ernst von Dobschütz. His 'transmuted eschatology', though he did not put all the eschatological sayings into this class, was an anticipation of Dodd's phrase 'realized eschatology'. Another line of approach was to admit an eschatological tension at the end of Christ's life, after Cæsarea Philippi, but to contrast with that an earlier, sunnier period. In 1931, T. W. Manson, in *The Teaching of Jesus*, put the distinction between these two periods of Christ's life quite differently. In the former period, the kingdom lay in the future; in the latter, Jesus speaks of entering the kingdom, thus showing that by then it had come. Some of the texts quoted for the earlier period, such as Mark 1_{15}, were differently interpreted by later scholars, as we shall see; but there are others, such as Mark 9_1, which seem to bear out this thesis. The kingdom came at the moment of Peter's confession at Cæsarea Philippi, because Peter recognized the kingdom in the person of Jesus;

[12] Deissmann, *Religion*, pp. 116, 117, 110, 122, 121.

and as the kingdom is a personal relation, Peter's confession was 'just that acknowledgement that was needed to make the Kingdom *de jure* into a Kingdom *de facto*'.[13] In one sense therefore the kingdom was always present, or rather it was as useless to ask whether it was present or future as it would be to ask the same question about the Fatherhood of God. After Peter's confession, however, the kingdom is present in a new sense, though even then the final consummation, which is the same as the Parousia, is still awaited.

In 1934 Otto took a decisive step forward when he maintained that Jesus 'already lived in the miracle of the new age which was active even in the present';[14] yet this new age was developing and growing; we enjoy now only its first-fruits. 'It is not Jesus who brings the kingdom—a conception which was completely foreign to Jesus himself; . . . the kingdom brings him with it.'[15] Dodd was largely responsible for introducing this point of view to English readers. He rejects the notion that Jesus meant that the kingdom was simply very near: Jesus unambiguously proclaimed that it had come. He regards the ministry of Jesus as 'realized eschatology'. There is to be no further, future coming of the kingdom. So far as history can contain it, it has come. But in its full meaning it is timeless, eternal, and 'that which cannot be experienced in history is symbolized by the picture of a coming event'. Dodd did not neglect to show the consequences of this for Christian piety. He showed that in the second century, apart from millenarian speculations, the main emphasis lay upon realized eschatology, and 'upon His [Christ's] abiding presence in the Church, especially guaranteed in the sacrament of the Eucharist', which may indeed be 'described as a sacrament of realized eschatology'.[16] Dodd represents almost the farthest length to which 'realized eschatology' has gone, the view of Cullmann being in essence similar, though Glasson has gone farther. He mostly explains away the predictions of the future in the Gospels altogether. Yet before Christ's death, the kingdom was 'present only in its initial stages';[17] and there is to be a progress, development, and evolution in subsequent history; this

[13] Manson, *Teaching*, p. 131; see pp. 116-41 and *passim*.
[14] Otto, p. 155.
[15] Otto, p. 103.
[16] Dodd, *Parables*, pp. 51, 108, 134n., 203. cf. Dodd in (ed.) Micklem, *Christian Worship*, pp. 68-82; Dodd, *History*, pp. 163-6, where he distinguishes these views from the mystic's denial of time. But *Maranatha* is found in the liturgy in the *Didache*.
[17] Glasson, p. 114.

might indeed be held to constitute a fuller coming of the kingdom. Thus the wheel has come full circle, and Glasson's views have an effect similar to that of those held before Schweitzer. But leaving aside this final complication, we see that 'realized eschatology' allows for a rich and intimate communion with God, though something richer must be kept for the eternal realm beyond history.

There is now, however, a certain reaction from Dodd, who does not seem to give a very satisfactory account of events from the resurrection till now. If *this* is the kingdom, it is not all that we had hoped. It is true that this is said to be the kingdom only 'so far as history can contain it': there is also the eternal kingdom. But this provokes the reply that in that case history does not contain it to any great extent; the kingdom is not very fully realized in time. And when perfection is ascribed to another world or sphere rather than to future time, then we are using Hellenic rather than Hebraic categories.[18] Dodd, as has been sometimes said, has platonized his eschatology, as is almost the inevitable fate of those who speak paradoxically of realized eschatology while in fact time continues. Starting from the Hebraic categories, they too easily arrive at the Hellenic, though Cullmann avoids this peril.

Flew is typical of this reaction, and rightly protests that the logia about the future coming 'are too much coloured by eschatology to be interpreted in a Platonic rather than a Hebraic way'.[19] He calls the Church 'The Community of the Interval'; for this interval the ethical teaching of Jesus was meant. 'In another sense than that of Schweitzer we may use the phrase *Interimsethik*.'[20] What is true of ethics is true also of piety. Communion with God must then be piety of the interval, and one of its characteristics is likely to be expectation.

Yet another position is represented by Barrett, who, unimpressed by Dodd, thinks rather in the manner of Schweitzer. In the lifetime of Jesus the kingdom was 'germinal';[21] but as Jesus did not distinguish between the resurrection and the Parousia,

[18] Quick, pp. 238-40.

[19] Flew, *Church*, p. 44n. (on p. 45); cf. Cadoux, pp. 133 n.1, 197 n.1, 296 n.3, 198 n.4 (on ἤγγικεν and ἔφθασεν), an old-fashioned 'liberal' contending against the use of Hellenic categories! (So did Harnack, but in a different connexion.)

[20] Flew, *Church*, p. 46.

[21] Barrett, p. 160; and see pp. 135-9 for his criticisms of Flew and of Johnston.

there could be no thought in His mind of the community of the interval. But we may deduce that so long as the kingdom was germinal and the Messiahship hidden, the communion with God would also be incomplete.

To sum up, when the kingdom is conceived as having come, communion with God is likely to be felt to be intimate: and if it be added that it came more fully with the resurrection and Pentecost, then we should expect a corresponding increase after those events in the intimacy felt. Realized eschatology saves piety from wistfulness. Yet we must concede that the kingdom is not fully realized, and our piety will be the piety (to use a later distinction) of those who are *in via*, not yet *in patria*; and even Dodd would admit that, though the fatherland does not lie before us in time, nevertheless we are not there; it is in another sphere, and indeed, for the individual, entry into that sphere (if he ever enters it) can only be future. In this tension Christian piety continually lives. At one moment the believer is in Babylon; at the next he is enjoying an antepast of heaven.[22] This tension is recalled by a phrase of Horton (p. 216), who is summarizing an article by Patrick:[23] 'The Anglo-Saxon faith in an "ontological" presence of God in church and sacrament and Christian life, *versus* the Continental insistence that God's presence with man is only "eschatological", a promise rather than a realized fact.' This is the contrast between the Catholic and Protestant formulations of Christian doctrine, and this fact, as Horton points out, makes the use of 'Continental' and 'Anglo-Saxon' far too sweeping. We are reminded also of the contrast which we have already seen in Heiler between mystical and prophetic piety, even though that must not be identified with the contrast between Catholic and Protestant. Enough has been said to show that a great deal of theology hangs on the question: realized or futurist eschatology? Patrick indeed said in the article quoted that Anglicans could not 'hope to settle their differences with the Continent by any conciliatory "both . . . and"; for it is the very genius of contemporary Continental thought to take its stand upon an uncompromising "either . . . or", with Luther, Calvin, and Kierkegaard'. More important than these is the Bible; it has been remarked that it was Christ who started the attack on 'both . . .

[22] cf. Howard, pp. 201-4.

[23] In *The Student World* (2nd Quarter, 1937), pp. 129-41.

and' with the phrase 'Ye cannot serve God and mammon' (Mt 6_{24}); but a consideration of the eschatology of the Gospels shows that the principle of 'both . . . and' goes back to Christ. He says *both* 'Thy kingdom come' *and* 'The kingdom of God has come upon you' (Lk $11_{2,\ 20}$).[24] It is the utterance of One who was *both* Very God *and* Very Man. These matters cannot be settled by phrases like 'either . . . or', but it is clear that two different types of piety find their justification in Christ's teaching about the kingdom of God, or rather that a tension between two types is suggested there.

A related but not identical question is whether the teaching of Jesus was primarily ethical or eschatological. When the kingdom was conceived as the Church, or, very differently, as an earthly Utopia, the ethical precepts of the Gospel contained a mode of conduct suitable to that kingdom, conduct which would moreover tend to promote the realization of the kingdom in a greater intensity. But Schweitzer's eschatology, as we have seen, involved an interim-ethic. Now, however, the new view of eschatology carries with it a new view of ethics.[25] The ethical element has reasserted itself. The sayings in which an ethical element appears to predominate without any explicit eschatological reference are too plain and numerous for them all to be ignored or interpreted eschatologically. Indeed reflection shows that even interim-rules, though their content might be largely determined by their temporary nature, would yet have some relation to, or basis in, principles of eternal validity. Now, however, the ethical sayings are capable of being viewed in a different light. Some of them at least are surely the ethics of the realized kingdom. They describe the man who has entered the kingdom; they tell us what is the natural conduct, or rather the supernatural conduct, of the man in whose heart God rules. The eschatology is perhaps the framework in which the ethic is set, but it is an unobtrusive framework. The eschatology yields the prolegomena to the ethics, not its contents.

It must be admitted that this way of relating the ethical interest to the theory of realized eschatology is the reverse of that put forward by Dodd, who thinks that there is more ethical

[24] And indeed existential 'either . . . or' is compatible with paradoxical 'both . . . and': they are often found together in the same type of theology.

[25] Flew, *Church*, pp. 60-3; Cadoux, pp. 125-7.

interest in Matthew and Luke than in Mark (as indeed there is) *because* these Gospels were reverting to a futurist eschatology.[26] But it seems a more natural interpretation of much of the Gospel ethics to regard it as the mode of life of the man who is in the kingdom.

It must however be admitted that there are some parts of the ethics, and some of those the very parts with which the study of piety is most concerned, where the eschatology seems to determine the content and not merely provide an unobtrusive framework. When Jesus bids the disciples watch and pray (Mk 14_{38}), the exhortation to prayer is closely linked with an exhortation which is surely eschatological. It is true that γρηγορεῖτε means rather 'keep awake' than specifically 'look out for': it is also true that they were to keep awake not so much *for* something as *against* temptation. Nevertheless (even apart from the suggestion that πειρασμός refers to the eschatological woes) there is a suggestion of expectation. This may be the expectation of the future kingdom, or it may be the expectation of the final consummation of the kingdom already partly present, in which case we are back at an interval by another route; but it is still true that an ethic for an interval holds good even for that interval only because it is rooted in the eternal will of God. Indeed, much of any ethical system, religious or secular, must of necessity be concerned with an interval, the interval in which the good man has to deal with injustice and evil. The Sermon on the Mount is largely concerned with this very problem. It is sometimes asserted that the Sermon on the Mount is not a suitable guide to our actual conduct in the world, because it is the ethic of the redeemed society, an account of what we shall all do when we are perfect, a description of the life of heaven. But in such a society no one will strike our cheek or wish to take away our cloak. The notion that it is the ethic of a completely perfect society is as foolish as the opposite view which recommends the Sermon on the Mount to all and sundry without the slightest reference to the need for a changed heart. It is in fact an ethic for the man who is himself 'in the kingdom' in a society which is very far from being the kingdom. Secular ethics has the same problem, though it may or may not entertain a hope of the perfect society being realized.[27] Thus the eschatological

[26] Dodd, *Preaching*, pp. 52-5, 64-9; but see Cadoux, p. 127 n.2.

[27] Where it does so, as in Marxism, that hope is very often a kind of secularized version of the Christian, or of the Jewish, hope.

nature of Christian ethics is but an instance of the tension in which all ethics is at present involved. As much then as any other ethical system, it is ethics, existing in its own right, though of course Christian ethics has its basis in the character of God; and eschatology does not itself dictate the solution of the problems which it sets to ethics.

Another related question is whether Christ's ethic was world-renouncing or world-accepting. These alternatives have fought with each other through the whole history of Christian ethics. They have been combined in strange ways; one might, for instance, venture the generalization that the 'Catholic'[28] tradition has found room for the world-renouncing element in monasticism, and for the world-accepting element in the sacramental principle, while Protestantism has been world-renouncing in the Puritan attitude to the visual arts, but world-accepting in the Puritan attitude to money. The question whether the world supplied media for communion with God hinges on this issue, which is thus important for our study. But, perhaps inevitably, men have tended to draw their view of the teaching of Jesus from the practices of the Church rather than the reverse. The investigation of the life of Jesus is always liable to be influenced by systematic theology or even by the general spirit of the age. 'Liberal' theology tended to ascribe to Jesus a world-accepting ethic. So did Anglo-Catholic sacramentalism with its stress on the Incarnation. The eschatological school reacted against this, as against much else. And evangelical religion observes that Christ, who by His Incarnation may seem to have accepted the things of this world, by His death renounced them all for its salvation.

Wellhausen attempted a synthesis of these two points of view by saying that the outlook of Jesus is chronologically divided into two periods at Cæsarea Philippi.[29] But even before Cæsarea Philippi, Jesus proclaimed with a note of urgency the coming of the kingdom and the consequent call to decision; even after it, He had a certain joyous calm. This solution is not finally satisfactory.

Nor is it possible simply to sweep aside the evidence on the one side or the other. Jesus was contrasted as a gluttonous man and a

[28] Not in the sense used in the Creed.

[29] cf. Flew, *Perfection*, pp. 29-31; Farmer, pp. 226-7.

wine-bibber with the ascetic John the Baptist, and Himself said that His disciples need not fast so long as the Bridegroom was with them (Mt 11_{18-19}, Mk 2_{19}).[30] Moreover, the nature-parables seem to show a sunny disposition. The parables, of course, often proceed by the *argumentum a fortiori*[31] and thus there is not a precise correspondence between the ways of God and the ways of nature. But there is a certain similarity: else this type of argument would not be possible at all.

The most striking modern attempt to be rid of these passages is that of Bultmann. He admits that there are in Jesus' words 'many sayings which imply a childlike belief in providence and a naïve optimism in his view of nature and the world', but he thinks that both in their form and content they are of the type of wisdom-literature, and he therefore doubts their genuineness. Yet he admits that 'Jesus would not have repudiated such ideas, since they are consistent with the typically Jewish belief in God'. Only an exact understanding of their meaning would show whether these are really consistent with the eschatological faith (he continues) or whether the tradition is mistaken.[32] But the whole method and tone of Jesus' teaching, especially of the Parables, is not so lightly to be dismissed. There can be no doubt that Jesus did show a high degree of world-acceptance.

It is equally impossible to eliminate the world-renouncing sayings. This element is also criticized by Bultmann,[33] who goes so far as to say that Jesus 'in no sense desires asceticism'. 'Asceticism' has many varied meanings, and there is no difficulty in showing that some forms of it are alien to Jesus, but Bultmann goes rather too far in dismissing the word altogether, finally rejecting the story of the rich man and Lazarus (Lk 16_{19-26}) as unique and 'probably not a genuine part of the preaching of Jesus'.[34] The world-renouncing sayings are not indeed evenly distributed among the Gospels. Kirk has conclusively

[30] But is the whole verse genuine?

[31] As in Mt 7_{11}; cf. Lk 16_{1-8}, 18_{1-8}.

[32] Bultmann, pp. 160-4, esp. 161. In the same passage he assumes that the Evangelists have invented the contexts, and therefore 'it is impossible now to determine whether or how Jesus used such words'. There are general reasons for thinking that the *formgeschichtliche Methode* is often pressed too far, and we doubt the invention of the contexts; but if we grant this, it seems far more likely that they would invent contexts for genuine sayings than that they would invent both contexts and sayings. And see Kirk, pp. 65-8.

[33] Bultmann, pp. 98-101.

[34] Bultmann, p. 104.

shown that Luke, despite a certain tenderness which characterizes his narrative, is more rigorist than the other two.[35] The contrast between Matthew's 'Blessed are the poor in spirit' and Luke's 'Blessed are ye poor' is typical of much else (Mt 5_3, Lk 6_{20}). It is not indeed clear which is the original and which the modification. To spiritualize and soften an apparently harsh demand seems a more likely process than the opposite, but Kirk is of the opposite opinion. In any case there is enough that is common to all the synoptic writers about taking up the Cross and denying oneself for it to be perfectly plain that Jesus' ethic had its sterner side; if it was not asceticism for asceticism's sake, at least it called for sacrifice for the sake of the goal, an ethic of which Jesus' own death was the supreme illustration.

It seems then that both rigorism and humanism, world-renouncing and world-accepting elements, form part of the teaching of Jesus Himself. Neither element is to be set down as simply a casual intrusion from the environment, whether Jewish or pagan.[36] In the synthesis of them or tension between them lies the path for Christian ethics.

We have now considered three questions. Is the kingdom of God future or present? Is the teaching of Jesus eschatological or ethical? Is the ethic of Jesus world-renouncing or world-accepting? In each case we have rejected the answer 'either . . . or', and said 'both'. But the relation of these three questions to each other must be considered. It might be thought that it was possible so to combine the questions that we have only two alternatives to consider. Is the teaching of Jesus the eschatological world-renouncing proclamation of a future kingdom or is it the ethical world-accepting proclamation of a present kingdom? But this overlooks many distinctions. The proclamation of the kingdom, whether as future or as present, is in any case eschatological; even a present kingdom would be the expected *end*. Similarly, the kingdom, whether present or future, cannot be divorced from ethics, if only interim-ethics. But it is also an unjustifiable, though not uncommon, assumption that there is a close connexion between eschatology and world-renouncing asceticism. In fact, the eschatological outlook expects events in time and thus values the time-process. It is this-worldly, not other-worldly. Heiler regards prayer for the coming of the kingdom as

[35] Kirk, pp. 68-74; Underhill, p. 80. [36] Kirk, pp. 67, 85.

the highest and most important prayer of prophetic piety, and prophetic piety is essentially life-affirming.[37] This outlook is only ascetic when the end is thought to be imminent. Asceticism is then simple and the most practical line of conduct, which is one of the reasons for Paul's view of marriage (1 Co 7_{29-32}). Jewish eschatology at any rate is not fundamentally ascetic:[38] the origin of the ascetic element in the teaching of Jesus does not lie here. In any case these three sets of alternatives are not to be merged into one.

In the light of these contrasts we may draw certain conclusions as to the type of piety which Jesus might be expected, as it were *a priori*, to practise and teach. They show what types were possible to Him. We shall subsequently consider *a posteriori* how far His utterances bear out these expectations. But in view of the comparative paucity of utterances on this subject, the principles to be reached in this general way must themselves be regarded as in a large measure an account of the subject.

The question of piety may thus be related to each of the three problems which we have so far considered. First, what kind of piety is consistent with the proclamation of a kingdom at once present and future? At this question we have already glanced. There is a piety which is proper to a future eschatology. In so far as the kingdom is future, it lays on man one salient duty, to watch.[39] This is particularly linked with prayer.[40] We thus get a clue to the content of Christian prayer, which is borne out by the model Prayer: 'Thy kingdom come' (Mt 6_{10}). There is about this an air of tension and of expectancy inconsistent with mystic absorption. But we find in the Gospels also the proclamation of a kingdom which has just come; and this, even though it is not fully consummated, carries with it the suggestion of a richer intimacy of communion than man has hitherto enjoyed.

Second, what type of piety is consistent with a proclamation at once eschatological and ethical? We have just dealt with its eschatological aspects. The ethical element in the teaching of Jesus precludes not only an exclusive stress on eschatology, but also any trace of antinomianism. Now, ethical questions interest the prophet rather than the mystic; not that the mystic is

[37] Heiler, pp. 248, 250.
[38] Kirk, pp. 59-63.
[39] e.g. Mk 13_{33-7} (Markan source); Lk 12_{35-8} (source L), 12_{39-46} (Q); Mt 25_{1-13} (M).
[40] e.g. Mk 14_{38}.

antinomian, but he regards good conduct rather as a remote preparation for the mystical experience,[41] a view quite alien to Jesus, for whom 'The Kingdom of God clearly involved a certain Way of Life for men.'[42] Thus the ethical teaching, as much as the eschatological proclamation with which it in other respects contrasted, is opposed to the notion of mystical absorption. The obedience of the will is more stressed than any sort of union. Prophetic religion sometimes indeed shows antinomian tendencies. But the teaching of Jesus gives no support to a piety which cares nothing about a man's conduct so long as he is 'saved', nor to that extreme anti-perfectionism which so stresses man's impotence that it expects nothing at all in the realm of moral achievement. We may also gather from the ethical element in the teaching of Jesus that He would have supported the prophets in their preference of moral conduct to ceremonial observance. Indeed, with His usual ability for picking the salient passages of the Old Testament for quotation (an ability which the first Evangelist, at least, did not share), He quotes: 'I desire mercy, and not sacrifice' (Mt 9_{13}, 12_{7}, Hos 6_{6}).[43] The Hebrew idiom may perhaps mean, 'I desire mercy rather than sacrifice', and in any case is a flimsy basis for supposing that Jesus wholly rejected the sacrificial system, but it shows Jesus to share the preference of the prophets for morality. We may imagine that, though He does not say so, He would have approved the maxim *laborare est orare* (to work is to pray) and would have extended it over the whole ethical field; to do the Will of God is the true worship.[44] But this rejection of ceremonial observance is not necessarily absolute; 'These ought ye to have done, and not to have left the other undone' (Mt 23_{23}).[45] We must not be surprised if we find some stress on ceremonial observance also.

Third, what kind of piety is consistent with an ethic at once world-denying and world-accepting? In so far as Christ called for a renunciation of the world, we might appear to have a type of

[41] Heiler, pp. 157-60.
[42] Cadoux, p. 115.
[43] In each case the sentence is peculiar to Matthew, but it bears the stamp of genuineness. cf. Taylor, *JS.*, pp. 68-9, which also deals with Mk 12_{33f}.
[44] cf. Mk 2_{23-8} (one of the contexts into which Matthew inserts the quotation from Hosea), $3_{1-6,\ 35}$, 7, 12_{28-34} (Why do Matthew and Luke agree in omitting the last part of this? Did they not like the contents?) (All these are from the Markan source); Mt 23_{1-12}, 5-7, especially 5_{23-4} (partly Q and partly M); Lk 11_{37}-12_{1} (Q); Mt 21_{28-32} (M); cf. also the Cleansing of the Temple; cf. Ja 1_{27}.
[45] cf. Cadoux, pp. 120-2.

piety often associated with mysticism, and the death of Christ might seem to be the supreme example of the *via negativa*.[46] But Christ's asceticism, if indeed that is the proper name for it, does not go so far. It is rather that of the stern prophetic moralist, who sees service in the world, though not the worldly spirit, as the supreme service of God. But apart from the 'ascetic', or at least austere, element, thus shown to be itself capable of two interpretations, we have also to allow for the non-ascetic, world-accepting element. In so far as Jesus accepts the world, and particularly nature, He is on the way toward a sacramentalist outlook, which is as much a characteristic of some mystics as it is totally lacking in others.[47] His words do not indeed go far, but they are compatible with that type of piety which apprehends God in the natural world, treats nature as a sacrament, and finds God in all His handiwork. Such a view does not necessarily lapse into a purely immanentist pantheism.

The contrasts which we have noted in the teaching of Jesus have thus suggested a considerable range of types of piety. It would be as mistaken to stress one of these to the exclusion of its rivals as it would be to stress either of the alternatives unduly in the original series of contrasts. The piety of Jesus is not one-sided. So at least these considerations suggest. We must now examine the detailed evidence, to see whether this probability is realized.

JESUS AS A MAN OF PRAYER

Jesus was not only a Teacher about prayer: He was also a Man of prayer. He both described and had communion with God. Naturally there is no disharmony between His experience and His teaching, but they may conveniently be discussed separately. As Deissmann well put it: 'As if face to face we can see the praying One in His own prayers. In the words to His disciples which deal with prayer we see Him again as in a mirror'.[48] The whole method of treatment used by Deissmann and Heiler implies this distinction. Deissmann makes it vivid by his contrast between white-hot, glittering metal, and iron bands which are sold all

[46] cf. Heiler, pp. 165-6, 159.

[47] It is remarkable that Heiler's description of the main characteristics of mystical piety lacks an account of its attitude to nature (*Das Gebet*, pp. 248-83; E.T., pp. 135-71), as his account of the variants of mystical prayer lacks any mention of nature-mysticism (*Das Gebet*, pp. 322-46; E.T., pp. 203-26).

[48] Deissmann, *Religion*, p. 63; cf. 25, 39.

ready for use. It is an illustration peculiarly apt to this particular subject, though Deissmann goes too far when he supposes that the teaching of Jesus on other subjects, e.g. the Law, could be ascertained without reference to His actions.

We must therefore consider with particular care the very strong objections which Bultmann has brought against this consideration of the prayers of Jesus. After saying that modern interpretations of prayer as an inner reconciliation with fate, a reverent submission to the purpose of God, are far removed from Jesus, he continues:

> 'It is therefore a great mistake to discuss the prayer life of Jesus, to speak of Him as a praying man, to call Him the greatest man of prayer in history; even historically one has no right to do this. How a man prayed concerns no other man, not even the historian. And whoever allows himself to judge how fervently or deeply Jesus prayed, proves only that he neither understands nor respects Jesus' conception of prayer. . . . For according to Jesus, prayer is talking with God; whoever assumes he can evaluate any prayer presumes to stand in the place of God.'[49]

We must first face the question, parenthetic in the German, whether we have any historical right to make such judgements. This must be read in connexion with passages in the Introduction, in which he disclaims all interest in the 'personality' of Jesus. He defends this on the ground that the sources are not interested in this question: even such a question as whether He thought Himself to be the Messiah is obscure. The obscurity of a subject is, however, no reason for abandoning it. It is true that 'the examination of history is no neutral orientation about objectively determined past events', but that is no excuse for ignoring them or asserting that there are no facts when there are. The frequent modern assertion, doubtless true, that the Gospels are not biographies or memoirs, but 'expanded kerygma', equally must not exempt us from historical investigation. And in fact recorded prayers of Jesus do exist. They are not the main interest of the writers, but they are nevertheless available. Indeed what they record thus incidentally is less likely to be distorted than the rest of the tradition. Bultmann's more particular objection, already quoted, against the discussion of Jesus' prayers is a dangerous half-truth. Nobody would deny that not only 'according

[49] Bultmann, pp. 188-9 (*Jesus*, pp. 158-9), 8-10.

to Jesus', but according to anyone who knows at all what prayer is, 'prayer is talking with God', but it is possible to overhear the conversation, and to judge it by what we overhear. Bultmann says, in a passage omitted from the middle of our former citation, 'Whoever so judges [i.e. judges how fervently or deeply Jesus prayed] either sees in prayer merely a psychological phenomenon, which can become the object of interesting analysis, or he arrogates to himself God's own right'.[50] But the prayers of Jesus *are*, in one of their aspects, a psychical phenomenon capable of analysis; and we no more usurp the functions of God in reading and judging them than we usurp the functions of the Roman Church of the first century by reading and discussing the Epistle to the Romans. Indeed we cannot help reading these prayers, if we regard it as the duty of Christians to read the whole Bible; and may we not learn from what we read?

It must not of course be supposed that by considering the prayer-life of Jesus as we do that of other men we are putting Him 'on a level' with them. Jesus is certainly the 'Object' of Christian faith,[51] but He is also its Author, a Subject who gives us an example of faith (He 12_2).[52] Or (to avoid making Christ 'Object') He is the God to whom we speak, but also the One who speaks to God. That He should be both is part of the mystery of the Trinity. To neglect the example which He afforded to us by His godly life is a Christological heresy. There may indeed be instances in which His status as God makes His conduct inapplicable as an example (some of the arguments about pacifism turn on this point), but there is no reason for supposing that to be so here. We may lack the intimacy which Christ had with His Father, but there is no reason why we should not profit by the study of it.[53]

[50] Bultmann, p. 189 (*Jesus*, 159). The syntax of the German shows a slight anacoluthon. It is probably aimed directly at Heiler, whose whole method it undermines. The sub-title of his *Das Gebet* is *Eine religionsgeschichtliche und religionspsychologische Untersuchung*.

[51] I use this phrase only in a limited sense. It has recently been insisted that God is always the Subject who must be spoken to. Cf. J. Baillie, pp. 219-27. Put in those categories, the truth mentioned in the text can be re-stated as I have subsequently shown.

[52] cf. A. E. Garvie, 'The Author and Finisher of Faith', in *LQR*, April 1940, pp. 184-94.

[53] cf. the characteristic complaint of Deissmann, *Evangelium und Urchristentum*, p. 95 (quoted in Heiler, *Das Gebet*, p. 5), that not a hundredth part of the literature devoted to the life of Jesus has dealt with His prayers. On the other hand, support for the view that we know next to nothing of the prayer-life of Jesus, though not for the view that it is improper to investigate it, can be found in Cadbury, esp. p. 189.

Let us then reverently consider the prayer-life of Jesus. Jesus lived in the midst of a praying people, and we may safely assume that He followed their customs in this respect.[54] He practised the pious custom of giving thanks before meals (Mk 6_{41}, 8_{6}, 14_{22-3} and parallels; Lk 24_{30}).[55] He referred to the 'Hear, O Israel' which was daily recited by the pious Jew, and most probably recited it Himself (Mk 12_{29-30}, Dt 6_{4-9}).[56] The Psalms and other Scriptures sprang readily to His lips. He seems to have worn in the 'hem of his garment' the reminders of the obligation to piety prescribed by the Law. His attitude to them was a blend of conservatism and innovation,[57] but they do not seem to have entered deeply into His life (Mt 9_{20}, Lk 8_{44}).[58] We have various accounts of His attendance at synagogues, and His attendance there on the Sabbath-day is once mentioned with the words 'as his custom was' (Lk 4_{16}).[59] Moreover, He took a part in the service by reading the Scriptures even though His subsequent exposition led to a tumult.[60] He also visited the Temple, probably not only at the 'Cleansing' of the Temple (Mk 11_{11}, Mt 21_{12}, Lk 19_{45}, Jn 2_{14}), but on the other visits to Jerusalem recorded in the Fourth Gospel.[61] We may with safety infer, moreover, from the practice of the early Church in attending the Temple and preaching, as long as it was possible, in the Synagogues that Jesus had left them an example of so doing (Ac 2_{46}, 3_{1}, 13_{5}, $_{15}$, 14_{1}, 17_{2}). He had come 'not to destroy, but to fulfil' (Mt 5_{17}) the religion of Israel, and His religion was a corporate, not a solitary, thing. There is also other evidence, not concerned with corporate worship, that He did not disregard the ceremonial observances required by the Law, though he

[54] So Deissmann, *Religion*, pp. 48-50, who cites Lk 18_{9-14}. The OT affords ample evidence. Not to pray seems largely a modern custom. The ancient world prayed.

[55] We need not here go into the eucharistic significance of some or all of these.

[56] Rawlinson, *Mark*, ad loc.

[57] cf. Cadoux, pp. 120-3.

[58] This is a 'minor agreement' against Mark. But in Luke it is omitted by some of the authorities for the Western text, and may be in the other MSS. by assimilation to Matthew, in whom it may well be due to a Judaizing tendency.

[59] This seems to correspond to the visit to the synagogue in Mk $6_{1ff.}$ (=Mt $13_{53ff.}$). But Luke here has material of his own, and probably the whole passage Lk 4_{16-30} is derived from L.

[60] cf. Jn 6_{59}, Ac 13_{15}.

[61] His going to the Temple on such a visit is specifically mentioned in Jn 7_{14} (cf. Jn 10_{23}). The number of such visits is affected by theories of dislocation in the text of this Gospel. Probably there were some such visits despite the silence of the synoptists about them, for even the synoptists contained hints that there must have been such visits, e.g. Lk 13_{34}.

certainly attacked the legalist religion of the Scribes and Pharisees. We do not read of corporate prayer with the disciples, though the Last Supper was the corporate act of a religious fellowship.

He also engaged in private prayer, withdrawing from the disciples, sometimes for whole nights (Mk 1_{35}, 6_{46}). Luke has a special fondness for mentioning this, even when he is otherwise following Mark (Lk 3_{21}, 5_{16}, 6_{12}, $9_{18, 28}$).[62] It has sometimes been remarked that Jesus is recorded as having prayed chiefly at great crises of His life, from which it is inferred that He did not generally pray with any unusual frequency. This is not entirely true. The prayer at His Baptism indeed marked a special crisis.[63] The prayer at the choice of the disciples was indeed a prayer at a great turning-point. The same may perhaps be said about the fact that Jesus was praying at the Transfiguration; but we do not know that Jesus was praying then because He was about to be transfigured (Lk 3_{21}, 6_{12}, 9_{28-9}).[64] The same may be said of the occasion when He gave the disciples the model prayer (Lk 11_1). This was indeed a great occasion, but unless we invoke the divine omniscience, Jesus did not know that it was going to be; it was the initiative of the disciples in making a request when Jesus was already praying which led to the great event.[65]

It was, further, pointed out by Dibelius[66] that Jesus is recorded as praying, apart from Gethsemane, only twice in Mark (Mk 1_{35}, 6_{46}).[67] Neither of the Markan instances, he says, seems to be a part of the pericope. The narratives did not consider it essential; it did not pertain to the history of salvation. He is not example, but instrument, of God's revelation. Now it is true that in each case the reference to prayer is in a sense incidental to the story. In Mark 1_{35} it could easily be omitted, as it is in the Lukan parallel (Lk 4_{42}), surprisingly, in view of Luke's general fondness for these references. But in each case a departure by Himself

[62] Also in Lk 11_1 he mentions that Jesus was praying in a context where Matthew does not do so.

[63] cf. *infra*, p. 100.

[64] Transfiguration is almost represented as the effect of prayer.

[65] Nor is there anything remarkable about the circumstances of Lk 5_{16}. We omit here the prayers in Gethsemane, which are integral to the whole story, and the prayers from the Cross. These were obviously crises.

[66] Dibelius, pp. 52-5.

[67] But prayer is implied at Mk 7_{34}, as well as grace before meals. Dibelius adds that it is only once recorded in Matthew, but Matthew is so largely dependent on Mark for the framework of his narrative (as opposed to his sayings) that we may safely ignore him.

apart or to a desert place was fairly obviously for the purpose of prayer. Yet the fact that it is not essential to the pericope does not mean that it is not true or that it ought not to be of interest to us or even that it was of no interest to the Evangelist; for he goes out of his way to record it when there is no strict need to do so. Dibelius finds the same attitude in John. But Luke, as is well known, has a biographical interest in the human qualities of Jesus, and his biographical picture calls for some instances of Jesus' piety. For the others, a belief in Christ as Revelation naturally assumes that Jesus was in touch with God, and is not interested in the point. This no doubt is a sound account of the motive which led Luke to record the instances which we have already enumerated, but it does nothing to show that they are false. Indeed, Dibelius implies that the others assumed (presumably rightly) that He was in touch with God. To make the lack of interest in this shown by the other Evangelists normative for us is simply to repeat Bultmann's error. A certain slight argument for the frequency of Jesus' prayers can perhaps be based on the words 'according to custom', which Luke inserts into the sentence which describes His going out on to the Mount of Olives after the Last Supper, for it soon becomes clear that His purpose on this occasion was to pray, and we may plausibly infer that He had done so on other occasions also.[68] Taking all these considerations into account we may conclude that Jesus prayed frequently. On the other hand He seems never to have been discovered in anything like a trance or ecstasy (unless the Baptism or Transfiguration could be so considered), and does not seem to have spent an abnormal amount of the daytime in prayer.

The recorded prayers of Jesus are very few. This is not surprising; He prayed alone, and had no occasion to tell others what He had said. But His recorded prayers bear the stamp of genuineness: their brevity and directness vouch for them. They were prayers of such a character that the disciples could easily remember them years afterwards.[69] In two cases the actual Aramaic was

[68] Lk 22_{39} 'inserts' it in the sense that a very similar sentence in the parallels (Mk 14_{26}, Mt 26_{30}) lacks it. But Luke has his own sources for the Passion-Narrative, and the context shows that he is using one of them here. Are we to understand that this had been His custom in the few days subsequent to the Triumphal Entry, or is this a reference to earlier visits to Jerusalem?

[69] Deissmann, *Religion*, p. 54; Heiler, pp. xviii-xix.

transliterated as well as translated (Mk 14_{36}, 15_{34}).[70] The recorded prayers of Jesus are best reckoned as five in number.[71]

(I) THE PRAYER OF JOY

I thank thee, O Father, Lord of heaven and earth, that thou didst hide these things from the wise and understanding, and didst reveal them unto babes: yea, Father, for so it was well-pleasing in thy sight (Mt 11_{25-6}, Lk 10_{21}).

The same translation serves for both passages, for the differences are insignificant.

This may confidently be ascribed to Q. Despite a note of time in Matthew ('at that season'), the Matthaean context has no particular appropriateness. Luke records the situation.[72] The seventy (or seventy-two) had returned from their successful mission-tour, rejoicing in their power over the demons. Jesus calls attention to a deeper motive for rejoicing: their names are written in heaven. Jesus Himself, as He sees the power given to simple men, is filled with a new confidence and trust in His heavenly Father. Moreover, Luke introduces the prayer with a stronger phrase than Matthew—'he exulted (ἠγαλλιάσατο) in the Holy Spirit'. The word for 'exult' is a strong one: it is interesting to note that the Holy Spirit, so closely connected in later theology with Christian prayer, is mentioned here. That is, of course, part of the framework supplied by the Evangelist, who perhaps had Pauline teaching in mind. To turn to the contents of the prayer, the two vocative phrases are interesting. 'Father' and 'Lord of heaven and earth' express complementary aspects of the divine Nature, but it is interesting that it is 'Father' which is chosen for repetition. We mention here a matter which applies to some of the other prayers of Jesus. The Jews had avoided addressing God simply as 'Father' (Abba). This was the intimate, homely, familiar mode of address which Jewish children used to their fathers.[73] For God, the more reverential form 'our Father'

[70] cf. *infra*, p. 43.

[71] Heiler reckons four, apparently omitting Lk 23_{46}. We can scarcely reckon 'Ephphatha' (Mk 7_{34}), though Deissmann, *Religion*, pp. 66-7 does so. In Lk 22_{32} Jesus speaks of an intercessory prayer which He has offered. We are not, of course, here considering the Fourth Gospel.

[72] '. . . one of the many jewels which he has added to our knowledge of the life of Jesus. Only through the situation do we clearly understand the prayer'. Deissmann, *Religion*, p. 56.

[73] cf. Lk $15_{18, 21}$.

was preferred. Jesus was an innovator in using the more familiar form, an evident proof of the intimacy of His communion with God.[74] Heiler regards the filial relationship as very characteristic of prophetic religion. In the Old Testament this relationship is combined with the relationship of a subject to a king. But in mystical religion the terms are more erotic; of these terms there is no trace in the prayers of Jesus. The use of 'Father' is prominent again in Luther.

Of the phrase 'Lord of heaven and earth', it has been remarked that it is 'clearly inconsistent with any limitation of the divine interest to Israel';[75] and of the prayer as a whole that 'Jesus was thankful, not that the σοφοί were ignorant, but that the νήπιοι knew'.[76]

Heiler[77] points out that only one of the prayers of Jesus is a prayer of joy: the others are all cries of petition, intercession, and the like. He finds the same characteristic in Luther, and sees in it one of the marks of prophetic as against mystical piety. In mysticism, contemplative adoration is the heart of prayer; in prophetic piety, adoration and thanksgiving are subordinate to petition and intercession. This may be true in general, but we may doubt whether the prayers of Jesus are rightly used as evidence on this point, for, however much we are justified (against Bultmann) in making use of the prayers of Jesus as far as they go, it is perhaps a little precarious to assume that the proportions of His prayers are accurately represented by the proportions of those that have survived to us. The cries of Jesus in Gethsemane and on the Cross (in which class all the other recorded prayers are to be put) were naturally more public than the normal prayers of Jesus; moreover, they cover only two days of crisis; they cannot be taken as typical, though they may be instructive. Thus it may well be that this cry of joy and thanksgiving, though itself uttered (according to Luke) at a turning-point in our Lord's ministry, is more typical of the normal unrecorded prayers of Jesus than any other recorded prayer is.

[74] cf. Cadoux, pp. 28-9; T. W. Manson in (ed.) Micklem, *Christian Worship*, p. 42; Kittel, *KTW*, I.5; Manson, *Sayings*, p. 168; Heiler, *Das Gebet*, p. 401 (more briefly in E.T., p. 280); Dalman, pp. 190-3.

[75] Cadoux, p. 152.

[76] McNeile, ad loc. (p. 161b); cf. Cadoux, p. 202 n.2.

[77] Heiler, p. 230.

(2) THE PRAYER FOR HELP

My[78] *Father, if it be possible, let this cup pass away from me; nevertheless, not as I will, but as thou wilt* (Mt 26_{39}).

Abba, Father, all things are possible to thee; remove this cup from me; yet not what I will but what thou wilt (Mk 14_{36}).

Father, if thou art willing, remove this cup from me; nevertheless not my will, but thine, be done (Lk 22_{42}).

Later comes a second prayer:

My Father, if this cannot pass away unless I drink it, thy will be done (Mt 26_{42}).

We may assume that the Markan version is more original than the Matthaean: Matthew introduces modifications of no great importance for our purpose. They are, however, instructive, not as throwing any light on what really happened, but as showing how the story appeared to the more cautious and 'orthodox' mind of the writer of the First Gospel. He often softens the more human characteristics of Jesus into what the orthodoxy of his age thought more fitting for the Son of God, and this is such an instance. He omits 'Abba', a word which Mark is the only Evangelist to use.[79] He would indeed be interested in anything Jewish, but probably he felt that Abba was too intimate; or else he saw no point in the transliteration. He replaces 'All things are possible to thee; remove this cup from me' by 'If it be possible, let this cup pass from me', which is more tentative.[80] Not content with the spirit of resignation in the latter part of the prayer, he wishes to make the attitude of Jesus plain from the start. Not content with this, he puts a slightly different prayer on the lips of Jesus the second time, where Mark simply says He said the same words. The note of obedience and resignation is here even more strongly stressed. This throws no light on what Jesus said: it does show that the Markan narrative was held to be a little startling; it is all the more likely to be significant.

78 Some MSS. omit 'My'.

79 The statement of Cadoux, p. 32, that Matthew substitutes 'My Father' depends on the reading.

80 He also improves Mark's grammar. ὡς is better than τί: but see Taylor, *Mark*, ad loc.

The prayer in Luke is roughly similar, but the passage as a whole is different, and is no doubt taken from Luke's special source for the Passion-Narrative. The prayer, like Mark's, contains an imperative 'take away', but, like Matthew, he qualifies it with a condition, not however Matthew's 'if it be possible', but 'if thou art willing'.[81] Luke also has a more vivid account of the Agony, and mentions the Angel.[82] There is no account of the prayer being repeated. In the prayer itself the phrase, 'not my will, but thine, be done' is closer than the other Evangelists to the usual (Matthaean) version of the Lord's Prayer: not, however, to the Lukan version.[83]

Behind the source-criticism lies the question of the genuineness of the prayer. It has been asked, 'somewhat prosaically', says Rawlinson,[84] how the disciples could have known what Jesus said when He was away from them or when they were asleep. It is not the kind of prayer which Jesus would be likely to narrate subsequently to the disciples. The fact that He was a short distance away might not prove an insuperable difficulty,[85] but the fact that they were asleep is awkward[86]. Deissmann[87] suggests 'it is not the prayer that is a secondary feature of the story, but the sleeping disciples. That detail has probably arisen through a misunderstanding of the word of Jesus: 'Watch and pray, that ye enter not into temptation.' It has been assumed that the command, 'watch', was to be taken literally, and the conclusion was drawn from it that the disciples had already slept.[88] H. G. Wood

[81] But the variants are here important. Some of the authorities for the Western text alter the order of the clauses; more important is the doubt about παρένεγκε (remove). Some MSS. read the infinitive παρενεγκεῖν. Then the translation could only be: 'If thou art willing to remove this cup from me.' The sentence must then be regarded as broken off (aposiopesis). This represents a softening tendency in so far as it avoids the imperative, and that may be the origin of the variant; but it is hardly a successful softening, for an aposiopesis would suggest that our Lord changed His attitude. The third reading παρενεγκαι (we omit the accent in order not to prejudge the issue), found, among other MSS., in Sinaiticus, might be 'remove' or 'to remove', according to whether it is parsed as First Aorist Infinitive Active or First Aorist Imperative Middle.

[82] But some MSS. insert it in Matthew instead, or omit it.

[83] So Creed, ad loc.

[84] Rawlinson, ad loc.; cf. Dibelius, p. 60.

[85] So Matthew and Mark, but Luke has 'about a stone's throw', which is certainly difficult.

[86] But see Manson, *Teaching*, p. 104n.

[87] Deissmann, *Religion*, p. 58 n.4.

[88] Another suggestion is that the prayer was overheard by the young man who subsequently fled naked (Mk 14_{51-2}), who may have been near at hand at the time. The curious irrelevance of the two verses about him, found only in Mark, further

suggests that the disciples 'must have been spiritually close enough to interpret the scene aright'.[89] This is tantamount to asserting that we do not know what words Jesus used. A quite different line is taken by Deissmann, who says 'The content of the prayer in Gethsemane fits so badly into a dogmatic conception of Christ, that we can scarcely assume that in the later times of the Christ-cult it was first ascribed to Jesus'.[90] That this is not a merely subjective impression is shown by the fact that the author of Matthew felt it necessary to soften it. This tells strongly in favour of its genuineness. Why should the early Church invent what the early Church found it necessary to soften? We may conclude that the words are probably genuine, in their Markan form.

The occurrence of a somewhat similar passage in John 12_{27-8}, though not placed in Gethsemane, is some confirmation of the synoptic story.[91]

We take then the Markan form of the prayer to be genuine; it remains to consider its contents. The context is clear enough. The shrinking which Jesus felt we can well understand. Such crises evoke fervent prayer. This is 'the highest moment in the history of prayer'.[92] Its importance lies in the light which it throws upon a well-known controversy: should we in prayer ask God for particular goods? Some will pray for spiritual blessings, as for the conversion of a friend, but not for something 'material', such as success in an examination; some will pray for good health, but not for good weather; some will ask something for themselves, but not for others. But behind all these distinctions there lies the question: 'What is the use of asking God for anything? He has already made up His mind what is best for us.'

'We are not, in our prayers, trying to suggest to God something He has not thought of. That would plainly be ridiculous. Nor are we trying to change His mind. That would be an enterprise blasphemous

suggest that he was Mark himself. This is a possible, but precarious, hypothesis; if so, Mark must himself have contributed the prayer to the oral tradition before he wrote his Gospel; otherwise the Lukan account would have had to be wholly dependent on Mark's Gospel, which it is not.

[89] H. G. Wood in (ed.) Peake, *A Commentary on the Bible*, p. 697, quoted with approval by Rawlinson.

[90] Deissmann, *Religion*, p. 58, n.4 (on p. 59). cf. Taylor, *Mark*, p. 551, who strongly argues for its historicity.

[91] cf. Temple, *Readings in St John's Gospel*, p. 198. 'What took place in the Garden was not an isolated crisis; it was the focus of a lifelong temptation and of a lifelong victory over temptation.' cf. *infra*, p. 199.

[92] Heiler, p. 123; cf. 228-9.

in the attempt, and calamitous in the accomplishment. He knows what we want before we ask it. Then why ask?'[93]

This question has received two main answers. The first is given by the prophetic tradition. Prayer of this type is full of petition, even for material goods. No doubt in origin such prayer was quite naïve. The philosophical difficulties did not occur to the mind. If those who uttered these prayers had been asked whether they hoped that God would change His mind, they would have said 'Yes', and perceived no difficulty. Though the concept of the immutability of God is at least as old as Plato,[94] it is by no means a part of the Hebraic conception of God, though indeed the Hebrews had the idea of 'steadfastness'. But in the course of Christian history, immutability has found a place among the attributes of God. Many would think this a part of the baleful influence which they deem Greek philosophy to have exercised on Christianity: but even so, we cannot quite go back to the naïve attitude of former days. The supporters of the prophetic tradition, however, are ready with new lines of defence. 'There may be blessings which are only effectively blessings to those who are in the right condition of mind.'[95] Or again, the statement that God has already decided what to do may be met by the reply that God has decided to do something through your prayers if you pray. The prayer is a channel for God's blessing (not merely to yourself) just as is some physical action. But why does God withhold a blessing, which He surely longs to give, simply because a prayer is omitted? One might equally well ask why He withholds a blessing such as physical health, simply because a necessary surgical operation is omitted. God's way of 'waiting' till we do something is simply part of His dealings with our fallen world. Even if it be asserted, in Calvinistic fashion, that He Himself ordains whether we perform or omit the prayer or other action, the point is not affected that petitionary prayer may be necessary for the receipt of a blessing. Nor does the consideration that God foreknows, or, more accurately, knows in eternity or in His transcendence of time whether we shall omit it or not substantially affect the issue.[96] A case is thus made out for petitionary and intercessory prayer. Moreover, it is asserted that

[93] Temple, *Christian Faith and Life*, p. 107; cf. Farmer, pp. 127-44, 260-74; C. F. D'Arcy on 'Prayer (Christian, Theological)', *ERE*, X.171-7. See *infra*, p. 82, on Mt 6_8.

[94] *Republic*, 380. [95] Temple, loc. cit. [96] cf. Lewis, *Miracles*, pp. 208-16.

petition is the heart of prayer (*beten* is akin to *bitten*), and that the proposed alternatives are hardly prayer at all. Better to be a somewhat naïve man of prayer than a philosophic doubter who does not really pray at all. It is fitting that our relation to God should be that of children to a Father, and indeed in the relation of children to their earthly father we see a parallel to what happens in prayer. The father is glad to hear the requests of the child, made in a spirit of loving trust, even though he was already aware of the need and intended to meet it.

The other main answer comes from the mystical tradition. There is, it is claimed, something assertive and selfish about petitions; the heart of prayer is adoration and communion with God. We do not think highly of an earthly friendship in which the sole conversation consists of requests made by one to the other. No one should wish to set his will against the will of God: the only proper form of prayer about a particular point is that God's will may be done. Submission and resignation are the dominant notes. To make any suggestions as to what we should wish the will of God to be only qualifies the surrender which we make. Far better to confine oneself to submission. So the argument runs.

On this controversy, this prayer of Jesus, wrung from a heart too deeply moved to be thinking of controversy, affords the perfect comment. The Old Testament (says Heiler)[97] knows nothing of such prayer; prayer which begins with a wish and ends with surrender to the will of God is a creation of Jesus. He begins (in the Markan version) with 'Abba Father', an expression of confident trust. We have already commented, in connexion with the 'Prayer of Joy' on Jesus' use of the term 'Father': we have here to add that the word 'Abba', found only here in the Gospels, made such an impression on the mind of Paul that he twice used the Aramaic word transliterated (Ro 8_{15}, Gal 4_{6}).[98] This prayer may thus be said to begin with a note of intimacy and confidence. Then there is an expression of confidence that God is able to answer His request; then the request itself, expressed with a plain imperative; then submission to the will of God. Submission it may

[97] This point is well made by Heiler, pp. 266-7, but unfortunately he ignores source-criticism and uses the inferior, i.e. the Matthaean, version, which is the most commonly quoted in the Church today; the modern Church shares the reluctance of the early Church to believe in the Humanity of Christ.

[98] cf. Deissmann, *Religion*, p. 54; Taylor, *Mark*, p. 553; Kittel, *KTW*, I.5; *supra*, p. 37.

be called, or even resignation, but it cannot be called sad or reluctant resignation; it breathes the spirit of confidence. Yet we may believe that the prayer was repeated (apparently three times, though that is not explicit in the Markan version), not for emphasis, but because it was not until the third time that Jesus had firmly overcome temptation and made the sacrifice complete.

This prayer was, in a memorable phrase of Deissmann,[99] 'an appeal for help so poignant and yet so simple that the gods of Oedipus and the God of Job never received one like it, a petition and at the same time a submission'. Yet it is a common type of prayer in Christian piety, both in the course of prayers of a mystical type and among prayers of a prophetic type. How then is the prayer to be classified? Which of the two conceptions of prayer does it support? In one sense it effects a synthesis, as its imitation in all types of subsequent Christian piety shows; in another sense it transcends the distinction. It cannot be said simply to lend its support to the prophetic type of prayer, for, as we have seen, it strikes a note hitherto unheard in prayers of that type. On the other hand we have here more than a juxtaposition of phrases, the first of the prophetic and the second of the mystical type. The prayer does not take, as it were, a neutral position in this conflict. We must agree that Heiler applies his own principles of classification quite rightly when he implies[100] that though all Christian mystics have seen in this prayer the prototype of Christian resignation, it is fundamentally of the prophetic type. Resignation, whether in a Stoic, a Buddhist, or a Christian mystic, is passive, negative, an emotionless lack of will. There is indeed a certain inconsistency in even speaking at all of the submission to the will of God, for it is only in prophetic piety that will is strongly ascribed to God. The prayer of Jesus, on the other hand, is an active, positive trust in the will of God. He who thus prays, in the prophetic manner, as modified by Christ, actually asserts his own will in a spontaneous way, but subordinates it to the will of God. The prayer of Jesus might be described as an example of mystical piety if it consisted only of the last clause; but the typical prayer of mysticism would never contain the first part of this prayer. Jesus' prayer is a paradoxical combination of two indispensable elements.

We may indeed wonder whether this paradox is not connected

[99] Deissmann, *Religion*, p. 58. [100] Heiler, p. 269.

with paradoxes even more fundamental and profound. We are concerned here with the whole question of Jesus' temptations. The more we abandon the idea that this was a passive resignation (and surely the whole trend of the narrative, rightly called the Agony in the Garden, supports such an abandonment), the more it is plain that we have here a real struggle with temptation. The assertion of His own will which the first part of this prayer contains involves temptation, and, had it been persisted in, would have been sinful; yet we can hardly say that the mere expression of it was sinful. It was nevertheless an expression of the Humanity of Christ. So we go on to the question, canvassed by the Cappadocian Fathers and more recently, in a surprising way, by Barth, whether Christ assumed fallen or unfallen human nature.[101] To say that He had unfallen nature, but was tempted *ab extra* in the same way as 'Adam' is hardly a complete solution; but there are grave difficulties about referring to His Human Nature as fallen. But this is, of course, not an isolated question about Christ; it is a form of the fundamental Christological question. As it is raised here in connexion with His human will, we may recall that the Church condemned Monothelitism, and that the Catholic Faith is that Christ had two wills, one divine and one human, the human always perfectly following the divine. It is easy to condemn the artificiality of such a formula; but it is clear that a serious question lay at the heart of the controversy. The two parts of this prayer do indeed suggest two wills; but the weakness of the formula lies in the fact that it does not even hint at the cost of the surrender; indeed this prayer shows that the human will did not 'always' follow the divine, but sometimes expressed, if not asserted, itself first.

It may be said that all this only emphasizes the point that Christ's case is not ours; His Deity sets Him apart, and we cannot discuss the operations of our wills, or our use of petitionary prayer, in the same categories at all. There are two answers to this. First, as Donald Baillie has shown,[102] the paradox of grace in ourselves is a derivative paradox which is not unconnected with the greater paradox of the Incarnation itself. It is clearly not Baillie's intention to present a minimizing Christology, or to say that the Incarnation is but the supreme instance of something common among men, but we sometimes fear that that might be the

[101] cf. D. M. Baillie, p. 16. [102] D. M. Baillie, pp. 106-32.

ultimate issue of this line of thought. Probably, however, a stress on the word 'derivative' robs this criticism of its sting. Some words which he applies to Christology could indeed be applied to this question. 'A toned-down Christology is absurd. It must be all or nothing—all or nothing on both the divine and the human side.'[103] So it is with this prayer; neither clause is toned down. To stress only the first clause would be Nestorian or Pelagian; to stress only the second would be Docetic and Monophysite.[104] Secondly, if the connexion suggested by Donald Baillie be denied, the argument can proceed equally well *a fortiori*. If Jesus, with His perfect submission to the Father, yet found it necessary to express His own human will first, how much more shall *we* find it necessary? The servant is not above his Lord, and it is not right for us to try to outdo Christ in this respect. We may moreover deduce that, whether or not this human will flows from the possession of fallen human nature, the expression of it does not in itself involve actual sin. It is of course true that in our case the nature from which the will flows certainly is sinful, and therefore the expression of it in prayer, like all else that we do, is tainted with sin. But that is no reason why we should refrain from thus expressing our will; and that, not because 'a little sin keeps us humble', as the opponents of Methodist views of perfection like Zinzendorf and Forsyth declare, but because such expression is not itself sinful.

This prayer has proved to be the most instructive of the prayers of Jesus. We learn from it that petition is by no means to be excluded from Christian prayer. 'Ask, till true prayer makes you forget your asking', said Schleiermacher.[105] The stress on asking is right, but the antithesis between asking and 'true prayer' is misleading. Paradoxically one must combine the naïve expression of one's own will with an active, joyful surrender to the will of God. This paradox lies at the heart of Christian prayer, and thus all sound instruction on how to pray is also necessarily paradoxical.

[103] D. M. Baillie, p. 132.

[104] But we must not allow 'motif-research' to run away with us. It does not follow that an Alexandrian theology goes hand in hand with mystical religion, and an Antiochene with prophetic.

[105] The word-play is clearer in the original, in which 'prayer' is akin to 'ask'. *Bittet, bis das wahre Gebet euch des Bittens vergessen macht. Predigten*, I.35. I owe the quotation to Heiler, *Das Gebet*, p. 601 (not in E.T.). cf. Herrmann quoted in *Das Gebet*, p. 389 (part of it in E.T., p. 271).

(3) THE PRAYER OF INTERCESSION

Father, forgive them; for they know not what they do (Lk 23_{34}).

This, like the fifth prayer in this series, is to be found only in Luke, and forms part of his special passion-narrative.

It is unique among these prayers in that serious doubts are cast on its authenticity by textual criticism. It is omitted by ℵ^a B D* Θ and some other Greek MSS., the Old Latin a b^b and some other versions, notably the Sinaitic Syriac. But it is found in ℵ* and in many Greek MSS., including the important A C L, many versions, including the Old Latin MSS. b* c e, and the Curetonian Syriac: it is also attested by many Fathers. This is a fairly equal division of evidence. The Egyptian evidence is divided (B against ℵ): so is the Antiochene (Syriac versions); so is the Western (D a against b* c e). It is true that the Caesarean tradition (Θ) is powerfully against it. Thus on textual grounds the omission is not certain. Is the omission or the insertion of such a prayer the more explicable? It was argued by Harnack, supported by Streeter,[106] that the prayer was deleted because the early Church found it hard to forgive the Jews, and indeed concluded from their sufferings that God had not forgiven them. To this defence it is sometimes added that the real application of the words was to the soldiers. On the other hand it may be said that 'the omission of a prayer so sublime and so Christ-like seems less probable than its insertion'.[107] It has also been argued: 'The "ordinary" Christian knows that, if anyone hurts him without knowing what he has done, he is generally closer to the mind of Christ if he does not express his forgiveness.'[108] But the crucifixion of Christ was hardly a slight accident to which there was no need to call attention; they did not know what they were doing, but they ought to have known. Moreover, our Lord was not telling them that He forgave them. He was praying for their forgiveness.[109] The prayer is of course in harmony with our Lord's teaching (Mt 5_{44}), and may therefore have been invented to illustrate His command; but the words 'they know not what they do' go beyond that which the teaching of Jesus would itself

[106] Streeter, pp. 138-9.
[107] Creed, ad loc.
[108] A. H. Dammers, in *Theology*, LII.138 (April 1949).
[109] cf. H. A. Blair, in *Theology*, LII.224-5 (June 1949).

suggest.[110] It seems more likely to be due to His insight than to that of the early Church.[111]

The content of this prayer calls for little comment. The contrast between its spirit and that of many of the Psalms is obvious. Few would be so bold as to criticize these words as going too far; yet the Christian Church has not always gone beyond lip-service to them. There have, however, been some famous examples of such prayers; on the lips of the martyrs, such words had in them sometimes a certain proud defiance; perhaps the most beautiful instance is the first, that of the first martyr Stephen: 'Lord, lay not this sin to their charge' (Ac 7_{60}).[112] The Christian here receives a warrant for intercessory prayer. God is eager to forgive them; yet it is right for us to pray for it. We have also here a warrant for praying for those who are not Christians. The liturgical prayer of Christendom has been a good deal influenced by Christ's words, as recorded in the Fourth Gospel: 'I pray not for the world, but for those whom thou hast given me' (Jn. 17_9). Since Christianity became an official religion, this has not imposed any very great restriction. Thus, for instance, the intercessory prayer at the Holy Communion in the Anglican and Methodist rites is not a prayer for the Church *and* for those in authority *and* for those in distress; as the bidding shows, it is a prayer for 'Christ's Church militant here on earth', and those in authority or in distress are assumed to belong to it. How far this practice ought to continue in our present so-called post-Christian society is a further question, and one that is complicated by the question of Baptism. Traditionally, however, the prayer for the Church has covered everyone except the Jews and the heathen, and it has often not been felt necessary to pray for them very regularly. Our Lord's example has not, however, entirely been forgotten,[113] and Good Friday is thus marked in the Roman, Anglican, and Methodist rites by prayers of this kind. The tone of the Roman prayer

110 Creed, ad loc. points out that the idea that ignorance is a ground for forgiveness is not infrequent in ancient literature, but the transposition of that thought into such a prayer is in peculiar harmony with the spirit of Christ.

111 cf. Deissmann, *Religion*, pp. 59-60; Heiler, *Das Gebet*, p. 534 (note 104; not in E.T.).

112 To argue that this prayer shows the early Church to have possessed sufficient insight to have invented such a prayer for the lips of Jesus begs the question entirely, for if our Lord's prayer was genuine, then that of Stephen is not due to spontaneous insight, but was no doubt a conscious echo of it.

113 Nor that of Stephen. The Anglican Collect for his Feast refers to, though it does not exactly follow, his example. And cf. *infra*, p. 202.

('who repellest not from thy mercy even the perfidious Jews') perhaps leaves something to be desired.[114] However that may be, our duty to pray even for our enemies is clear.

(4) THE PRAYER OF DESPAIR

My God, my God, why hast thou forsaken me? (Mt 27_{46}, Mk 15_{34}).

This is found in Mark, and in Matthew, who no doubt took it from Mark: it is not in Luke, who follows his own Passion-narrative. As would be expected, the MSS. vary considerably in the spelling of those words which are foreign to Greek. These variations sort themselves out into two main alternatives, representing the Hebrew and the Aramaic forms of the words. It is a difficult question which Christ used, but not important for our purpose.[115] We may also leave aside the eccentric variant in the Apocryphal Gospel of Peter,[116] 'My power, my power, thou hast forsaken me', which involves a very curious Christology, but is not likely to be genuine. Much more important is it that in Mark, D, supported by some of the Old Latin MSS., has 'reproached' (ὠνείδισας) instead of 'forsaken' (ἐγκατέλιπες), and it can be argued that Mark's transliteration of the Aramaic corresponds to the Aramaic word which that reading would involve.[117] Moreover, such a variant is not likely to have been invented. It is of course a mis-quotation if Jesus was quoting Psalm 22, as is usually assumed, but we cannot be sure that He was. It is true that the double 'My God' is reminiscent of it, but even this is not certain; the MSS. are indeed almost overwhelmingly in favour of it, and the omission of the repetition by two important MSS. (B 565) is usually regarded as an accidental haplography. But it seems just possible that what Jesus said was, 'My God, why hast thou reviled me?', and that this was subsequently assimilated to the Psalm. On the whole, however, it seems more likely that the common reading is correct, and this we shall assume.

The verse is one of Schmiedel's pillar passages, and is quite unlikely to have been invented.[118] The fact that Luke, after he had

[114] The Roman Mass on that day is archaic in form, so that these or similar intercessions originally stood in the Mass daily. But their retention on Good Friday, though due to various reasons (for the liturgy on that day has many peculiarities), is perhaps partly due to Christ's word from the Cross.

[115] cf. Deissmann, *Religion*, p. 61; W. F. Lofthouse in *Expository Times*, LIII.188-92.

[116] *Ev. Petri*, V.19.

[117] Cadoux, p. 258; cf. Lofthouse, op. cit.

[118] But Dibelius, *Religion*, p. 59, thinks it may be interpretative rather than historical.

read Mark, did not see fit to insert it in his Gospel strengthens this line of argument. Difficult as the passage is, we feel that some deep secret is contained there, and we should not wish for its omission. This line of defence is however challenged by those who say that we are to think not of the opening verse, but of the whole of Psalm 22. Whether or not that is a true explanation of the words if they are genuine, it would be a very precarious basis on which to invent them. It would be certain to cause difficulties and misunderstandings.[119]

If the words are genuine, what do they mean? This question has been widely discussed, because the theory of the Atonement largely hangs on the answer. There is hardly any major theologian who has not given his view of these words. An excellent summary of the present state of the question will be found in Taylor.[120] We shall treat first that which he takes second, the view that the whole Psalm is here meant or implied. It is sometimes said that Christ simply quoted the first words, meaning the whole Psalm, as we might say *Te Deum*. (This is to be distinguished from the view, already considered, that it was invented by the early Church with that in mind.) Now no doubt our Lord, even in that moment of anguish, was well aware of the context; and, even on the gloomiest view, there may be held to be some undercurrent of hope. Nevertheless it seems likely that He chose the verse which most clearly represented what He felt at that moment. Incidentally, this is the classic example of the use of a quotation in a prayer which is yet highly spontaneous.[121] Unless therefore we give up the attempt to ascertain what was in the mind of Christ,[122] we must conclude that He was referring to a desolation, real or vicarious or imagined. Leaving out, for the moment, the second of these possibilities, we have this difficulty, trenchantly put by Lofthouse: if we say that Jesus was wrong, in thinking that He was forsaken, then at the supreme moment of His ministry He was deluded; and we can hardly know when He can be trusted to be right. But that He was in fact forsaken by God is hardly credible. That last view has been so much attacked that

[119] cf. Taylor, *JS*, pp. 157-63; *Mark*, pp. 593-4.

[120] Taylor, *JS*, loc. cit.

[121] Heiler, p. 236.

[122] Instances in Taylor, *JS*, p. 162. We should perhaps distinguish from this the view of Cadoux that it was a cry of anguish, spontaneously cast into familiar words, throwing no clear light on the death of Jesus.

it is hardly necessary to add to the criticisms here, though we must not forget that it has the support of powerful names, including that of Dale.[123] Moreover, the evidence of the other Words from the Cross shows that the period of desolation, if such it was, was brief, perhaps only momentary: and, further, it was not the concluding mood. If our salvation really does depend on Jesus bearing our sin in the sense that He is literally abandoned by God, it seems strange that such an experience was so short-lived and isolated. 'Why did human sin fail to produce this effect on Him before? . . . And would the sacrifice of obedience have been more complete if this crowning bitterness had not been so mercifully transient?'[124] And had He, at the moment of death, really emerged from the central, crucial experience?

We are left with the possibility, usually neglected, that Jesus was entering in some way into that experience of dereliction which is the lot of sinners. The word 'vicarious' has been used to cover this theory, but it is not essential to it. Lofthouse is clearly no lover of the phrase 'vicarious penitence',[125] which is indeed one of the least defensible phrases in R. C. Moberly's *Atonement and Personality*. He therefore takes the view that Christ entered into the experience of being alienated from God, though He knew no alienation: 'Such an imaginative *Einfühlung* does not imply actual dereliction'. He quotes Ryder Smith[126] as saying 'He is so closely one with the alienated that He experiences their alienation' and adds: 'But it is their alienation; not His.' We might equally well add: 'But He does experience it.' Taylor stands more fully in the Moberly tradition, and says: 'Jesus so closely identified Himself with sinners, and experienced the horror of sin to such a degree, that for a time the closeness of His communion with the Father was broken, so that His face was obscured and He seemed to be forsaken by Him.'[127]

The positions of Lofthouse and Taylor, not really so divergent as they might appear, may be strengthened by the point clearly

[123] It often goes hand in hand with what we believe, despite Calvin, to be a clear misinterpretation of 'He descended into Hell'.

[124] Lofthouse, op. cit.

[125] Lofthouse, op. cit., p. 190 n.1, makes the most of the disagreement between the Moberlys, father and son. After all, they were united on the main issue.

[126] C. Ryder Smith, p. 254; quoted in Lofthouse, op. cit., p. 192.

[127] Taylor, *JS*, p. 162. Note the 'seemed', which brings this position closer to that of Lofthouse than might at first sight appear.

made by Heiler that complaint is a common feature of prophetic prayer. Numerous examples may be found in the Old Testament.[128] It is indeed one of the most striking examples of the naïve spontaneity which characterizes that type of prayer. It is characteristic of human childlike prayer to complain of desolation. Jesus was truly Man, and He shared this attitude with other men. It is indeed hard to understand how this was possible, just as it is hard to understand how He was tempted, but it is part of the greater paradox of the Incarnation. We have already dealt with this problem in connexion with another aspect of 'naïve' prophetic prayer, the frank expression of His own wishes: 'Remove this cup from me.' There the following words, 'Not what I will, but what thou wilt', modify the total impression, without constituting a withdrawal. Similarly, this prayer must be read in the light of other cries from the Cross, notably: 'Father, into thy hands I commend my spirit.' Nevertheless, the complaint was perfectly real. It was not a mere demonstration of solidarity with men coming from One who knew that He was in communion with God all the time. It was an actual effect of His self-identification with men in their sin. The penalty of sin was not simply transferred to Him, but He entered fully into the situation with all its penal consequences. Yet the other side of the paradox remains: in all this He did not sin.

The linking of this to the Incarnation throws light on the momentariness of this experience. Jesus was always and in all things God and Man. Yet, as many writers on Christology have observed, we discern His Deity in such facts as that He worked miracles, His Humanity in such facts as that He prayed or was hungry.[129] This is often taken to involve a somewhat artificial theory of 'alternating consciousnesses', but that does not necessarily follow.[130] It is quite possible to maintain that His consciousness was always consistently divine-human, while admitting (what it would be difficult to deny) that the aspect of His consciousness most apparent, at least to the observer, was now the divine, now the human. Thus the question why Jesus did not feel

[128] Heiler, *Das Gebet*, pp. 359-60 (more briefly in E.T., pp. 240-1), who quotes Jer 14_{19}, 15_{18}, Hab 1_3, Ps 43_2, 88_{14}, as well as, of course, Ps 22, which Jesus is here quoting. From such questions we pass to instances where positive charges are brought, e.g. Jer 4_{10}, 20_7. We omit Job, which is rather a special case.

[129] cf. *Tome of Leo*, end of cap. IV.

[130] cf. Quick, p. 124.

this dereliction before is to some extent undermined. Jesus as the Second Person of the Trinity was always in the most intimate communion with God the Father; as Man, he enjoyed communion in prayer; and yet as One who had identified Himself as fully as a sinless Being could with sinful man, He was always cut off from God. We must not suppose that sin now produced this effect for the first time. We have already seen another prayer in which the human side is clear; we know that His life was one of temptation: in so far as He was a Man of sorrows and acquainted with grief, it was because of this crushing burden. This is not as difficult as it may sound, for human experience affords faint analogies. We know what it is to have alternating moods of joy and sorrow: we also know what it is to have an emotion which strangely combines the two. Indeed there are nearer parallels, such as writers of the 'vicarious penitence' school have used. He who seeks by love and sympathy to win back a degraded sinner has a joy, as well as an innocence (despite the fact that we are all sinners), which the sinner lacks, and yet he feels something which is best called 'vicarious shame', an expression which is not open to the same objections as 'vicarious penitence' and is perhaps our best clue to this experience of Jesus. (By this we do not mean to suggest a minimizing Christology, to the effect that the two natures in Christ are simply analogous to two human moods or that Christ differs only in degree from a good man who sympathizes with sinners. But human nature, which for all its corruption is yet the recipient of grace, may be some faint shadow of this profound mystery.) But however paradoxical and complex this state may be, one cannot always give equal expression to both sides of it. In the case of men, we should speak of varying moods, and there seems no reason why we should not say the same of the Perfect Man. To suppose that He merely *displayed* different sides of the matter to the beholder would have a somewhat docetic flavour. He would indeed be bound to express such a paradoxical state in varying words: He could not be for ever employing the figure of speech known as oxymoron. Thus even if the relation between communion and dereliction in the mind of Jesus was ever constant, He would give expression first to one and then to the other. It is, however, simpler to think that there was in His consciousness an actual variation in emphasis. But the point is that both were continually present; even the strongest expression of the one did not (we may reverently conjecture) eliminate from His consciousness altogether the other. Thus in this cry from the Cross, our Lord may indeed have touched a new depth of woe; He may have realized fully for the first time what Incarnation involved; but it was not (as some seem to imply, evoking very natural protests from others) a sudden reversal of all that He had hitherto known, a sudden cessation of a hitherto unclouded intimacy. It was the bitterest dregs of the Cup that He had begun to drink as soon as He became incarnate, when He first 'emptied himself'.

And as His life had never been free from what we may call an undercurrent of dereliction, so is this utterance not free from an undercurrent of communion. We must admit that, not unnaturally, the word 'Father' is here lacking. This is the only prayer of Jesus, including those in the Fourth Gospel, where it does not occur—a striking testimony to the intimacy which Jesus usually enjoyed.[131] But He still uses the vocative 'My God'. While it is a clear sign that the relation of Jesus to the Father (despite the unity of substance) was not one of identity as many of the mystics felt it to be, yet it has not sunk, under the stress of dereliction, to a third-personal relationship. Jesus does not say, 'God has forsaken me', still less of course draw atheistic inferences from His feelings. The fact that He prays at all is proof that He regards God as accessible to His prayer. This is not of course peculiar to Jesus. It is part of the whole paradox of prophetic complaint.

What may we deduce as to the proper nature of Christian prayer? We may reflect, both here and in connexion with Gethsemane: 'It is enough for the disciple that he be as his master' (Mt 10_{25}).[132] Yet we may also remember that our Lord's prayer in the Garden changed the course of prophetic piety. Here indeed on the Cross His utterance is not of a new type. It has not in fact eliminated this kind of prayer from Christendom: so long as the Psalms are the model of Christian devotion, and indeed form a large part of its material, such prayers are likely to continue. Nevertheless some elements in the Psalter now cause a good deal of embarrassment to a Christian congregation,[133] and their use can only be defended by the employment of mystical and allegorical exegesis. There has indeed been some diminution

[131] Heiler, *Das Gebet*, p. 401; not in E.T.

[132] cf. *supra*, p. 46.

[133] cf. John Wesley, who in the Preface to *The Sunday Service of the Methodists*, said that many of them are 'highly improper for the mouths of a Christian congregation.'

of this kind of prayer; yet it is remarkable that the Reformers included complaint among the proper contents of prayer.[134]

The conclusion that the Christian may complain of desolation follows also from the nature of the work of Christ. On the view, indeed, known as penal substitution, Christ suffered pain on the Cross instead of us that we might be free from pain. But two objections to this are well set out by Quick.[135] The sufferings of Christ are not the same as those which repentant sinners on this theory escape. For physical pain and death they do not escape, and as for the rest, 'However we interpret the cry, "My God, why hast thou forsaken me?", it can hardly be denied that the suffering here expressed is that of a love which feels itself deserted by God—and that is precisely the kind of suffering which the hardened sinner could never know'. Secondly, the effect of the Cross on the Christian is not simply the negative one that he is relieved of something which otherwise he would have had to do or undergo. Such considerations have rightly (we think) led Quick and others to the theory which in various forms is known as the representative, sacrificial, or vicarious penitence theory. On this view Christ made an offering in which we are to participate.[136] Whatever we may think of the actual phrase 'vicarious penitence', it seems true that Jesus submitted to this experience, not as a Substitute instead of us, but as a Representative on our behalf. Thus it is to be expected that Christians should share the desolation, and indeed at the outset of the Christian life, the Christian does often pass through a season of penitence and desolation before he is assured of salvation. He is crucified with Christ. It might, however, be argued that this is but the initial experience, and that what follows is of a different kind. The Christian life itself, it might be said, is one of joy and assurance. This is partly true; yet it is also a life of penitence. Methodists, who have laid the most stress both on Assurance and Perfection, have in Charles Wesley's hymns a testimony of the fact that the Christian life is an oscillation between penitence and assurance. The penitence

[134] The evidence that they said so is in Heiler, *Das Gebet*, p. 359 (not in E.T.). The actual examples quoted ibid. (E.T., pp. 240-1) are purely biblical, but there are later examples in *Das Gebet*, p. 382 (E.T., pp. 262-3), e.g. Luther: 'O God, dost Thou not hear? My God, art Thou dead? . . . Where art Thou, O my God?'

[135] Quick, pp. 228-9. There are of course other objections to this theory less immediately relevant to the present question.

[136] cf. Taylor, *ANTT*, pp. 292-3, and McLeod Campbell and R. C. Moberly there quoted.

of the Christian is very far from being a hopeless remorse, such as we may suppose that of Judas to have been. The penitence and the confidence are subtly intermingled; they are not mutually exclusive states: but it is inevitable that first one, then the other, should be expressed.[137] This is a paradox which is sometimes expressed by saying that we are not Christians, but we are continually becoming Christians. In this world we are always on the frontier, as it were, between darkness and light. We thus conclude that the Cry of Dereliction, though not to be artificially imitated by Christians, yet represents an element in prayer which Christians may rightly use. It was because of the world's sin that Christ felt forsaken: it is because of the world's sin and his own that the Christian feels forsaken, but it is no sin for him to express that feeling of being forsaken; and he is never forsaken altogether.

(5) THE PRAYER OF TRUST

Father, into thy hands I commend my spirit (Lk 23_{46}).

Luke's independent account of the Passion preserves this prayer, as it does Luke 23_{34}, Matthew and Mark mention a loud cry, but do not say what it was. There are no textual problems; it was undoubtedly part of the original text of Luke. It is possible, however, that it arises out of a pious attempt to find some words of which the loud cry might consist. Cadoux, though regarding it as historically reliable, yet regards it as 'somewhat more dubious'[138] than Luke 23_{34}. The fact that it is a more conventional prayer than the others makes it possible, though by no means certain, that it was subsequently ascribed to Jesus.

This prayer, like the last, is taken from a Psalm (31_5).[139] But one word is added, and the addition is that characteristic word which is in all the prayers of Jesus save one. 'These words, expressing the experience of the nation in extreme peril . . .', says Briggs,[140] 'have also been found appropriate in all ages to pious individuals, such as Polycarp, Bernard, Luther; for the generic experiences of Israel were, in the unfolding of the

[137] No doubt the Dark Night of the Soul is something similar, but that is an expression proper to mystical piety.

[138] Cadoux, p. 32. Dibelius, p. 61, thinks it part of an attempt to turn the story into something like a martyr-legend.

[139] The Hebrew has 'hand'. Luke's 'hands' follows LXX.

[140] Briggs, ad loc.

divine purpose of redemption, preparatory to the personal experiences of individuals'. This prayer breathes a very different spirit from that of the Cry of Dereliction, which does not, of course, occur in the same Gospel. Yet they can be reconciled, and in our treatment of that prayer we have sought to show that the combination of these two attitudes is part of the essential paradox of Christian prayer.

What have we learnt from the prayers of Jesus? They are in their brevity of form and in their content, of the prophetic rather than the mystical type. They show a spirit of intimacy which among the Jews had been unusual, but there is no trace of mystical absorption. They are deeply rooted in the Old Testament Scriptures. They combine a warm trust and confidence with an extreme frankness of utterance. They do not shrink from petition and intercession, including intercession for enemies. Their combination of petition with acceptance of the Divine Will is something new and creative in the history of prayer. This combination, like that of dereliction and trust, arises out of the paradox of the Incarnation, and yet points forward to the tensions which should mark the earnest prayer of all Christians.

CHAPTER THREE

THE SYNOPTIC GOSPELS (*continued*)

THE TEACHING OF JESUS ON PRAYER

WE turn now from the practice to the teaching of Jesus; and having considered already its general principles, proceed at once to particular passages, grouped according to sources.

Mark

As we should expect, we do not find a great deal in a source which is more concerned with the proclamation of the kingdom and with works of healing than with teaching.

In Mark 11_{22-5} there are three sayings on prayer, which have become attached to the story of the withered fig-tree (Mk $11_{12-14, 20-5}$). As for the sayings, 'The motives of composition are apologetic and catechetical. . . . The sayings themselves are genuine utterances of Jesus, but the manner in which they are introduced is artificial.'[1] The sayings begin

'*Have faith in God: verily I say to you that whosoever says to this mountain, Be taken up and cast into the sea, and does not doubt in his heart but has faith that what he says comes to pass, it will be done for him. Therefore I say to you, all things whatsoever you pray and ask for, have faith that you have received them, and you shall have them.*'

Probably the parable later recorded in Luke 13_{6-9} (where the fig-tree represents the Jews or Jerusalem) generated the story of the withered fig-tree;[2] the significance of this was then forgotten, but it was felt that some 'moral' must be attached. A recollection of a saying now in Luke 17_6 (which may have been available to Mark as a piece of floating oral tradition), not about the cursing, but about the removing of a tree, may have reminded Mark, by way of the idea of removal, of a piece of oral tradition about removing mountains. He awkwardly attached this, as if the point

[1] Taylor, *Mark*, p. 465.
[2] See Deissmann, *Religion*, pp. 98-100; Cadoux, p. 271 n.2; Taylor, *Mark*, pp. 458-9.

of the fig-tree story had always been believing prayer. Matthew presumably copied him (Mt 21_{21-2}), and tried to make the connexion clearer by writing 'If you have faith and doubt not, you shall not only do the thing of the fig-tree, but even if you say to this mountain, Be thou taken up and cast into the sea, it shall be done'. This is ingenious, for the connexion between the fig-tree and believing prayer is intrinsically difficult to make, but the expression 'the thing of the fig-tree' is as awkward in the Greek as it is in the English. But Matthew had also to deal with the passage about the removal of the tree, which he would find in Q. He kept the main form of it, including the reference to faith as a grain of mustard-seed, but replaced the tree by this mountain from Mark (Mt 17_{20}), so that he has the removal of the mountain twice. Mark, having heard of the removal of the tree in the oral tradition, and not having it before him in Q (which he did not possess), made no further use of it after it had suggested to him the connexion here.

This at least we may conjecture to have been the history of these sayings; however that may be, the references to the mountain and the fig-tree are instances of hyperbole.[3] J. Weiss draws attention to the phrase 'believe that ye have received them', i.e. that your request has been granted before ever your prayer is uttered, and adds 'The prayer, then, is after all not so much an attempt to bring influence to bear, so as to determine or alter God's purpose, as a trustful submission to God's hand.[4] This seems somewhat forced and takes this verse too literally: it would make no sense if literally applied to the mountain in the preceding verse. The words should be understood as a strong and hyperbolic exhortation to believing, prophetic, intercessory prayer.

The next verse in Mark (11_{25}) also concerns prayer:

'*And whenever you stand praying, forgive, if you have anything against anyone; that your Father also which is in heaven may forgive you your trespasses.*'

This has every appearance of being a disconnected logion, attached here only because it has the idea of prayer in common with the preceding verse, for in Matthew it is found in a different place and in a somewhat different form in connexion with the Lord's Prayer (Mt 6_{14}). (It reflects a knowledge of the Lord's

[3] Cadoux, p. 202 n.2. [4] Weiss, *Mark*, p. 179, cited by Rawlinson, ad loc.

Prayer and suggests that that prayer was known to Mark.)[5] The passage may have stood there in M. That also was probably not its original position; it was probably at first an isolated fragment. Its position here in Mark, however, has been quite appropriately chosen, 'as if to guard against the idea that the Divine resources available through prayer could be exploited for purposes other than those of love'.[6] The saying refers to the ethical background necessary to prophetic prayer,[7] and particularly to the requirement that we should forgive our fellows. Thus this verse and the preceding one, taken together, require faith and a forgiving spirit.

This ethical tendency is also clear in the depreciation of a purely external worship. A clear example of this is to be found in the words of a scribe, which our Lord approved: 'To love him [God] with all the heart, and with all the understanding, and with all the strength, and to love one's neighbour as oneself, is much more than all whole burnt offerings and sacrifices' (Mk 12_{33}). The passage is one of the few found only in Mark, but it would be precarious to draw any adverse inference from that. This view of the cult is in the prophetic tradition, and in harmony with the best teaching of the Old Testament, being reminiscent of 1 Samuel 15_{22}. It will be noticed that it does not actually condemn the cult; it merely gives it a secondary place.

A somewhat similar warning against an unethical external piety is contained in these words spoken against the scribes:

'*They that devour widows' houses and for a pretence make long prayers; these shall receive greater condemnation*' Mk 12_{40}.[8]

In the form in which Mark has it, the fact that the same Greek definite article covers both participles makes it quite clear that he is not attacking two separate sins of the scribes: the offence which He is attacking lies in the hypocrisy of making long prayers when engaged in evil conduct.

[5] Taylor, *Mark*, ad loc. [6] Rawlinson, ad loc.

[7] The next verse (Mk 11_{26}) is omitted by many MSS., and is probably a harmonizing addition, being similar to Mt 6_{15}.

[8] The general sense seems to require that the first part should go with what precedes rather than (by a different punctuation) with what follows; so we have an anacoluthon, avoided in some MSS. of Mark, as in Lk 20_{47}. (It is not in the best MSS. of Matthew, but occurs in some, either before or after Mt 23_{13}, in a form only slightly different from that in Luke, no doubt by assimilation from him: it is reckoned as Mt 23_{14}.) Possibly Mark wrote οι, meaning it was the relative pronoun οἵ, and then absent-mindedly thinking he had written the article οἱ, was betrayed into the anacoluthon that we find.

The Markan source also contains the Agony in the Garden. We have already considered the Prayers of Jesus on this occasion, but we must also note that the passage contains an exhortation addressed by Jesus to the disciples:

'*Watch and pray that you may not enter into temptation*' Mk 14_{38}.[9]

Prayer is here, as sometimes elsewhere, connected with watching. Now 'watch' (γρηγορεῖτε) might be taken to mean 'keep awake'. (Luke's 'Rise up' clearly sees no more than that.) It is, of course, clear that it had that sense in the preceding verse (37) 'Couldest thou not keep awake one hour?', but by a sort of play on words this is made the occasion for an eschatological exhortation, 'Watch (keep awake)', i.e. for the kingdom. γρηγορέω frequently bears this eschatological sense. To confine ourselves to this Gospel, we find it in 13_{35}, where there is just such a word-play with the literal meaning of the word. The doorkeeper in the Parable, in the previous verse, is bidden to watch, or keep awake, literally; and this is the basis for an exhortation to watch, 'for you do not know when the lord of the house is coming'. The context is quite clearly eschatological; and in this passage also some MSS. have an explicit reference to prayer (Mk 13_{33}).[10] Thus, to revert to 14_{38}, we may say that the exhortation to pray is eschatological, which is an important step forward in our investigation. Moreover, the content of the prayer (not the purpose, as some translations suggest[11]) is not to enter into temptation, and this also has eschatological connexions. Some indeed think that the word πειρασμός, 'temptation' or 'trial', always has reference to the tribulations that were expected to precede the coming of the kingdom; and this might be the meaning here, when the

[9] Mt 26_{41} is substantially the same. Lk 22_{46}, though following another account here, has 'Rise up and pray that etc.' But he also has, earlier in the same passage (verse 40), 'Pray not to enter into temptation'.

[10] After the words 'Take heed, watch' (here ἀγρυπνεῖτε), some MSS. add 'and pray'. As it is doubtful, I have not referred to it in my discussion of the Markan passages, except here. There is wide MSS. support for it, but it is lacking in the important B D k.

[11] In the English versions, as in the Greek editions, there is usually a comma after 'pray'. This is, of course, a possible construction, and in Attic Greek would be almost certainly the construction. Then προσεύχεσθε is used absolutely, and followed by a negative final clause 'lest ye enter'. But we are not bound by the punctuation of the editors, and we should probably delete the comma. Then the ἵνα clause is a substantival clause, the object of προσεύχεσθε, a quite possible way in Hellenistic Greek of expressing content or purport, in this case an indirect command. It is a fine point, as the purport and the purpose of a prayer are usually identical. Lk 22_{40} has the infinitive in a similar sentence, and this is surely not the infinitive of purpose.

passage is considered in the light of realized eschatology. In some other passages the word could hardly bear this meaning, and must simply mean 'trial' in a more general sense, 'a time of testing and crisis': and that equally well might be the meaning here.[12] The disciples were to watch for the coming kingdom: they would not be able to watch if they succumbed to temptation in the hour of trial. In either case, they are to watch, and thus prayer is set in an eschatological context.

The same source also contains a reference to the importance of prayer in exorcisms. To the question of the disciples why they had not been able to achieve the success which Jesus had achieved in this, He replies:

'*This kind can come out by nothing save by prayer*' Mk 9_{29}.[13]

Also in Mark (13_{18})[14] are the words 'Pray that it be not in the winter', referring to the flight which will be necessary amid the eschatological disasters. This is a striking example of a definite prayer enjoined for a particular 'material' blessing.

To sum up Mark's rather scanty teaching on prayer, Jesus refers to its theological, ethical, and eschatological setting. It springs from faith in God, it must not be combined with unsocial conduct, and it is accompanied by watching for the kingdom. Moreover, its character is strikingly intercessory. Every one of these points suggests prophetic rather than mystical piety. Here is no absorption. We have here a communion which, though intimate, is yet expectant.

Q

The source Q, as we might expect of a source consisting largely of the sayings of Jesus, contains some valuable treasures. After the Prayer of Joy with which we have already dealt, Jesus, turning to His disciples, as Luke records, said:

'*All things have been delivered to me by my Father, and no one knows the Son save the Father, nor does anyone know the Father save the Son, and anyone to whom the Son wills to reveal him*' Mt 11_{27}.

[12] cf. Cadoux, p. 256; Taylor, *Mark*, ad loc; *infra*, p. 76.

[13] It is not necessary for us to consider the genuineness of 'and fasting', added by some MSS. Matthew does not contain the sentence, save in some MSS., no doubt by assimilation, in a slightly altered form, from Mark (Mt 17_{21}). Matthew has instead the removal of the mountain (Mt 17_{20}), discussed *supra*, p. 59.

[14] cf. Mt 24_{20}.

'*All things have been delivered to me by my Father, and no one knows who is the Son save the Father, and who is the Father save the Son, and anyone to whom the Son wills to reveal him*' Lk 10_{22}.

Fortunately, this passage has been greatly discussed because of its importance for Christology. It is not therefore necessary to do more than to refer to the main results of the critical discussions.[15] There are practically no variants in the Greek MSS., and those in the Latin versions are very slight. But the patristic quotations are very various, particularly as regards the order of the clauses. But as this famous passage was probably usually quoted from memory, which is not so easy as it sounds, these variations may be easily explained; and there is not much modern support for such re-arrangements of the text as those of Harnack and Easton. Not only is the evidence for them extremely slight, but as Norden and others have shown, they upset the rhythm. Nor is there any real ground for attacking the genuineness of the passage. It is undoubtedly a Q passage, and it seems likely that the Matthaean form is the better, the variations in Luke being but slight stylistic improvements. The fact that it is, in the well-known phrase, like a meteorite from the Johannine sky is not in itself any reason for doubting its genuineness. Nor are the alleged parallels from other classes of literature. The Old Testament provides sufficient parallel to make the genuineness of the passage perfectly plausible.

Of the contents of the logion, the first clause is important for Christological purposes, but not for us. The next clause speaks of the Father's knowledge of the Son. That God knows men is nothing new. We may compare Amos 3_2; 'You only have I known of all the families of the earth'. It is therefore not surprising that He should be said to know the Son.[16] To be known of God is a mark of every Christian. More important for our purposes is the Son's knowledge of the Father. Two points are important here;

[15] The earlier discussions, the chief of which are those of Harnack, Weiss, Chapman, and Norden are summarized in the commentaries, and most admirably in McNeile, ad loc. See also Rawlinson, *The New Testament Doctrine of the Christ*, pp. 251-69; Dibelius, *From Tradition to Gospel*, pp. 279-83; Otto, pp. 393-5; Manson, *Teaching*, pp. 109-12; N. P. Williams, in *Expository Times*, LI.182-6, 215-20, which contains a full answer to Norden, and also to Dibelius; Taylor, *JS*, pp. 35-7 (to those whom he cites at p. 37 n.2, add Cadoux, p. 33); W. Manson, pp. 71-6, who deals also with Bultmann and Arvedson.

[16] cf. 1 Co 8_3, 13_{12}, Gal 4_9; *infra*, p. 165; cf. the use of the noun γνῶσις in Ro 11_{33}.

the Mediatorship of the Son, and the use of the word 'know'. The former point is of supreme importance to Christology, but only on the verge of our task. We are concerned with communion with God in general, and not with the respective parts (to put it crudely) played by the Persons of the Trinity; with the mode of the communion, not with its *terminus* within the Godhead. Nevertheless it is worth pointing out that the highest possible place is here ascribed to the Son. John Baillie speaks with disapproval of that christocentrism, common to Luther, Ritschl, Herrmann, and Barth which makes Christ the Mediator no less of knowledge than of salvation, and which seizes eagerly on this text.[17] He quotes with approval a possible solution by D. S. Cairns: 'He does not say, "No man knoweth God save the Son". That would be to deny the truth of the Old Testament revelation. What He does say is that He alone has a deeper secret, the essential Fatherhood of the Sovereign Power.'[18] Another possible solution is to include the revealing work of the Son, the Logos, the Second Person of the Trinity, outside the Incarnation. It may be said that wherever a man knows God, whether or not that knowledge is mediated through any knowledge of the historic Jesus, that knowledge is in fact mediated to him through the Eternal Christ. It is difficult to say how far this thought could have been in the mind of Jesus as He uttered these words.

The other point[19] is the use of the word 'know'. This word, which is important because of its part in the Gnostic heresies, has been fully investigated by Bultmann.[20] The words γινώσκω and ידע (which is usually translated in LXX by γινώσκω and οἶδα) both roughly mean 'know', but knowledge was differently conceived by the Greeks and by the Hebrews. The former laid stress on seeing, though sight was not, of course, the only organ of knowledge. The Hebrews conceived God rather as a Will, with a definite aim. Thus the knowledge of God is not a knowledge of God's eternal Being, but of His claim; the obedient and reverent

[17] J. Baillie, pp. 17-18.

[18] D. S. Cairns, *The Riddle of the World*, p. 321, cited in J. Baillie, p. 18 n.1.

[19] A subordinate point is whether there is any difference between Matthew's ἐπιγινώσκει and Luke's γινώσκει. (I omit the variant ἔγνω in Matthew.) See J. A. Robinson, *Ephesians*, pp. 248-54; Moulton-Howard, I.113; Lightfoot, p. 204; Mayor, pp. 171-4; Bultmann, *KTW*, I.703. Possibly ἐπιγινώσκω speaks of a fuller or more definite knowledge than γινώσκω; but in this context the difference is negligible.

[20] Bultmann, *KTW*, I.688-719.

recognition of God's power, grace, and demand. This knowledge is thus not a personal 'possession'; it exists, in so far as one exercises it. It has nothing to do with the βίος θεωρητικός or the mystical vision of God. Not to know is not only an error; it is morally culpable. Knowledge is almost the same as the fear of God.[21] Thus Manson says:

'What is meant by knowledge of God is to be looked for in the Old Testament rather than in Western ideas of Knowledge. The broad distinction is that knowledge of God is there an essential part of religion, whereas our tendency is rather to look upon it as a branch of science and philosophy. The Cartesian division of all truth into Rational Theology, Cosmology, and Psychology still lingers with us. In Hebrew thought דעת אלהים is not theological but religious. It can be put alongside יראת אלהים, "the fear of God"—which is another name for religion—and classed with חסד and אמת, "mercy" and "faithfulness".'[22]

The New Testament largely follows the Old Testament usage, the Greek words being used in the sense of the Hebrew words which they translate in LXX. Knowledge means insight into the Will of God.[23] It means also the acknowledgment (*Anerkennung*) of God Himself; but the New Testament is not directed simply against the practical denial of God by those who are theoretically monotheists (as was the message of the prophets); it was also directed to those who did not know one God at all. Thus theoretical knowledge crept into the meaning of the word, though the practical element is still predominant.[24] The word is also used of God's knowledge of us, a usage which is the most remote from the Greek usage, but this usage (to which we have already referred)[25] tends to disappear. But in the Johannine Gospel and First Epistle the meaning of the word is further modified by the Hellenistic-gnostic use of the word, as we shall have to consider later.[26]

The question thus arises whether the word ἐπιγινώσκω (if we assume the Matthaean form to be correct) is here used in the sense of ידע or in a sense more akin to that of the Fourth Gospel. Bultmann argues that the relationship between the Father and the Son is described in a Johannine way and therefore the conception of knowledge (*Erkenntnisbegriff*) must be Johannine. The phrase

[21] This is largely taken from Bultmann.
[22] Manson, *Teaching*, p. 111 n.2. He compares Hos $4_{1, 6}$, Is 11_2, Jer 22_{16}.
[23] e.g. Lk 19_{42}.
[24] cf. Ro 1_{21}, 1 Co 1_{21}, Gal 4_{8-9}.
[25] cf. *supra*, p. 63.
[26] cf. *infra*, p. 208.

'and anyone to whom the Son wishes to reveal him' shows that the verb cannot have the sense of ידע. He points out that Strack-Billerbeck produces no parallels to this verse, and concludes that the question of its genuineness must be settled by whatever decision is reached as to the relation of the words of Jesus in the Fourth Gospel to those in the Synoptics.[27] Similarly a statement that the logion was Greek had been made by Bousset,[28] but the parallels from Hellenistic circles which he and others who reject the saying quote are not close. On the other side many have been satisfied that the tone of the words is predominantly Jewish. Thus for instance Manson writes that this is a knowledge 'in which all that the Old Testament writers mean by "knowledge of God" finds full scope and expression'.[29] 'The knowledge of God implied,' says Taylor, 'is nearer to that which is described in the Old Testament than it is to the utterances of Hellenistic piety.'[30] It may moreover be observed in more specific reply to Bultmann's points that none of the characteristics which he adduces[31] to point out the difference of the Johannine use of γινώσκω from the Old Testament use is present here. It is not combined with a verb of seeing; the content of γινώσκω is not described by a ὅτι clause; obedience and love are not regarded as the criteria of γινώσκω; nor is γινώσκω connected with πιστεύω. Nor is it clear that the clause 'and anyone to whom the Son wishes to reveal him' necessitates an interpretation other than that of the Old Testament. It is true that if 'obey' were taken to be the chief content of γινώσκω, then there would be a certain difficulty in the thought of a revealed obedience; but if it be rather a recognition (*Anerkennung*), there is no reason why that should not be conferred by a revelation; after all, it is God who confers the knowledge of Himself in the Old Testament sense of knowledge also. 'And I will give them an heart to know me, that I am the Lord.'[32] It must however be admitted that the use of the word

[27] Actually he is opposed to the genuineness of the passage, as can be gathered from his *Die Geschichte der synoptischen Tradition*, pp. 171-2.

[28] Bousset, p. 50, calls it *ein griechisches Werk*, and possibly *ein dogmatisches Wanderwort hellenistischer Gemeindeüberlieferung*.

[29] Manson, *Sayings*, p. 79. Moreover the passage cited *supra*, p. 65, from Manson, *Teaching*, p. 111 n.2, in connexion with the meaning of γινώσκω in general, was in Manson's work, p. 111, used in special reference to this passage.

[30] Taylor, *JS*, p. 36.

[31] Bultmann, *KTW*, I.712-3; cf. *infra*, p. 208.

[32] Jer. 24_7. The root ידע is involved. Incidentally the כִּי ('that') clause seems to diminish the value of Bultmann's point that ὅτι ('that') clauses reveal a use of 'know' other than that of the Old Testament.

ἀποκαλύπτω gives a slightly non-Hebraic flavour to the passage. But Bultmann's conclusion seems too sharply drawn. It is not merely that the Judaism of Christ's day may have been coloured by mystical ideas, and that therefore the sentence may well be genuine.[33] There is really nothing in the logion which is markedly non-Jewish or 'mystical', unless 'mystical' be used in so broad a sense as to cover the whole Old Testament. But whatever the precise nuance of the word 'know' in this important logion, there can be no doubt that 'know' is one of the most important of the words by which the relation of Christians to God may legitimately be described.

The remaining relevant logia in Q deal more specifically with prayer, and are mostly to be found in Matthew's Sermon on the Mount and Luke's Sermon on the Plain, which are composed of a mixture of Q material with material from M and L respectively. Thus prayer is mentioned as one of the forms which the love of our enemies should take.

'Pray for them that persecute you' Mt 5_{44}.[34]

Matthew adds 'that you may be sons of your Father which is in heaven'. This is the height of intercessory prayer. Heiler cites a not very close Buddhist parallel,[35] referring to the religion of Jesus and the Buddha's doctrine of deliverance as the purest expressions of the higher religious spirit, and contrasting them with the frank wish of Greek piety for the destruction of the enemy. But such wishes are common in Old Testament piety also, for the use of such passages from the Psalms in Christian devotion, with the aid of some sort of mystical exegesis, must not blind us to their original meaning. Moreover, the Buddhist ideal, as Heiler says in the same passage, is freedom from feeling, a very different thing from the universal love of our neighbour which animates the Christian. The real contrast is not that of Jesus and the Buddha against the Greeks; Jesus stands out alone against all other types of religion. This might seem a contrast with the principle previously stated that in prayer the Christian is to set forth with a childlike simplicity whatever is in his heart. The answer is that

[33] So W. Manson, p. 75; Otto, pp. 235-6, 393-5.

[34] cf. the parallel, Lk 6_{28}, 'Pray for them that despitefully use you'. In Matthew some MSS. have the familiar reading 'them that despitefully use you and persecute you', which may be due to assimilation from Luke.

[35] Heiler, p. 82.

the heart of the Christian, though not freed from naïve petition and even shrinking from pain, can by grace be freed from personal enmity. We have already seen, of course, in the prayer for the forgiveness of His enemies uttered from the Cross, how faithful the practice of Jesus was to His teaching on this point.[36]

The Sermon on the Mount contains also a passage on anxiety, towards the end of which occur these words:

'*Do not then be anxious, saying: What are we to eat? or What are we to drink? or What are we to put on? For all these things do the Gentiles seek: for your heavenly Father knows that you need all these things. But seek first his kingdom and his righteousness, and all these things will be added to you*' Mt 6_{31-3}.[37]

These words breathe the spirit of simple trust, which Jesus stressed in His teaching on prayer. The suggestion that we should concentrate in petitionary or intercessory prayer on God's kingdom and righteousness corresponds to the prayer which Jesus Himself uttered in Gethsemane, 'not what I will but what thou wilt' (Mk 14_{36}); we are to pray only in accordance with God's will: nevertheless, as that example shows, we are not to refrain from the frank expression of our own desire for a particular benefit: but 'all these things' are to be sought only in so far as they are in harmony with God's will, God's rule, God's righteousness.

The Sermon on the Mount also contains a great passage on the goodness of God in answer to prayer, beginning 'Ask, and it shall be given you' (Mt 7_{7-11}, Lk 11_{9-13}). The passage passes from the thought of the reliability of a human father's answer to the requests of his children to the thought of the divine Father, with the words,

'*If ye then, being evil, know how to give good gifts to your children, how much more will your Father in heaven give good things to them that ask him*' Mt 7_{11}.[38]

The argument proceeds on the πόσῳ μᾶλλον (how much more) principle, also described as the *argumentum a minore ad maius* (from

[36] Manson, *Sayings*, pp. 52-3, deals with a charge brought by C. G. Montefiore that the practice of Jesus was inconsistent with this passage.

[37] Lk 12_{29-31} is the parallel; cf. Mt 6_{8}.

[38] Luke substitutes 'Holy Spirit' for 'good things'. Most scholars are agreed that Matthew represents the reading of Q; e.g. Barrett, pp. 126-7. This is slightly confirmed by the fact that the MSS. of Luke show a tendency to assimilation to Matthew here, and not vice versa.

lesser to greater), which is really a form of the *argumentum a fortiori* (from the more striking case). This type of argument is frequently found in the Parables, and to understand it from this particularly clear example will give us a clue to the understanding of some Lukan parables on prayer. This passage, like the Lukan parables on prayer and some of the passages on faith (e.g. Mk $11_{22ff.}$) speaks most clearly of prayer as having a real effect on God: it affords no support to the rationalizing notion that the effect of prayer is simply on the person who prays.

A passage which shortly afterwards follows in Matthew lays down, after some illustrations, the great principle by which piety may be tested,

'*By their fruits ye shall know them*' Mt 7_{20}.[39]

This may not be actually from Q, but is conveniently mentioned here together with its context and parallels. We must notice also

'*Why do you call me Lord, Lord, and not do the things that I say?*' Lk 6_{46}.

As in the Markan source, piety is strongly connected with ethics. A mere outward observance is valueless.

To sum up the teaching of Q on prayer, we find, as in Mark, that it is sometimes intercessory, and that it has an ethical setting. But instead of the eschatological associations which we found in Mark, we have the idea of 'knowing' God. This may have a 'Johannine' flavour, but is not necessarily Hellenistic or Gnostic; it is entirely compatible with Old Testament and prophetic religion; nevertheless, it more vividly suggests communion with God here and now than those passages where prayer is always associated with watching.

M and L

We deal now with passages ascribed to M and L, beginning with those which occur in both, but are nevertheless not found in Mark or ascribed to Q. One of these is the Lord's Prayer (Mt 6_{9-13}, Lk 11_{2-4}), the greatest of the passages on prayer, which demands as full a treatment as anything which we have to consider.

[39] There is a roughly similar passage in a rather different context in Mt 12_{33}, which corresponds to Lk 6_{43-5}. But the following verse, Lk 6_{46}, corresponds roughly to the verse which follows the first Matthaean passage, Mt 7_{21}. The Matthaean version of this verse is probably secondary; thus Luke here is Q: Matthew is M. cf. Manson, *Teaching*, pp. 121-2; Cadoux, pp. 231-2. Thus Mt 7_{20} is not itself paralleled in Luke, and is probably an addition to Q made by the Matthaean editor.

In Matthew there are no textual variants of any real importance, save that the Doxology, though found in many inferior MSS. and some quite important ones, is lacking in the best. It was doubtless an addition from later liturgical use, though it is to this day lacking in some liturgical contexts.

It is far different in Luke. Here the prayer in the better MSS. is considerably shorter than in Matthew, but every one of the passages thus omitted is found, no doubt by assimilation, in at least some of the MSS. The clauses which are common in substance to both Gospels are found in varying forms, but here again assimilation has been at work. In the clause about the forgiveness of sins, the true text of Luke is not difficult to disentangle. In the petition about the bread, Luke, in the best MSS., has the Present Imperative (δίδου), and correspondingly 'each day' (τὸ καθ' ἡμέραν), whereas Matthew has the Aorist Imperative (δός), and correspondingly 'this day' (σήμερον). Some of the MSS. of Luke have shown a grasp of Greek grammar inferior to that of the author of the Gospel by making one of these assimilations without the other. In this clause Marcion has 'thy daily bread'. But far the most striking variant in the texts of Luke lies in the words 'Let thy Holy Spirit come upon us and cleanse us'. This is implied in Marcion for 'Hallowed be thy name', and it is substituted for 'Thy kingdom come' in 162 (with a variation in the order of words and the omission of 'upon us'), 700, Gregory of Nyssa and Maximus of Turin (omitting 'upon us'). The reading of D, which has 'upon us' before 'Thy kingdom come', or after 'Hallowed be thy name', might be a survival of this.[40] This is a very slender attestation of the variant, but the great weight of authority on the other side might be accounted for by the great tendency to assimilation to Matthew which we have already noted. A further strong argument that this variant may have stood in the original text of Luke, though not in the words of Jesus, is that he inserted a reference to the Holy Spirit into the Q tradition at Luke 11_{13}. He may well have made a similar alteration here. Some scholars therefore, notably Streeter, think that this variant represents what Luke wrote.[41] If that is so, we must probably also

[40] Streeter, p. 277.

[41] Creed, ad loc., points out that 'the textual evidence is less homogeneous than Streeter states'. There is not only Creed's point that Streeter does not state the different position of this variant in Marcion; there is the minor point, not in Creed, that Streeter did not mention the slight omissions in 162, and Maximus.

accept Streeter's opinion that Matthew's version is here more original, and that will then probably apply to the whole prayer. On the whole, however, the greater probability lies with the non-Marcionite text of Luke, and we may perhaps accept Burkitt's suggestion that the origin of the variant lay in Marcionite liturgical usage.[42] That view would leave us free, if on other grounds it were desired, to accept the Lukan version of the whole prayer as the original.

We can now come to the source-criticism. Matthew and Luke differ so much (quite apart from the Marcionite variant) that it is impossible that the passage should have stood in Q. It must therefore be assigned to M and L. Which version, then, is to be preferred? This is not easy to determine. Of the verses which undoubtedly form part of the prayer, the Matthaean version (except for 'Our Father', which we shall consider later) is to be preferred as the more pointed; but possibly the briefer version, i.e. the Lukan, is a surer guide to the number of the clauses.[43] If these suggestions be followed, the original form of the prayer (in Greek) would be thus, though the reconstruction cannot be certain.

> Πάτερ,
> ἁγιασθήτω τὸ ὄνομά σου·
> ἐλθάτω ἡ βασιλεία σου·
> τὸν ἄρτον ἡμῶν τὸν ἐπιούσιον δὸς ἡμῖν σήμερον·
> καὶ ἄφες ἡμῖν τὰ ὀφειλήματα ἡμῶν, ὡς καὶ ἡμεῖς ἀφήκαμεν τοῖς ὀφειλέταις ἡμῶν·
> καὶ μὴ εἰσενέγκῃς ἡμᾶς εἰς πειρασμόν.

Before this can be translated, it is necessary to determine the meaning of the exceedingly rare word ἐπιούσιον. A careful discussion by Foerster yields 'that we need'.[44] The translation would thus be as follows:

[42] So Chase thought it was a liturgical alteration when the Prayer was used at the imposition of hands (confirmation).

[43] cf. Kittel, *KTW*, I.5 n.14; cf. Manson, *Sayings*, p. 266. The tendency of liturgical forms is probably to grow rather than shrink through use. Experiments show that this is not true of narrative, but the addition of the doxology in Matthew would suggest that liturgy may operate differently. But Cadoux, p. 166, prefers the Matthaean form of the prayer.

[44] Foerster, *KTW*, II.587-95, but see Moulton-Howard II.313-4. Streeter, p. 277 n.1, thought that this word, a remarkable point of contact between our two versions, might be due to an assimilation of Luke to Matthew which has infected all our authorities.

Father,
Hallowed be thy name;
Thy kingdom come;
Give us to-day the bread that we need;
And forgive us our debts, as we also have forgiven our debtors;
And lead us not into temptation.

The context differs in the two sources. In Matthew, it occurs in the Sermon on the Mount, and follows without a break some words on prayer also apparently from M: it is introduced simply by the words 'After this manner therefore pray ye'. Prophetic prayer, unlike mystical, has no elaborate technique or 'method', based on psychological analysis. Its instructions are as terse as its prayers.[45] The Lukan account seems more original: it is not there part of the Sermon on the Plain; Jesus was praying in a certain place, and when He stopped, one of the disciples said 'Lord, teach us to pray, as John also taught his disciples' (Lk 11_1). In Matthew it is followed by some verses on the forgiveness of others of a type found also elsewhere in the Gospels. These are probably floating logia, attached here because of the obvious connexion of thought. In Luke it is immediately followed by a parable about prayer from L. Probably it was already attached to the preceding verses in M and the following verses in L before these sources reached the Evangelists, but we cannot be sure that either of these connexions is original.

Its contents are obviously of supreme importance. Whatever may be thought of the value for us of the overheard prayers of Jesus, there can be no objection to our basing our prayers on this model, designed for this very purpose. We have to remember that it is not a prayer of Jesus, but a prayer which He gave to His disciples (for He would not Himself have needed to pray for forgiveness); we can therefore fittingly use it in liturgical prayer, so long as that use does not become mechanical. On the other hand, Deissmann warns us not to separate this prayer too sharply from the actual prayer-life of Jesus; He 'has given His best, the ripe fruits of His own prayer-experience'. 'The Lord's Prayer was not given by Jesus as the foundation stone of an impersonal liturgy for a new cult.'[46] The idea of giving a model prayer was

[45] cf. Heiler, p. 281.

[46] Deissmann, *Religion*, pp. 63-4; cf. Heiler, p. xxii.

not new. Luke refers to John the Baptist, and it was a common custom of the Rabbis.

It would be as impertinent to praise this prayer as it would be to praise the actual prayers of Jesus; but it may be said that it shows the same qualities that they show: it is terse, natural, and spontaneous. In one sense it is not original, for the separate clauses can all be paralleled from Jewish sources. In this respect also, of course, it resembles the actual prayers of Jesus, which drew, as we have seen, on the Psalter. But the choice and arrangement of these petitions and their brevity make a powerful impression of originality.[47]

The word 'Father' is the opening word which we have already found in the prayers of Jesus Himself. If it were thought that the true version of what Jesus said was 'Our Father', then the question would arise why Jesus taught His followers to use a mode of address other than that which He employed Himself. The point has been used in the interests of a high Christology; Jesus had God as His Father in a different sense from that in which we have. A reply is sometimes made that Jesus said 'Our Father', thus including Himself with the disciples, but this is easily countered by the fact that He taught the prayer to them; they did not say it together.[48] The Johannine phrase 'My Father and your Father' (Jn 20_{17}) is held to reveal the mind of Jesus on this point.[49] Manson's assertion that 'the originality of Luke is shown by the recorded prayer of Jesus Himself (Mk 14_{36}) and the testimony of Paul (Ro 8_{15}, Gal 4_6)'[50] simply assumes without argument in the first part of the sentence that the same form would be taught to the disciples as was used by Jesus Himself, but there is substance in Manson's point about the testimony of Paul.[51] Paul had somehow learnt that it was right for Christians to use the form 'Father'. This is strong evidence for the Lukan reading here, and affords the justification of this reading which we deferred previously.[52] Thus the Christological question is not affected by what we believe to be the true reading here, though of course a difference between the filial relationship of Christ and that of the Christian may be

[47] cf. Manson, *Sayings*, pp. 167-8.

[48] cf. Cadoux, p. 32.

[49] Contrast Deissmann, *Religion*, p. 64. 'It is a dogmatic affectation to make a deep chasm between "my Father" and "our Father" in the words of Jesus'.

[50] Manson, *Sayings*, p. 168; cf. Dalman, p. 192.

[51] cf. *supra*, p. 43.

[52] cf. *supra*, p. 71.

established on other grounds. Our version also omits 'which art in heaven', a reverential and liturgical addition which also hints at the idea of God as King.

We must next notice that the prayer begins with adoration and with such petitions as are concerned with God's glory rather than man's need. The first person pronoun (or possessive adjective) does not occur, if we follow the readings we have adopted, till the fourth clause. Thereafter more personal needs are mentioned. This does not mean that the first part of the prayer consists of mystical adoration rather than prophetic petition. It is significant that the adoration is cast, as it were, into the form of petition. The first of these petitions is 'Hallowed be thy name'. The name is to the Hebrew mind more than a mere word, as many instances show. This is really analogous to, or an instance of, prophetic symbolism. The name stands for God Himself, just as the symbolic acts of the prophets stand for the events which it is desired to produce; and just as those symbolic acts are not mere symbols but (in the opinion of the prophets) help to effect the events, so the hallowing of the Name is to ascribe holiness to God, to acknowledge God as what He is. This petition 'seems to mean both that God should hallow His name by His mighty acts and that men should hallow it by their acknowledgement of Him as the one true God, and by living in accordance with His will'.[53]

The next petition 'Thy Kingdom come', which may be regarded as a way of hallowing God's Name, is, as the former petition was not, definitely eschatological. It reveals 'unambiguously his [Jesus'] belief in a future "coming" of the Kingdom, distinguishable from any presence of it already realized, and apparently capable of being hastened on by his followers' prayers'.[54] This harmonizes with, and is important evidence for, the position we have already adopted, that Jesus' eschatology was in part futurist. It might indeed be contended that in the view of Jesus the kingdom would come wholly with the resurrection, ascension, and gift of the Holy Spirit; and that the prayer was only (to coin a phrase) an interim-prayer until that time, though this does not seem very likely; but at least the kingdom was not wholly present when Jesus taught it to them. It may possibly have been some hesitation

[53] Manson, *Sayings*, p. 169.

[54] Cadoux, p. 201, who also remarks that Dodd nowhere reconciles this with his contention that Jesus taught only 'realized eschatology'.

about the meaning of this clause which produced the variant reading about the Holy Spirit. The fact that these readings are rivals for the same place is no proof that they have the same meaning. If the petition about doing God's will, which we have rejected, were retained here, it would no doubt acquire an eschatological flavour from its context, though not exclusively so. God's will can be done here and now.

We now turn from petitions concerned primarily with God's glory to personal petitions of the kind which we more normally associate with the word 'petition'. Here simple human requests are made, and the common Christian practice of petition receives the highest sanction. The first such request is 'Give us to-day the bread that we need'. There seems no need to read any eschatological significance into that, nor to take it primarily, still less exclusively, of spiritual food. The simplicity of the prayer seems to preclude such a view, and only erroneous presuppositions could make such an exegesis necessary.[55] No doubt, as at the Last Supper, the simplest type of food is chosen to represent all sustenance, and it may be that spiritual food is not wholly excluded.

Then comes the prayer for forgiveness. This has been thought by some Evangelicals to constitute the chief part of prayer. 'God, be merciful to me a sinner' (Lk 18_{13}) has been thought to be the typical prayer. This is something of an exaggeration. If this note were indeed essential to prayer, then our Lord would Himself have been unable to pray, which is clearly a wrong view. Nevertheless in the prayers of sinful humanity it does play an important part, on the prophetic view. 'In the centre of prophetic-evangelical prayer stands petition for the forgiveness of sins, which in mysticism belongs to the periphery of prayer'.[56] It is significant that in so short a prayer as this it finds a prominent place. To this is added the remarkable qualification 'as we also have forgiven our debtors'. The Lukan assertion that we do forgive all our debtors is perhaps even more striking, both because of its form and because it is slightly less familiar to us. But the Matthaean form clearly implies the same thing; otherwise it would be unsafe to utter the petition at all. Jesus laid much emphasis

[55] Heiler, p. 251. We omit various ingenious theories based on the translations of ἐπιούσιον.

[56] Heiler, *Das Gebet*, p. 362 (my translation; cf. E.T. 243).

on the duty of forgiving others (Mt 18_{23-35}). There are Rabbinic parallels to this, but Jesus laid more emphasis on the duty of offering forgiveness than was common in Jewish circles, which usually stressed the duty of seeking it. But this advance on customary Jewish teaching is itself dangerous. It may suggest that God forgives us *because* we forgive others, rather than by grace. The words which follow the Lord's Prayer in Matthew seem to fall into this peril: 'For if ye forgive men their trespasses, your heavenly Father will also forgive you.'[57]

The prayer, in what we judge to be its original form, concludes with the words 'And lead us not into temptation'. The precise meaning of the word πειρασμός, here found in the accusative and translated 'temptation', is open to dispute. Schweitzer held that the word refers to 'the general eschatological time of tribulation'.[58] But the word could not have this meaning in the verse 'But ye are they which have continued with me in my temptations' (Lk 22_{28}); unless indeed in the light of realized eschatology, we should regard the 'trials' of Jesus' whole ministry as those of the end. Otto,[59] while not making any reference to Schweitzer's view of the meaning of the word, yet regards this Lukan verse as a redactional supplement on the ground that Jesus' πειρασμοί had not yet begun, still less those of His disciples. But nothing is said about πειρασμοί for the disciples, only that they continued with Jesus in His, and these can be found in His conflicts with the scribes. It seems therefore a very arbitrary proceeding to omit the verse.[60] If therefore in this Lukan verse the word does not bear this eschatological meaning, there seems no necessity for it to do so here in the Lord's Prayer. There are plenty of trials or testings in the religious life, into which the disciples might well pray not to be led.

The verse has however occasioned a good deal of rather unnecessary difficulty on other grounds. It is felt to be a rather odd thing to say in prayer, and Schweitzer's translation is sometimes felt to mitigate the difficulty. The difficulties usually alleged, however, are incompatible with each other. One is that there is

[57] cf. Manson, *Sayings*, p. 171, 'It is *quid pro quo*'. Probably the parallel, Mk 11_{25}, is more original.

[58] Schweitzer, *Quest*, p. 362. Of course it does sometimes undoubtedly have this meaning, e.g. Rev 3_{10}.

[59] Otto, p. 273.

[60] So Taylor, *JS*, pp. 177, 188; cf. Cadoux, p. 256; cf. *supra*, p. 25.

no need to pray against trial, which should be a joyful experience; the other is that there is no need to pray against it, as God would not be so cruel or so foolish as to lead us into it unnecessarily. The first of these views rests almost entirely on a single verse, 'Count it all joy, my brethren, whenever you fall into various πειρασμοί (Ja 1_2; cf. Ro 5_{3-5}). It does not much matter whether the word is translated 'trials' or 'temptations'. Neither is to be sought deliberately; they are unpleasant experiences, but they are not the worst thing that can happen to a man. The only ultimate evil is that a man should sin, and this he may by grace avoid in a time of temptation or trial. The paradox is familiar in connexion with physical pain, which is indeed often called a 'trial' in popular piety. It is morbid to desire it; nor need we suppose that God's absolute will or original purpose for man includes it. It is a result of the Fall. Nevertheless when it comes, it is, relatively at least, His will. It is permitted by Him, and is therefore in a sense to be accepted at His hand. We may then rejoice in it, in the sense that we rejoice that God is able to transform it (as the experience of many Christians has shown) into a means of closer communion with Himself. But to count these experiences as joy when we have fallen into them is not the same as to court them deliberately; we need not pray for them, nor refrain from praying against them. And what is thus said of physical pain applies equally to those experiences, whether of trial or temptation, which are referred to here. Hunger may also be a salutary experience; yet it is in a sense an evil, and we pray against it in this very prayer. Some Latin writers add a gloss[61] 'which we cannot bear', which is based on the promise in 1 Corinthians 10_{13} that God will not allow us to be tempted more than we are able (sc. to bear).

The second and more sweeping objection, which has to some extent affected some Latin texts of the prayer, is that God would not allow us to be tempted, and therefore there is no point in praying against it. 'What should we think,' it is asked, 'of a human father who deliberately put temptation in his children's way?' Some people see relief from this in the idea that 'Lead us not' has an Aramaic original which would be better translated 'Do not cause us to enter' or 'Do not allow us to enter'. This may be so, but it would not relieve the difficulty, such as it is. Presumably the idea is that God would never *lead* us into temptation,

[61] So McNeile, ad loc.

and therefore we must not pray that He will not, but that He might *allow* us to enter it, unless we pray against it.[62] The most fatuous of these explanations is the notion sometimes found in popular works that a pause or dash should be inserted, thus: 'Lead us—not into temptation.' This is no help at all. All these explanations rest on the assumption that there is no need to pray against that which God will not do anyway, or, more simply, that to ask God not to do something implies that He is likely to do it. In its positive form this would mean that to ask God to do something implies that He is likely not to do it. This would imperil petition altogether. One might as well expunge the petition about bread with the remark 'What should we think of an earthly father who let his children starve?' The negative form of this petition, together with the opposite objection arising out of the point that trial is not wholly evil, has given plausibility to an attack which few would make on a positive petition. Even so, this objection, even when made only to the negative petition, is really derived from philosophical doubt about all petitionary and intercessory prayer. The underlying thought is that God is in any case resolved to do whatever is best, and therefore it is both wrong and unnecessary to ask Him to do or not to do anything. With the answer to this objection we are not here concerned, but we must point out that it is a characteristic of what we have called prophetic prayer quite to ignore this objection. He who prays pours forth his requests in a frank, childlike (one might almost say naïve) way. We have already seen this tendency at work in the prayers of Jesus Himself. This disputed petition here has the same childlike quality. A child, being taken across the road by his father, is reported to have said 'Don't let me get run over'. Such a prayer is very similar in form and spirit to this one; and he would be a foolish earthly father indeed who rejected such an expression of childlike trust or thought that it conveyed an innuendo that he was at all likely to let the child be run over. (The parallel, of course, deals only with the second objection.) Thus this verse brings out more clearly than any other how markedly this prayer stands in the prophetic tradition. We have already rejected the petition 'but deliver us from evil (or, from the evil one)'. Possibly

[62] A further development of this view is that 'enter into' means 'yield to'; in this form it is really an attempted answer to the first objection that trial in itself is really a joyful experience.

some unnecessary doubt of the kind we have been discussing led to the amplification of the negative petition by this positive one.

What conclusions emerge when we survey the proportions and shape of the prayer as a whole? It is predominantly petitionary; some would say, exclusively so. 'The Lord's prayer, the model prayer of Christianity, is exclusively petition. Its contrast with the mystic's prayer is evident.'[63] The petitions at the beginning have indeed an admixture of adoration, but neither their content nor their context makes it possible to treat them as examples of mystical prayer. We may nevertheless see some significance in that those which contain adoration and are less concerned with personal blessings precede the others.

Perhaps we may also attach some importance to the fact that the prayer for forgiveness of sins does not stand at the beginning, where it stands in many liturgies. Some Presbyterian liturgiologists see an element in which their liturgy is superior to the Anglican in the fact that it begins with adoration and not confession. But the matter is not as simple as that. The Presbyterian and Reformed Liturgies ought properly to be compared with the Eucharist, not with Morning and Evening Prayer. The Anglican Eucharist, though it begins on a somewhat subdued and penitential note, has its confession considerably later. The Reformed rite, on the other hand, as we have it in, say, Calvin, does begin with confession. It is true that this may be preceded by a Psalm or Hymn, but the Anglican rite may also be preceded by the Introit Psalm, which stands, however, later in the Roman rite. It is true that the penitential introductions to Morning and Evening Prayer cannot well be preceded by any act of praise, because of the versicle 'O Lord, open Thou our lips', which follows them. (Despite this, a Hymn is often sung first.) But the Reformed rite is not here intrinsically superior to the Anglican. It is rather true that in practice all rites feel the need of starting with adoration, and supply this need in various ways, thus conforming to the pattern of the Lord's Prayer.

A more important question is, whether a survey of the parts justifies the claim often made that the whole prayer is eschatological. Heiler, for instance, is of the opinion that the petition for the coming of the kingdom of God in its fulness, that is 'for the realization of the sum of all good, the transformation of all the

[63] Heiler, p. 242.

actual into a perfect ideal reality' (perhaps a somewhat Ritschlian conception of the kingdom) is 'the supremely important petition of prophetic prayer, into which merge all other desires. Jesus' prayer is essentially eschatological'.[64] That this is true of the central petition 'Thy Kingdom come' is clear, but for the rest, Heiler relies largely on 'Thy will be done' and 'Deliver us from the evil one', neither of which we have included in the text. He does not mention the argument from the word πειρασμοί, which argument we have rejected. No doubt it is true, in a general sense, that the prayer hopes for better times, as any petition necessarily must; but that does not mean that it is eschatological in the usual sense. Mingled with the fundamental petition for the coming of the kingdom are petitions which relate equally, at least, to the interim period, before the kingdom is established, as, for instance, the petition about bread. We may thus characterize the prayer as wholly prophetic, but only partly eschatological.

M

When we turn from the Lord's Prayer to those passages in M which are not paralleled in L, we can best begin with the context of the Lord's Prayer. We have here, in the Sermon on the Mount, a triple warning against ostentatious piety (Mt 6_{1-18}). It deals with almsgiving, prayer, and fasting. At first we should be inclined to treat only the second of these as relevant to our subject, regarding almsgiving as the ethical fruit of piety and fasting as a very doubtful form of it. But that would be to impose our modern point of view upon the passage. No distinction is there made between these three religious exercises, and presumably each of them is regarded as a form of communion with God. There is a notable omission of any mention of the Temple. The balance of clauses, however, is disturbed by the addition, to the second part, of verses 7-8 as well as the Lord's Prayer. The general form of these three warnings is, When you give alms (pray, fast), do not be ostentatious as the hypocrites are, that they may be seen of men; verily I say unto you, they receive in full their reward; but when you give alms (pray, fast), do it in secret, that you may not appear to men to be doing it, and your Father, who sees what you do in secret, will reward you. There is no need to accept the reading which would add to this the word 'openly'.

[64] Heiler, p. 248.

The general meaning of this passage is plain enough without going into further detail; with regard to prayer, it is clear that the passage is not intended to discourage attendance at the Temple or Synagogue, as was the custom of Jesus and His disciples. It refers to ostentation in what is supposed to be private devotion. The 'chamber' may be supposed to be figurative, and in this sense Jesus fulfilled His own injunction, by praying alone in remote places at night (Mk 1_{35}). Indeed the scarcity of His recorded prayers testifies to His practice. A reluctance to be seen in public offering private prayers (except immediately before or after Divine Service) is common in England, and variously ascribed to Protestantism, to lack of courage, and to the reserved national temperament; may it not equally well be due to the desire to avoid ostentation in accordance with this passage?

To the section on ostentation in prayer is attached another logion of considerable importance.

'*And when you pray do not heap up empty phrases as the Gentiles do; for they think that they will be heard for their many words*' Mt 6_7.

The word βατταλογέω is clearly a strong and sarcastic word, but it is very rare, and its meaning is uncertain. It is possibly onomatopoeic. The translation 'heap up empty phrases' is only a guess (taken from the Revised Standard Version), which combines mention of quantity and of quality; it owes something to the reading of the Sinaitic Syriac and to a supposed derivation from the Aramaic בטל 'idle, useless'.[65] The familiar rendering 'vain repetitions' is really similar, but must not be understood to forbid all repetition of a prayer. The repetition of a prayer under the stress of deep emotion may claim the sanction of Christ Himself in Gethsemane (Mk 14_{39}, Mt 26_{44}). Nor can it be intended to discourage lengthy prayers or importunity in prayer. Prolixity is here condemned, and the heaping-up of numerous epithets as if to make sure of pleasing the Deity, almost as one says much in the hope of stumbling across some magic formula. Prolixity is sometimes a mark of liturgical prayer, though not when that is at its best: mystical piety also sometimes heaps up expressions of adoration,[66] though sometimes a mystic will dwell long on a single phrase, or contemplate the ineffable mystery

[65] cf. McNeile, ad loc.; Moulton-Howard, II.272.
[66] e.g. Heiler, *Das Gebet*, p. 296.

without any use of words at all; prophetic prayer, at its best, is always terse and direct.[67] The Lord's Prayer, the prayers which Jesus uttered, and the prayers which He approved (e.g. Lk 18_{13}) emerge unscathed from this condemnation of prolixity.

The reason for the injunction which we have been considering is given in the next verse,

'*Therefore do not be like them, for your Father knows the things of which you have need before you ask him*' Mt 6_8.[68]

These words contain within themselves the whole paradox of petitionary prayer. It is the fact that God knows our needs which encourages us to pray with confidence; yet it may easily provoke the retort, 'Then why ask Him?' In itself, apart from its context, this verse sounds like a familiar part of the argument of those, whether of a philosophical or mystical bent of mind, who would discourage petition altogether and make adoration the heart of prayer. The immediate context (with the Lord's Prayer following), as well as the general tenor of Christ's teaching, utterly forbids such an interpretation. It is the more striking that Christ, while fully grasping this consideration about God's knowledge, should yet be an unambiguous supporter of petitionary prayer. We have already considered this paradox in other passages;[69] the importance of this verse is that it shows how clearly Jesus was aware of one side of the paradox, of which indeed it is the perfect expression. Human analogies, drawn from the relation of child to father, may help with this problem, as may other considerations which belong rather to the realm of apologetics or philosophy of religion; it is part of the general problem of the relation of God to the world, which involves the questions of deism and pantheism, transcendence and immanence, monism and pluralism, and underlies the questions, not only of prayer, but of miracle and providence. But the man of prayer will not allow erroneous inferences from the omniscience of God to force his prayer into an unnatural silence; nor will he wait for the permission of the philosopher before he continues on his accustomed way. The

[67] cf. Heiler, *Das Gebet*, p. 356 (E.T. 237).

[68] With most MSS., I omit 'God' before 'your Father', though it is found in ℵ* B and the Sahidic version. cf. Mt 6_{31-3}, Lk 12_{29-31}. For the thought, cf. Jerome, cited McNeile, ad loc., '*Aliud est enim narrare ignoranti, aliud scientem petere*'. cf. Is 65_{24}.

[69] cf. *supra*, p. 42; Heiler, p. 270.

fact that such a man prays and cannot but pray is one of the data with which philosophy must come to terms.

Another very definite assurance that our prayers will be heard is contained in the remaining passage on prayer which is to be found in M, viz. Matthew 18_{18-20}. The authenticity of these sayings has been a good deal disputed. We need not pause here over the first verse, about binding and loosing, for there was probably no original connexion between this and the rest. Its precise sense is hard to determine, but it is not primarily concerned with prayer, though indeed those whose actions on earth are effective in heaven might well pray with confidence.[70] Then, loosely connected, there follows this verse,

'*Again verily I say to you, that if two of you agree on earth about anything that they ask, it shall be done for them by my Father who is in heaven*' Mt 18_{19}.

What is meant is not any sort of agreement such as evil men might make for their own ends, but such an agreement as the next verse describes in oft-quoted words,

'*For where two or three are gathered together in my name, there am I in the midst of them*' Mt 18_{20}.

A possible variant is 'For there are not two or three gathered together in my name, with whom I am not in the midst of them'.[71] The saying is of a strongly ecclesiastical flavour; two constitute a community. It is in the Christian community that the presence of Christ is known. The saying contrives at once to stress the corporate nature of the Christian religion and yet to give some encouragement to separatists. But before we consider further the significance of the saying, we may take with it another one, also peculiar to Matthew. At the very end of the Gospel, after the command to teach and to baptize, Jesus says

'*And lo, I am with you all the days until the end of the age*' Mt 28_{20}.

This saying is less ecclesiastical in form, but equally so by virtue of its context. The two passages are often both taken to be not genuine. In each case difficulty arises from the context, but

[70] cf. Mt 16_{19}; Flew, *Church*, pp. 133-5.

[71] This is found in D, some versions, and Clement of Alexandria, and is supported, among others, by Cadoux, p. 78, and Manson, *Sayings*, p. 211, who also quotes Jewish parallels to the whole saying.

particularly in the latter saying. The command to baptize in the preceding verse has been much discussed, and we are driven to the view that the words cannot be regarded as a verbatim record or literal transcript of the words of Jesus.[72] This has an adverse effect on our estimate of the genuineness of the verse we are considering. Moreover, both Matthew 18_{20} and Matthew 28_{20} are peculiar to Matthew, and it is remarkable that so important a trend of thought should be confined to this Gospel. This argument from silence is however somewhat dangerous, and verges on the next argument commonly used, which is the *a priori* assumption that this is not the sort of thing that Jesus could have said.[73] A good example of this kind of argument is to be found in Cadoux.[74] He is willing to allow that Jesus ascribed to Himself a 'quasi-ubiquity' in that those who believed on Him or worked for Him were His representatives; of this there are other examples.[75] But he asserts that the idea that Christ would be spiritually or mystically present 'belongs to a different range of thought, one remote from Palestinian habits, and hardly likely to have dwelt in the same mind alongside the notion of a period of absence to be terminated by a triumphant and glorious visible return'. He concedes that such experiences were enjoyed by Paul and the Fourth Evangelist, and occupied a prominent position in their religious outlook, but they reflect a different order of thought from that which was customary with Jesus. Against this several points may be made. The phrase 'mystically present' is an interpretation of the saying (in which the word 'mystically' does not occur) and serves to excite suspicion against it. As for its being remote from Palestinian habits, without raising the supposed Jewish parallels (which are indeed only remote), we may observe

[72] cf. Flemington, pp. 105-9.

[73] Those who decide against these sayings do not usually ascribe them to M (in the sense of the supposedly written source thus designated), as we have hitherto done, but suppose them to have been added by the writer of the Gospel.

[74] Cadoux, pp. 315-17; also 77-8.

[75] Lk 10_{16}, Mk 9_{37} and parallels, Mt 10_{40}, 25_{40-5}. This goes back to the Jewish maxim that a man's representative (שָׁלִיחַ) shall be as himself, in which a considerable literature has now sprung up, in view of its connexion with the Christian ministry. cf. Rengstorf, *KTW*, I.415, 426. An attempt to read a particularly high view of the ministry into such a verse as Mt 10_{40} is defeated by such a verse as Mk 9_{37}, where the same character of 'representing Christ' is ascribed to little children. (Taylor, *Mark*, ad loc., thinks that by 'children' is meant 'the weaker members of the community': but this does not vitally affect the point, for it is to be hoped that that is not a possible description for the ministry.)

that the originality of Jesus naturally led to many innovations. That which came quite naturally to the minds of Paul and the Fourth Evangelist only a few years later (though admittedly on the basis of a different experience) might not unreasonably have occurred to the mind of Christ Himself. But the main argument relies on the alleged incompatibility between this mode of thought and the eschatological. But that these can be found together in the same mind can be shown from the cases of Paul and the Fourth Evangelist themselves. This paradoxical combination is the heart of Christian piety, and it is important to know whether it can claim the authority of Christ Himself; at least it cannot be ruled out simply on the ground that the ideas are incompatible. We might perhaps admit with McNeile[76] that the saying about the two or three, if genuine, could not mean to the hearers 'all that it could to Christians of a later date—the universal presence of the Divine Humanity expressing itself in the Church'; but that is a very different thing from denying that Christ could ever have said it.

If the saying be genuine, even though Christ did not mean all that the Church has read into it, we may perhaps see here a trace at least of a mode of thought other than the eschatological, a hint of a deeper intimacy than prophetic piety would allow. There were in the early Church, as there still are, two main conceptions of the activity of Christ after the ascension. One, based on such passages as Psalm 110, stressed His exaltation to the right hand of the Father; on this view He is absent rather than present, or at least He rules from a distance, though of course with this there goes the expectation that He will return at the Parousia. The other view depicts Christ as still present with His people, the Lord granting His real presence, especially through His sacraments, to His assembled people. This view is often called mystical, but might better be termed ecclesiastical. There is some rough truth in calling the former view Protestant, and the latter Catholic. But this can easily be exaggerated. Indeed some 'Catholic' theology can be criticized as implying the absence of Christ from His Church. The view of the apostolic ministry which stresses the word *shaliach* (an agent who acts in the absence of the principal) is particularly open to this criticism. It resembles the contrast between Christos and Kyrios made famous by Bousset in *Kyrios*

[76] McNeile, p. 267.

Christos; as also the contrast between Hebraic and Hellenic. We cannot rule out the possibility that the insertion of the text in the Gospel arises from wishful thinking unwilling to face the austerities of the eschatological message. But if it is genuine, then it is important that Christ Himself should give His support, however slightly, to this point of view, in the midst of many passages where He supports the other. It may well be that the idea of holding these two views in a fruitful tension goes back to Christ Himself. Of course, if the two views are considered separately, the views of communion with God that they imply are markedly different. If Christ be held to be in some sense absent till the Parousia, communion with God is doubtless possible, but it is of a less warm and intimate kind than that which is possible if Christ is present with His Church.

We may here mention a somewhat similar saying among the Agrapha, sayings of Christ handed on by oral tradition and not found in the Canonical Gospels, though of course ultimately written down. In the first collection of Oxyrhyncus papyri discovered by Grenfell and Hunt occur the words, so far as conjecture can restore them,

'*Jesus says, Wherever there are two, they are not without God, and where there is one alone, I say, I am with him. Raise the stone, and there thou shalt find me; cleave the wood, and I am there.*'

The thought, though relevant to the passages which we have been discussing because it speaks of the presence of Christ, is somewhat different. The stress on corporateness is lost; the individual can find God. The conclusion seems at first sight almost pantheist, but there are many other interpretations. For these reasons, as well as because the Agrapha generally speaking lack the authority of the Canonical Gospels, the genuineness of the saying is open to much dispute; and, though it has its defenders,[77] we shall not rely on it.

If then we summarize what we learn from M about Christ's teaching on prayer, we have first of all the Lord's Prayer, wholly prophetic and partly eschatological; then we have a considerable emphasis against ostentation and prolixity; we learn that God hears and welcomes our prayers, though He knows what we need,

[77] cf. Cadoux, p. 317, and literature there cited in n.2. For a list of possible interpretations, see W. A. Curtis, in *The Expositor*, Eighth Series, V.481-94.

and we have the sayings of a less eschatological and more ecclesiastical character, about which there is some room for doubt.

L

We come to the passages peculiar to the source L, of which we have already considered the L version of the Lord's Prayer. There are also in L two vivid parables about prayer. They both serve as good examples of the desirability of treating parables on the 'How much more?' principle, and not as allegories. One is the Parable of the Friend at Midnight (Lk $11_{5\text{-}8}$), which immediately follows the Lord's Prayer. It is possibly of special application to teachers, as a prayer for bread for others. The other is that of the Unjust Judge or Importunate Widow (Lk $18_{1\text{-}8}$). The aim of these, as is explicitly stated at the beginning in the case of the second, is that we 'ought always to pray and not grow weary'. The Syrophoenician woman (Mk $7_{24\text{-}30}$) would be a good example. Actually the contents of the second prayer do not entirely correspond to this. Even if we leave out 8b, as a saying only loosely attached, it still seems that the parable is not so much about prayer in general as about vindicating the elect. It might indeed be suggested that verses 7 and 8 are both additions to the original parable, and the idea that the two parables, the importunate friend and the unjust judge (or importunate widow) are parallel, having originally made a pair, would support that.[78] But the idea of avenging is deeply woven into the parable itself, so that the point is rather to do with prayer for vindication than with prayer in general; and perhaps it is rather that God will hear than that we should be importunate. But at any rate it is true that God is not like the man who says he *cannot* rise from his bed when he means he *will* not, nor, of course, like the judge who fears not God and reverences not men. But if importunity or 'shamelessness' in petition stirs even lazy or unjust men, then, *a fortiori*, it will avail with God. The tone is not indeed that which we have seen in the warning against vain repetitions (Mt 6_7), but the injunctions may fittingly be regarded as complementary. We are here at the furthest possible remove from those ideas of prayer which simply refer to the subjective effect on the person praying, and make no mention of God's answer. It is true that we are

[78] Thus McFadyen, p. 142, doubts if Lk $18_{7\text{-}8}$ is genuine, and thinks it is a product of later days of persecution.

dealing with One who knows what things we have need of before we ask Him (Mt 6_8), but, as Manson finely says in his commentary on the importunate friend,[79] 'we are not dealing with a mere combination of omniscience and omnipotence, but with a Father who cares for us as persons; . . . therefore our desires are His concern as much as our needs'. Yet even this passage in Manson concludes with a reference to the education of our desires. 'It may be that it is only by telling God frankly what we want that we can learn what we truly need.' We might add that it may be that it is only when we tell God what we want that He does some of the things which it is His will to do, inasmuch as He could not fittingly force them on us otherwise. It would be a transgression of our own warning that we should not turn the parable into an allegory to point out that the man gives bread and does not tell the importunate man what he ought to have asked for; but the parable is certainly, so far as it goes, compatible with 'naïve' notions of God answering prayer which may be not too far from the truth. Manson also observes that the one parable may be regarded as comment on the petition in the Lord's Prayer about bread, and the other as comment on 'Thy kingdom come'.[80]

This parable is immediately followed by that of the Pharisee and the Publican, also from L (Lk 18_{9-14}). This is deservedly one of the best known of Luke's parables. Its position here is no doubt due to its mention of prayer, which links it with the previous parable; but its message deals rather with the general attitude which Jesus requires than specifically with prayer, though it is in prayer that this spirit is expressed in the parable. The prayer of the Pharisee is really a piece of hypocritical self-congratulation; the terse words of the Publican 'God, be merciful to me a sinner' express the penitence and humility which is the true spirit of prayer, particularly of the prophetic type. But if we feel that our liturgies or our private devotions express something of this spirit, we must be careful lest for that very reason we say 'I thank Thee that I am not as that Pharisee'.

There is one other reference to prayer, and that a rather curious one, which we may mention here, for we owe it to Luke, though not to the source L. At Luke 5_{33}, Luke is following Mark, and

[79] Manson, *Sayings*, p. 267.

[80] Heiler, *Das Gebet*, pp. 368-9 (E.T. 249 omits the references to Luke), relates them both to the coming of the kingdom; cf. *Das Gebet*, p. 398 (E.T. 278, which is somewhat abbreviated). Importunity is a mark of 'prophetic' prayer.

adds to a reference to fasting the words 'and make petitions'. This is quite in harmony with the author's custom of inserting references to prayer; but unfortunately these words occur in the passage where the fasting of the disciples of John and of the Pharisees is contrasted with the absence of fasting on the part of the disciples of Jesus. The implication would seem to be that the disciples of Jesus do not pray, and moreover have no need to do so while the bridegroom is with them. But Luke verbally avoids this. Where Mark has 'but thy disciples fast not' (Mk 2_{18}), Luke ought logically to have 'but thy disciples neither fast nor pray', but instead he has 'but thine eat and drink', unless we accept the reading of D e 'but thine do none of these things'. But no great significance can be attached to Luke's mention of prayer here; it seems to be largely a matter of habit.

If we then sum up what are the main characteristics of the teaching on prayer contained in L,[81] leaving out the L version of the Lord's Prayer, already considered, we find importunity and humility, indeed penitence, to be the notes chiefly stressed; these notes are strongly characteristic of the prophetic view of prayer.

JESUS AND THE TEMPLE

There is one set of passages which throw light on Jesus' conception of piety, which can be grouped conveniently together as they deal with a single aspect of the theme, and have therefore been omitted in the foregoing passage based on the distinction of sources. These are the passages dealing with His attitude to the Temple. Mark $11_{11, 15-19}$, together with the Lukan parallel, (Lk 19_{45-6}) and the rather different account in Matthew 21_{10-17}, deals with the Cleansing of the Temple.[82] To go first, on arrival at Jerusalem, to the Temple was characteristically Jewish; to cleanse it implied an intimate connexion with it and authority in it. By His use of a quotation from Psalm 8_3 (LXX), He showed His approval of the children shouting their praises there.[83] It is more important that He quoted the verse 'My house shall be

[81] For completeness we should mention the worship of the angels (Lk 2_{14}), the prayer of Simeon (Lk 2_{29-32}), and other references to prayer and the Jewish cult in the Birth-narratives. Thanksgiving to God is commended in Lk 17_{11-19}.

[82] cf. Jn 2_{13-22}; cf. *supra*, p. 34.

[83] At least in the Matthaean version; but this has some improbability; see McNeile, ad loc.

called a house of prayer'.[84] This perhaps suggests that He did not condemn the Temple-cultus, but rather wished for its purification. (His stress, however, is not on sacrifice, but on prayer.) A similar conclusion might perhaps be drawn from Matthew 23_{21}, 'He that swears by the temple swears by it and by him that dwells therein'. On the other hand this may be one of those arguments which shows an opponent to be wrong on his own premisses. No very safe inferences can be drawn from the Lukan story of His being in the Temple at the age of twelve, especially as the translation of the crucial verse is uncertain. Is it 'in my Father's house' or 'about my Father's business'? (Lk 2_{49}). But it is clear that Jesus was no mere iconoclast; He did not set up a rival cultus. Indeed such is His conservatism here that, whereas in some other matters He shows Himself willing to condone what is technically desecration,[85] here, if we may judge from a single verse (Mk 11_{16}) standing in Mark only and not in the parallels (which is unusual), by His prohibition of carrying vessels through the Temple, He seems to have forbidden its use for a purpose good in itself, but not specifically religious. In view of all this, it is not surprising that for a time after the ascension the disciples continued to attend the Temple.[86] On the other hand, Jesus foretold the destruction of the Temple (Mk 13_{1-4} and parallels), and said 'A greater than the temple is here' (Mt 12_{6}), adding the well-chosen quotation from Hosea 6_{6}, 'I desire mercy and not sacrifice' (Mt 12_{7}, 9_{13}).[87] The twofold attitude thus taken towards the Temple is indeed only an aspect of a similar attitude taken towards its priesthood and indeed to the Law in general.[88] Here is one of those many tensions which we find in the life of Jesus.

JESUS AS THE OBJECT OF OUR PRAYER

We have now considered Jesus as a worshipping Subject, and also as Teacher about communion with God. He is also the

[84] Luke has 'be' for 'be called'. Only Mark finishes the quotation, which is from Is 56_{7}, with the words 'for all the nations'; cf. Marsh, pp. 114-15.

[85] Mk 2_{23}—3_{6}, and parallels, esp. Mt 12_{5-7}, a Matthaean addition to the parallel passage.

[86] Lk 24_{53}, as well as many passages in Acts; Mk 14_{58} is not really relevant to this subject.

[87] cf. *supra*, p. 30; cf. Mt 5_{23-4}.

[88] cf. Heiler, *Urkirche*, pp. 39-40.

Object of our worship, and it might be thought that we ought here to consider Jesus as the Object of worship in the synoptic Gospels. But that would throw no light on the precise subject which we are considering. The deepening recognition of the status of Jesus, the slow ascription to Him of such titles as Messiah, these and similar questions belong rather to Christology. In any case, Jesus was not clearly and unmistakably worshipped as God during His lifetime. Men had communion with Him by the ordinary channels of social intercourse, though their fellowship was accompanied, no doubt, by a deep sense of reverence. This reverence is expressed by the word προσκυνέω, worship. But this word does not always have a full theological meaning, any more than in our phrase 'His Worship the Mayor'. It is not indeed a courtesy rendered to ordinary men, but to men specially worthy of reverence, possibly because they were felt to have something divine or supernatural about them: it refers to some rather oriental outward act such as prostrating oneself, or the like. It is used in the LXX in connexion with kings (e.g. 2 K=2 S 18_{28}), by Christ, as recorded in Matthew (Mt 18_{26}), in speaking of the relation of slave to master (without any note of disapproval), and in Acts 10_{25} of the attitude of Cornelius to Peter, though indeed Peter protested that he also was a man. Thus, though it is sometimes used in the Gospels in contexts where it might bear a richer meaning (e.g. Lk 24_{52}) it need not involve adoration of Jesus as God in many passages where people make this sign of reverence (e.g. Mt 8_2). Once indeed it is used of mock adoration (Mk 15_{19}). In Matthew 14_{33} it seems to have a fairly full meaning.

A somewhat similar point arises from the fact that men came to Jesus in His lifetime with requests, notably for healing, which we with our present Christology are apt to regard as prayers. How far they were so regarded by those who made the requests, it is difficult to say. But certainly the way in which Jesus dealt with these requests must be regarded, by those who are Christians, as indicative of the way in which God answers prayer; and thus affords indirect teaching about the nature and spirit of the petitions which we ought to offer. Some of these requests do not meet with approval: 'Ye know not what ye ask' (Mk 10_{38});[89] some are at first refused in order to test character (Mk 7_{27}); many are granted, a striking instance being that of the Dying Thief

[89] cf. Ro 8_{26}.

(Lk 23_{42}): one at least is granted in order to show its presumptuousness (Mt 14_{28-31}). There is no need to enumerate these incidents here; most of the well-known healing miracles are amongst them, and a consideration of the details of them is not germane to our theme; but the way in which Jesus received these petitions is a strong support for the use of petition in prayer, and thus for prayer of the prophetic rather than the mystical type. The word most frequent in these narratives is faith; sometimes a lack of faith is condemned (Mt 14_{31}); often faith is commended. Faith, even if it be but little faith, or vicarious faith, like the faith of a parent for his child, is an indispensable condition for the proper offering of petition or intercession. Prophetic piety is aptly named also faith-piety.

CHAPTER FOUR

THE SYNOPTIC GOSPELS (*continued*)

VISION

WE NOW ask what words are most used in the synoptic Gospels to describe man's communion with God, and in view of the prominence often given to the phrase 'the vision of God' in subsequent theology, we shall begin with that.[1] The Old Testament lays greater stress on hearing[2] than on seeing, though 'seeing' is, of course, used in descriptions of prophetic ecstasy. It is commonly supposed that the Old Testament speaks occasionally of the vision of God, but Michaelis[3] disposes of most of the instances. Kirk[4] cites Genesis 32_{30}, but, as Michaelis points out, Jacob expresses here a certain astonishment that his life was preserved. Kirk's other instances can mostly be questioned by similar means.[5] The vision of Isaiah does indeed stand in a somewhat unique position. Some of the other prophetic visions of God must also be allowed, but they are not the result of any mystical striving after the vision of God; they are shown to men by God. Numbers 12_{6-8} depreciates the visions enjoyed by the prophets in comparison with the experience of Moses, and the account in Exodus 33_{17-23} of Moses seeing God's back turns on the point that man cannot see God and live.[6]

This does not, however, entirely dispose of the matter, for there is evidence that this caution was a later development, arising from motives of reverence and a fear that the vision of God might be taken too literally; probably references to seeing God have been actually removed from the tradition. Manson[7] observes that in

[1] cf. Michaelis, *KTW*, V.315-81; Blackman, *RTW*, p. 223; Kirk.
[2] Kittel, *KTW*, I.216-22.
[3] Michaelis, *KTW*, V.329-35.
[4] Kirk, p. 11.
[5] The references in Kirk, p. 11 are as follows, the page in Michaelis where the same passage is treated being added in brackets:—Gn 12_7 (p. 333), 18_1 (p. 333 n.91 on 18_2 bears on this point), Ex 6_3 (p. 331), 33_{11} (p. 331), Nu 12_{6-8} (p. 331), Dt 34_{10} (p. 331), Is $6_{1ff.}$ (pp. 330-1), Amos 7_7 (p. 330), 9_1 (p. 330), Mic 1_{1-3} (p. 329), Ezk 43_7 (p. 330 n.83). (Kirk's other Ezekiel references refer only to seeing glory), 1 K 22_{19} (p. 331).
[6] Instances of a similar caution are in Kirk, pp. 11-12.
[7] Manson, *Sayings*, p. 151.

Palestinian speech to 'see God' is another way of saying 'appear before God'; but it may well be that in early days the visitors to local shrines took the phrase 'see God' more literally. The phrase may have to some extent survived, with reference to attending the Temple worship, particularly at the Great Festivals. In many places the milder expression 'appear before God' is what we now find; but it is strongly suspected that this has been substituted for an original 'see God': the former expression is simply the Niph'al of ראה; and probably the vowel-points were simply altered from an original Qal.[8]

Despite this supposed characteristic of the primitive tradition, the Old Testament as we have it contains very little about the vision of God. We have already made use of Michaelis to attack the passages on which Kirk relies; it remains to say that Michaelis examines many other passages, both the instances of prophetic ecstasy and those of theophany, and shows that references to seeing God are exceedingly rare, and that there is a much greater stress on hearing. He goes so far as to criticize the view, expressed elsewhere in the same work, that the vision of God is there conceived eschatologically, i.e. was expected in the future.[9]

In the light of this the burden of proof surely lies on those who contend that seeing plays a prominent part in the synoptic Gospels. There are, of course, references to seeing the Son of Man coming in the future.[10] There are references to seeing Jesus in His lifetime, which mostly have no theological content at all, though after the resurrection, when they saw Him, they worshipped Him (Mt 28_{17}). The resurrection appearances constitute a special case of 'seeing'. They are a revelation from God rather than an ordinary instance of earthly sight. But they are not a vision of God the Father: and (even if we include the experience of Paul on the Damascus road) they only continued for a limited time. They could not constitute any general defence of the phrase 'vision of God'.[11] The similitude of the Sheep and the

[8] A typical passage is Is 1_{12}. Fuller details are in Kirk, pp. 12-14; Michaelis, *KTW*, V.324-5, Taylor, *FR*, p. 132.

[9] Kittel, *KTW*, I.218. Michaelis, *KTW*, V.334-5 considers Job 19_{26}, Ps 16_{15}, Is 60_2. He concludes '*Die Verheissung Mt* 5_8 *und die Gewissheit 1 Jn* 3_2 *haben somit keine unmittelbaren Vorläufer im AT*'.

[10] Mt 16_{28}, but probably this is an interpretation of the rather different wording in Mk 9_1. cf. Mt 23_{39} (=Lk 13_{35}), Mk 13_{26} (=Mt 24_{30}, Lk 21_{27}), Mk 14_{62} (=Mt 26_{64}) (avoided in Lk 22_{69}).

[11] Michaelis, *KTW*, V.355-62.

Goats (Mt 25_{31-46}) contains the verb 'see' in the question: 'When saw we thee hungry. . . ?' The answer 'Inasmuch as ye did it unto one of these my brethren, even these least, ye did it unto me' implies, though it does not use the word explicitly, that Christ is to be *seen* in the needs of others, but this is not what is usually meant by the vision of God. Nor are phrases about seeing angels relevant. But three passages call for further comment.

The first of these is the Beatitude, the genuineness of which we need not doubt, 'Blessed are the pure in heart, for they shall see God' (Mt 5_8, from M). This is often taken to mean a promise of the vision of God in this life to those who are pure in heart. But there is a good deal to be said for the view that this reward applies only to the future life. The reward must be considered in relation to the rewards mentioned in the other Beatitudes; some of these, as that the mourners shall be comforted and the merciful obtain mercy, are especially appropriate to the virtues involved, but there is nothing to show whether the reward occurs in this life or the next. The dating of others depends on the view taken of the kingdom of God. 'Theirs is the kingdom of heaven' is such a phrase, the interpretation of which depends on the view which is taken of eschatological questions in general. Manson[12] refers to the connexion between the phrase 'see God' and 'appear before God', speaks of the purifications required in the Jewish Law to remove physical disqualifications from joining in the Temple-worship, and then says, 'From this it is a simple matter to take the step that is taken in Psalm 24 and to think of an inward cleansing as the qualification for communion with God'. As far as the argument thus goes, the reward might be in this life, but, of course, the fact that the Temple-worship belongs to this life does not of itself necessitate the view that this reward in its spiritualized form is in this life. And one consideration tells strongly against the view that any of the Beatitudes refers to reward in this life. The last reward mentioned is 'Your reward is great in Heaven'. Here the reference to the future life and the exclusion of the present are quite clear. Further, though each of the rewards in the Beatitudes seems to be carefully chosen to fit the corresponding virtue, it seems likely that they all refer to the same kind of bliss, though they describe it in different phrases. There is none of them which *must* be referred to this life, but there is one (which we

12 Manson, *Sayings*, p. 151.

have quoted) which can only refer to the next life; the inference is that they all refer to the bliss of heaven. One consideration imperils this argument. The statement about the reward in heaven may mean that it is kept with God, ready to be conferred when the kingdom fully comes on earth.[13] But even so, eschatology is not so much 'realized' that the kingdom can be said to have come in this full sense; so that it still follows that this reward was not enjoyed on earth by the 'community of the interval'. Nor, on our argument, is the vision of God.

We thus approve the view of Michaelis, who regards the vision of God here, as also the parallel expression about being the children of God, as an entirely eschatological promise, whereas in 1 John 3_2 it is possible in this life to be a child of God, but seeing God is still future. The reserve of the New Testament on this subject distinguishes it plainly from the mystery-religions and Gnosis. We have here (he adds) a promise which rests solely on the authority of Jesus, a promise of such importance that it was not casually repeated, but only occasionally rang out, with restrained expressions of joy, as in 1 John 3_2.[14]

Thus the vision of God is in the synoptic Gospels neither here nor elsewhere promised to the Christian in this life. This conclusion has a profound effect, if it be correct, on Kirk's argument, which makes a very great use of this text, as indeed the title of his Bampton Lectures almost suggests. 'Christianity had come into the world,' he says, 'with a double purpose, to offer men the vision of God, and to call them to the pursuit of that vision.'[15] But the numerous reservations which, as he himself shows,[16] were applied by the Old Testament writers when they spoke of the vision of God, might have warned him not to read too much into the New Testament. And indeed he says of this Beatitude[17] 'It is extraordinary—especially in view of the prominence which the thought had attained in contemporary religion, and the high relief into which New Testament theology was about to throw it—that the sentence stands without an echo in the synoptic tradition. But this judgement is at best superficial'. To this it might be replied that the prominence which the thought attained was largely in pagan religion, with which we might expect some

[13] cf. Cadoux, p. 239, and Wellhausen, *Das Evangelium Matthaei*, p. 15, and McNeile, p. 54a, cited in Cadoux, p. 239 n.1.

[14] Michaelis, *KTW*, V.367-8. [15] Kirk, p. 1. [16] Kirk, pp. 10-14. [17] Kirk, p. 94.

contrast: 'the high relief into which New Testament thought was about to throw it' remains to be investigated; that it *seems* to stand without an echo is a fact; and the attempt to show that it does not really stand without an echo cannot be said to succeed; Kirk rests it on purely general considerations and on the Transfiguration,[18] which we have yet to consider. The other text which he greatly uses is the statement of Irenaeus 'the life of man is the vision of God',[19] but if our interpretation of the Beatitude is correct, then Irenaeus' point is quite different, and may indeed be the first explicit statement of this view in Christian writings.

VISION AT THE BAPTISM AND TRANSFIGURATION

The other passages to which reference must be made in connexion with Vision are the stories of the Baptism and the Transfiguration, both of which raise also the question, which we shall also examine at this point, whether Jesus was in an ecstasy.[20] It will be convenient to begin with the Transfiguration (Mk 9_{2-8}= Mt 17_{1-8}, Lk 9_{28-36}). The narrative seems to be derived from Mark, whom the other synoptists here follow, though with considerable freedom. The incident is so rich in symbolism, allusion, and allegory that the wealth of the material has long been 'the despair of commentators, as well as the whetstone of their ingenuity'.[21] Many of these lines of allusion have no particular relevance to our theme; detailed discussions of the whole incident can be found in the recent works of Boobyer and Ramsey.[22] They are agreed that Mark regarded it as a confirmation of the Messiahship of Christ in the form of a foretaste of His glory at the Parousia. We may next ask what actual experience lies behind the narrative. The view that it is a misplaced post-resurrection appearance has been argued or assumed by many liberal scholars and form-critics, especially on the Continent; but it is full of difficulties. Others see here Hellenistic ideas, either imported into an incident originally very different or worked up into a piece of symbolic writing which has no foundation in fact

[18] Kirk, pp. 94-101.

[19] *vita autem hominis visio Dei*; Irenaeus, *adv. haer.* IV.20.7, cited in Kirk, p. 1.

[20] cf. also Lk 10_{18}.

[21] Kirk, p. 98.

[22] Ramsey, pp. 101-47; cf. Michaelis, *KTW*, V.354-5; Taylor, *Mark*, ad loc.

at all. Thus Norden[23] thinks that the fundamental idea of the story is a mystical union between the Father and the Son, and sees in the word ἐπισκιάζω a reminder of a mystical experience described in Philo, whereas the obvious parallel is Exodus 40_{35}, where the overshadowing of a cloud symbolizes the divine presence.[24] In fact, there is nothing in the form which the experience took which could not readily be supplied by the Jewish mind; there are numerous parallels in the Old Testament, and to some extent in the New, to the items recorded.

Another theory, which sets the story in a rather curious light, is that of Bacon,[25] to which Kirk inclines, though indecisively. Paul holds that the converted Christian undergoes a metamorphosis in which his tabernacle, σκηνή (i.e. his mortal body), becomes less and less adequate; it is an earthly tabernacle soon to be laid aside;[26] so the story has reached its present form through Pauline influence. This, besides being in itself somewhat fantastic, harmonizes only imperfectly with Kirk's main contention that the life of man is the vision of God, for it ascribes to the vision a most disturbing effect.

Kirk's view is that a genuine incident lies behind the narrative, but before the writing of the earliest Gospel the Church had fixed on it as the central moment of Christ's earthly life, and had thus surrounded it with allusion and allegorism 'as though to remind itself that the *whole* gospel, from beginning to end, must be read and regarded as one great vision of God in Christ, akin to the vision given to the favoured three on the Mount of Transfiguration'.[27] We may reply to this with the words of Ramsey, who, deeply as he is concerned with the Transfiguration, yet admits, 'The Transfiguration does not belong to the central core of the Gospel. The apostolic *Kerygma* did not, so far as we know, include it'.[28] The vision, as indeed Kirk observes, was given only to the favoured three, and on the descent they were told to tell no one what they had seen till after the resurrection (Mk 9_9=Mt 17_9).[29] The whole stress is on the uniqueness of the incident; it

[23] cited in Creed, p. 133.

[24] A similar theory is that of Lohmeyer (see Boobyer, pp. 2-4; Ramsey, pp. 102-3) that the narrative combines a Jewish-Christian tradition about Moses and Elijah with a Hellenistic tradition of a metamorphosis.

[25] Bacon, pp. 253 ff.

[26] cf. 2 Co 5_{1-4}.

[27] Kirk, p. 101.

[28] Ramsey, p. 144.

[29] This secrecy is not sufficiently stressed either by Kirk or by Ramsey.

was abnormal; more than a foretaste of heaven, which all communion with God on earth is; it was an *exceptional* foretaste of heaven. Men did not usually see the glory of God in Christ. And this of course quite harmonizes with what we have described as Mark's own view of the incident. A foretaste of the Parousia is something unusual. Of course, what the disciples saw was eternally true; they had received a glimpse of reality, not of illusion; but their whole life was not to be spent in such a vision, but rather in *believing* what they there had *seen*. The attempt to extend the notion of vision from one exceptional incident to the whole Gospel we must deem completely erroneous.

We may reject such theories as those of Kirk and Bacon and yet hold that the incident was historic, a watershed, together with the incident at Caesarea Philippi, between the Galilean ministry and the way to the Cross. We may grant that some of the detail has been supplied in the interest of allegory, and yet ask what really happened. Presumably both Jesus and the disciples had an unusual spiritual experience. Such experiences have recently been closely studied as part of the psychology and phenomenology of religion. In the still more recent revival of Biblical theology, there has been a marked tendency to ignore the results of such investigations. It is certainly true that the inner experiences of Jesus must not be assessed simply by comparison with those of others; we must always remember that there was something unique about Him. But we have already rejected the idea that we must not investigate the devotional life of Jesus; and these parallels may be helpful. There are other instances of those who are enjoying intense communion with God seeing other objects glow.[30] This in itself would suffice as a parallel; the disciples had the experience, and thus saw Jesus glow. But further, there are many instances of those who are enjoying intense communion with God themselves glowing with a strange radiance;[31] on this view Jesus had the experience and the disciples saw it. This may well have been an 'objective' fact, though the words 'objective' and 'subjective' are somewhat imprecise in these contexts. It may well be that the disciples, being in an exalted spiritual state themselves, subjectively supplied some of the other details, or, in other words, that there was an element of hallucination, but of course, 'such experiences, however subjectively determined as regards their

[30] cf. James, pp. 241ff; Rawlinson, p. 119 n.2. [31] cf. Underhill, p. 116.

form and perceptual content, may yet have been the vehicles, in particular cases, of genuinely spiritual intimations from on high'.[32] It is also possible that the conversation with Moses and Elijah took place in the consciousness of Christ and was communicated in some way to the disciples.[33] The fact already mentioned that the items recorded were quite in the Jewish tradition makes it entirely possible that the disciples subjectively supplied some of them. The most interesting of the details probably thus supplied is the Voice from heaven.[34] This we may leave till we come to the Baptism. To sum up our conclusions on the Transfiguration, we may say that it affords no support for those theories which see the whole Christian life as a vision of God. But we do see here an intense degree of communion with God enjoyed by Jesus, and, to a lesser extent, by the disciples. Whether or not it deserves the title 'mystical ecstasy', we must defer till we have considered the incident in many ways parallel, the Baptism.

The Baptism (Mk 1_{9-11}, Mt 3_{13-17}, Lk 3_{21-2}),[35] source of embarrassment to Matthew and some of the apocryphal Gospels, crushed by Luke into the Genitive Absolute, largely ignored by the Fourth Gospel, denied by the Church a feast of its own and thrown in with the Epiphany, is a well-authenticated incident which serves as an initiation of Christ into His ministry, to some extent similar to the initiatory experiences of the prophets. Here, as in the Transfiguration story, we find a vision and a voice. As we proceed from Mark to Matthew and Luke, there is more stress on the 'objective' nature of the event, but in the most primitive version, the Markan, Jesus alone sees, and the voice is addressed to Jesus alone. The experience was thus a more private one than the Transfiguration, where the disciples are depicted as having a greater share. The symbolism is thoroughly Jewish; the Spirit, the dove, and the Voice (*Bath Qol*) are associated in the Rabbinic writings.[36] The *Bath Qol* is really an echo, inferior to the Holy Spirit which inspired the prophets. The fact that the *Bath Qol* and the Spirit are vouchsafed together here places Jesus at once

[32] Rawlinson, p. 119. And the disciples may have 'subconsciously' grasped the truths taught to them more fully than they normally realized; cf. McNeile, p. 252.

[33] So Maisie Spens and W. K. Lowther Clarke, both quoted in Ramsey, p. 108.

[34] Somewhat briefly treated by Boobyer, who links it with the shout at the Parousia, and Ramsey.

[35] cf. Flemington, pp. 25-33; Taylor, *Mark*, pp. 158-62, 617-19; Michaelis, *KTW*, V.353-4.

[36] cf. Barrett, pp. 39-40.

among the rabbis and the prophets. There is no need to regard them as external fact when the narrative itself (in its most primitive form) does not claim that the disciples saw and heard. Nor need we regard them as visual and auditory phenomena in the consciousness of Jesus, and yet they may have been, for a mildly kenotic view of His consciousness makes it possible to conceive that He received communications in this form. They might represent His own attempt to explain in categories familiar to His hearers what had occurred. But more probably it was deliberately intended at first as the expression in symbolic form of the experience which the disciples believed (and rightly so) to have come to Christ. It was the natural symbolism to use for that purpose. But by the time Mark wrote, it had become a miraculous sign, really visible and audible to Jesus, a development which the other synoptic writers continued further.[87] We are not bound to take a similar view of the *Bath Qol* in the Transfiguration story. We have already suggested that that is one of the items subjectively supplied rather than a matter of objective fact. Are we to go further in a minimizing direction and say that that was not an auditory phenomenon present in the consciousness of the disciples but merely the symbolic way in which they afterwards described what they had experienced? Not necessarily, for whereas in the story of the Baptism there is some little difficulty in thinking of Jesus receiving such an experience and describing it in that form (though it is not inconceivable), in the story of the Transfiguration there is no great difficulty in supposing that the *disciples* would have such an experience, particularly if their minds had dwelt on the narrative of the Baptism, even though they recognized that to be symbolic. In other words, the distinction drawn by Mark between Jesus hearing at the Baptism and the disciples hearing at the Transfiguration may well correspond to a difference in fact; only the difference in fact is (we suggest) between a consciously symbolic account and an actual (not objective) hallucinatory experience. If it be asked how three people could have the same subjective experience, there are many possible answers, among them telepathy.

On the view that we have taken of the Baptism, we have not to consider the question of the significance of vision which arose in connexion with the Transfiguration; but we must return to the

[87] cf. Rawlinson, p. 10.

question whether either of them was a mystical 'ecstasy'. Oepke, who refers also to the Temptations and the Cry of Joy (Mt $11_{25ff.}$) as well as to the word ἐξέστη in Mark 3_{21},[38] says that despite certain ecstatic features, Jesus shows a sobriety and willingness to return to human need which mark out his type of 'ecstasy' as distinctive.[39] The word is indeed ambiguous, but if a spiritual experience of quite abnormal intensity is thereby indicated, then we may allow it in the case of Christ both at the Baptism and at the Transfiguration, and in the case of the disciples also at the Transfiguration, where their confusion suggests that they were somewhat beside themselves or out of their mind, in a way which suggests the original meaning of the Greek word. There is, however, no need to class the experience as 'mystical' as Evelyn Underhill does, unless that word is broadened to cover every spiritual experience. We have, on the other hand, already noticed a certain resemblance between the Baptism and the call of the prophets, though, of course, the experience of Jesus was far greater and the comparison must not be pressed too far.[40] The presence of Elijah in the story reminds us that this experience of Jesus stood in the Jewish prophetic tradition, just as the mention of Moses reminds us that his face also shone (Ex 34_{29-35}). We must indeed be on our guard against over-hasty generalizations that the prophets heard while the mystics saw. But the ordinary visions of the prophets were not visions of God, but rather of symbolic objects,[41] and similarly the vision here at the Baptism (even if it was an actual experience of Jesus) is not a direct vision of God.[42] The greatest of these prophetic visions, that of Isaiah (Is 6), does indeed speak of seeing the Lord, but that is unusual. And whereas the mystics no doubt sometimes had clear auditions, they constantly speak of the communications they receive being ineffable,[43] the prophets, on the other hand, always speak clearly what they hear; here too the Baptism and the Temptation stand in the prophetic tradition, for what the *Bath Qol* said is perfectly

[38] cf. Lk 10_{18}.

[39] Oepke, *KTW*, II.454.

[40] cf. Bultmann, *Die Geschichte der synoptischen Tradition*, p. 263 f., quoted in Barrett, p. 44 n.2. For Jesus as a 'pneumatic' man, see Barrett, pp. 113-21.

[41] e.g. Jer $1_{11, 13}$.

[42] Michaelis, *KTW*, V.354 thinks that the verbal element in it is more prominent than the visual.

[43] cf. 2 Co 12_4.

clear (apart from textual variants!). It will thus perhaps be better to call these experiences 'prophetic ecstasies'.

MEANINGS OF THE WORD 'VISION'

But to return to our main theme, we have now dealt with the passages on which Kirk particularly relies in order to maintain the view that 'the idea of the vision dominates both our Lord's teaching and the synoptic presentation of His life'. That Jesus '*gave* a vision of God where others could only *speak* of it'[44] is true only in a general sense; it would be better if some word such as 'communion' or 'knowledge' were substituted for 'vision'. The fact is that Kirk always assumes without argument that 'vision' is the generic word. This comes out clearly in his summary of different conceptions of the vision of God.[45] He begins with this

'(1) The most primitive view is that God is *physically visible* in this life, though to see Him is death (older stages of the O.T.).'

With this we agree, with the remark that the life of man is clearly not yet the vision of God at this stage. He continues

'(2) God is *physically invisible*; but metaphorically visible (i.e. knowable), that is, *His character can be inferred* from His "works" (Rabbis and philosophers—but most representatives of both schools are touched by the next conception too).'

But if 'metaphorically visible' means simply 'knowable', why retain the word 'visible'? There is surely here a transition to another category. Indeed a 'knowledge' of God obtained by inference hardly deserves even the title 'communion', still less 'vision'. Kirk continues

'(3) God is comprehensible to reason, from His works, but *still more knowable by "faith", or mystic and ecstatic experience* (many representatives among the philosophers; also Philo and *Hermetica* in their best moments).'

On this we may comment that the word 'visible' has now fallen altogether out of this summary of 'the different conceptions of the vision of God'; we must also protest that to mention so closely together ' "faith", or mystic and ecstatic experience' is to confuse widely different types of piety. Kirk continues

[44] Kirk, pp. 94, 96. [45] Kirk, p. 110. The italics in what follows are his.

'(4) The N.T. position is analogous to (3), but enriches it . . .'

We need not pursue the quotation; the analogy between the New Testament on the one hand and Philo and the *Hermetica* on the other is, at best, exceedingly dubious. We proceed to the next point:

'(5) Most representatives of (2) to (4) insist that *moral affinity with God* is essential to the vision; the N.T. suggests that it is *more important* than "experience".'

It is not clear what is meant here by 'experience'; is the vision 'experience'? Kirk has two more such sections, in neither of which is the word 'visible' used. In fact, the paragraph abundantly shows that Kirk is not able to make that frequent use of the word 'vision' which his own thesis and that of Irenaeus require. Kirk has indeed looked briefly at this difficulty in these words:[46]

'In view of the passages cited above,[47] it seems ridiculous to say[48] that "the 'vision of God' in the New Testament is a privilege reserved almost exclusively for the future life"; still more to add that "this marks a great advance". The statements could only have a shadow of verisimilitude if by "seeing" God were meant *physical* vision alone; and even then they would be untrue, for it is impossible to suppose that New Testament writers conceived the risen saints (with their "spiritual bodies", 1 Co 15_{44}) to have physical vision.'

It seems only fair to quote this footnote of Kirk, because the position here described as ridiculous is (as far as concerns the synoptic Gospels at any rate) almost identical with our own. We should reply as follows: it is a profitless speculation what kind of vision the New Testament writers conceive spiritual bodies to have; but the main point is this: it does not follow that if you concede that no one has a physical vision of God, therefore you may claim that many people have a metaphorical vision. Because the use of a word is metaphorical, it does not follow that it must be uncontrolled; and the use of this particular metaphor ought to be governed largely by the use of it in the original documents. And there can be no doubt that the synoptic Gospels discourage the use of it. And the metaphor is the less necessary when other

[46] Kirk, p. 108 n.1; cf. p. 106 n.4.

[47] The reference in Kirk is mostly to Pauline and Johannine passages which we must consider in detail later.

[48] Here follow in Kirk some references which I omit.

words can easily be substituted for it, as in this case. The very passage to which this last quotation was a footnote runs as follows:

> 'That unbroken personal intercourse with the divine is the end for which man was created; that a foretaste of this experience is possible even in this life; . . . these are the pillars of the conception.'

This is perfectly true, but when a word like 'intercourse' is available, there is no need to defend a metaphor like 'vision', except where the New Testament usage itself explicitly warrants it.

OTHER WORDS USED TO DESCRIBE COMMUNION WITH GOD

We have examined at some length the popular word 'vision', and found that the synoptic Gospels do not afford an adequate basis for the current use of it. We now look more briefly at some possible alternatives.

The word 'knowledge' has much more to commend it, and has already been discussed in connexion with an important logion. The verb, with its Old Testament equivalent, has much to commend it as an expression of the synoptic type of piety, though its actual use is not common. But against it we must set the fact that there are other strands in its meaning, more Hellenistic in character, which are not appropriate here, that the noun γνῶσις seems to have been deliberately avoided by some of the New Testament writers[49] and that the use of the verb in this well-known synoptic logion has not been free from disputes as to which precise shade of meaning is to be put upon the word. 'Knowledge' has not the dangers of 'vision', and its modern use as in the title of John Baillie's book *Our Knowledge of God* is well calculated to bring out that character of 'encounter' or 'confrontation', the new emphasis on which is one of the most marked features of modern theology.

Another verb which must be considered is 'hear', though neither 'the hearing of God' nor 'the audition of God' would be a happy phrase in English. It is often said that hearing is a characteristic of Hebrew religion and seeing of Greek.[50] This is certainly true, as far as the prophets are concerned, but it is difficult to find

[49] This anticipates the discussion *infra*, p. 166. In the Gospels the noun is used only twice (Lk 1_{77}, 11_{52}) on which see Bultmann, *KTW*, I.706; ἐπίγνωσις does not occur.

[50] e.g. Quick, pp. 70-1.

passages in the synoptists which clearly support this point. It is indeed notable that at the great crises of the Baptism and the Transfiguration a voice is heard as well as a vision seen. There are, of course, many references to hearing Christ, but they can and mostly must be taken of physically hearing Him in His lifetime. There are various references to hearing the word, mostly in the Parable of the Sower (e.g. Mt 13_{19}, $_{23}$), or in such a verse as 'Blessed are they that hear the word of God and keep it' (Lk 11_{28}). But all these may refer to the physical hearing of the preached word. This is indeed a means of grace, but it cannot be said to follow that the same word is necessarily appropriate as a description of our interior intercourse with God. The phrase is harmless enough, but there is no particular warrant for it. On the other hand, such verses as Mark 4_9 contrast with physical hearing a non-physical and therefore metaphorical hearing, which might afford ground for a more general use of the word.[51]

We may here pause to inquire why hearing seems to us a weaker word than seeing. Quick, for instance, writes, quite correctly, of the Old Testament period,[52] 'Although the vision of God's face may belong to the hope of a redeemed world-order, the conviction prevails that for sinful man to see God would be death. "Hearing God" is the Hebrew way of expressing that less open and direct communion with God which is all that man can attain to in this world'. Now theoretically to hear someone's voice is as direct a means of communication as to see him. The one is (popularly speaking, at least) a matter of waves in the air; the other, a matter of waves in the ether. And indeed to hear a person's voice is usually more informative, and enables something with more intellectual content to be communicated. Indeed the Hebrews learnt more from the voices than from the visions that were vouchsafed to them, as Quick points out. And yet the feeling persists that we should keep the word 'vision' for the more direct communication; and the bearing of physics on the sentences quoted from Quick does not spring at once to the mind. Similarly, blindness is commonly, at any rate, counted a greater affliction than deafness. But, leaving aside this last point, we think the reason is partly this; when a person is near enough to be clearly seen, he is also near enough to be heard; but when a person is near enough to be heard, there may be some obstacle (or simply

[51] On the whole subject, see Kittel, *KTW*, I.216-22.

[52] Quick, p. 71.

darkness) which prevents him from being seen. The contrast is thus not between mere visibility and mere audibility, but between visibility which is assumed to include audibility on the one hand and mere audibility on the other. Also the eye takes in much more detail than the ear; it is much harder to simulate someone's appearance than to imitate his voice. Moreover, sight suggests a tangible object existing in space, which God, apart from the Incarnation, is not; hearing suggests a message in words, which God may easily be conceived as sending. It is true that God may be anthropomorphically pictured and that, on the other hand, He does not literally speak the words which we so readily ascribe to Him, partly because He does not utter them with physical lips and partly because presumably His thoughts are not originally in any particular human language. Nevertheless, to speak of 'seeing' God seems more metaphorical than to speak of 'hearing' Him. For all these reasons, 'hearing' is reckoned less than 'seeing', and thus there would be nothing extravagantly intimate about the use of the word 'hear', but there is no strong case for it.

There remains the possibility of using 'fellowship' or some translation of κοινωνία. Neither this nor κοινωνέω occurs in the synoptists, though κοινωνός appears twice (Mt 23_{30}, Lk 5_{10}) in uninstructive contexts. Nevertheless κοινωνία is not to be ruled sharply out. It is not a word like 'vision', where there is a risk of confusion between the physical and metaphorical meanings. It is found in some of the rest of the New Testament, though it remains of course to be investigated whether its presence there and absence here is due to any change of emphasis; there is however no *prima facie* case, as with 'vision', for confining it to the bliss of heaven. We shall consider the precise meaning of the word when we come to its occurrences in the later books, but we may say here that it has usually some flavour of 'partnership' (cf. Lk 5_{10}) or intimate 'fellowship', and, though the common translation 'fellowship' will need to be modified in certain passages, yet the word 'fellowship', expressing, as it does, an intimate human relationship, seems well fitted to describe that relationship with the Father which Jesus enjoyed and enjoined. If Jesus had spoken of Him solely as King, it would have been different: though it is possible to have personal relationships with an earthly king, there are comparatively few men who can describe them as intimate. But Jesus addresses God, and encourages us to address God, as

Father. This relationship contains within itself (though not as strongly as does the relationship with a king) the idea that the two are not equals. Yet the use of this word, indicating kinship between ourselves and God, is ample warrant for the use of such a word as 'fellowship'. It is moreover harmonious with Christ's stress on faith or trust.

There are, of course, other intimate personal relationships. There is friendship. The Lord spoke to Moses, as a man speaks to a friend (Ex 33_{11}). The idea occurs in the story of the importunate friend (Lk 11_{5-8}), but to stress this would be to allegorize the parable. The idea has no outstanding importance in the synoptic Gospels. There are also the relationships which form the basis of erotic or nuptial mysticism. There are indeed passages in which Christ speaks of a bridegroom in such a way as to imply that the bridegroom is Himself,[53] but He never addressed God the Father in erotic terms, and it would be absurd to speak of erotic or nuptial mysticism in the Gospels. The relationship spoken of in the Gospels is pre-eminently that of father and son, and to that relationship the word 'fellowship' is admirably suited.

THE CORPORATE ASPECT OF COMMUNION WITH GOD

We must briefly relate our theme to the conclusions reached in numerous existing works about Church, Ministry, and Sacraments, in order to determine how far this communion is corporate. This is on the fringe of our subject, but in any case so much work has already been done on it that it is necessary only to give a broad outline of the results. The old idea, characteristic of so-called 'liberal' scholarship, that Jesus did not intend to found a Church, has been exploded in the recent revival of Biblical scholarship. We can now say that Jesus intended His followers to be a society, and to enjoy communion with God within that framework. The most convenient account is to be found in Flew's *Jesus and His Church*, and there is a more recent survey of the large contemporary literature on this subject by Nelson.[54] In general we may agree with Heiler's verdict[55] when he claims that modern Biblical criticism, with its emphasis on eschatology, has not increased the

[53] e.g. Mk 2_{19-20}, Mt 25_{1-13} (but should this parable be thus allegorized?)

[54] cf. also G. Johnston; A. Raymond George in *Expository Times*, LVIII.312-16; Barrett, pp. 135-9.

[55] Heiler, *Urkirche*, p. 47.

gulf between Jesus and His Church; the Church is identical with the eschatological community which Jesus gathered by His preaching.

The phrase 'Son of Man' affords a particular complication. Manson, in *The Teaching of Jesus*, argued that in the earlier part of the ministry of Jesus, at any rate, it must bear a corporate meaning and indicate a community. The large recent literature does not support this.[56] If this were true, then it would speak of a very intimate communion between the Christians and Christ: to be part of the Son of Man would be a close contact with Him. This does not go beyond what the doctrine of the Church in other parts of the New Testament implies, but it would go further than the synoptic Gospels otherwise go. As its basis is so doubtful, we need not consider it in detail.

There is little agreement at present among New Testament scholars about the doctrine of the ministry. Since Kirk edited *The Apostolic Ministry*, there have been many replies, which it is perhaps too early to assess. The most notable is Manson's, of which this is typical, '. . . in so far as the Twelve had a special status conferred upon them by Christ, it was a personal thing and inalienable. It would be forfeited by misconduct; but it could not be transmitted to another. It did not pass at death'. But Christ's ministry continues, and the whole Church is its organ; 'the only "essential Ministry" in the Church is that involved in the continual presence of Christ Himself, and . . . all others are derivative, dependent, and functional'.[57] There is thus no reason, here or in the rest of the New Testament, for supposing that communion with God is mediated through Christian ministers in any special sense; it is also doubtful whether we should speak of it as *mediated by* the Church; but it is certainly right to say that the Christian enjoys communion with God in the Church and as a member of the Church.

On the sacraments, there is greater agreement. Recent controversies about some aspects of Baptism have only served to underline the widespread agreement that it was in some sense instituted by Christ, whatever we may think of Matthew 28_{19}. Thus Flemington says that 'Both the practice of the rite in early

[56] cf. Flew, *Church*, pp. 75ff.; Taylor, *JS*, pp. 21-32; *Mark*, pp. 119-20; M. Black, in *Expository Times*, LX.11-15, 32-6, which surveys the literature.

[57] Manson, *The Church's Ministry*, pp. 51, 31.

Christianity and the significance belonging to the rite seem alike to look back to Jesus himself and to find in his authority their most convincing explanation'. And again, 'Baptism in the New Testament was the gateway into the *koinonia*'.[58]

The problems connected with the Eucharist are more complex, and a wealth of scholarship has been lavished on the problems involved, which touch on every New Testament discipline from textual criticism to exegesis. There is as yet no standard work which sums up these findings with pre-eminent authority. But general assent would be given to Taylor's comment on the words 'Take ye; this is my Body' (Mk 14_{22}), that 'by His action and word Jesus intends the bread to be a means whereby the disciples may participate in the power of His surrendered life'. And similarly the words 'This is my blood of the covenant, which is shed for many' (Mk 14_{24}), evoke the comment 'the wine is offered as a symbol of the life and a means whereby it may be appropriated'.[59] Both these sayings thus suggest, as does also Christ's attitude to Baptism, that He contemplated the use of sacramental media of communion with God. These eucharistic sayings also suggest that that communion will be of a rich and intimate character. They favour an ecclesiastical rather than an eschatological view of communion with God, but there is no hint of mystical absorption or of any forgetting of the I-thou relationship. It so happens that the title by which this rite is often known to-day, the Holy Communion, uses the same word 'communion' which is the subject of this study; but the word κοινωνία is never used in connexion with it in the synoptic Gospels; it is used in connexion with it elsewhere, as we shall see, though never as a title of it. The Supper is a means, though not the sole means, of communion with God. There is however another saying which strikes a different note, 'Verily I say unto you, I will no more drink of the fruit of the vine, until that day when I drink it new in the kingdom of God' (Mk 14_{25}). This strikes the eschatological note. Its meaning is not indeed entirely clear, but perhaps the First Gospel interprets it rightly when it says 'until that day when I drink it new *with you* in my Father's kingdom' (Mt 26_{29}). Intimate as the communion of the Supper is when it is celebrated between the Last Supper

[58] Flemington, pp. 127-9; see also Barth, *The Teaching of the Church regarding Baptism*; Cullmann, *Baptism in the New Testament*; Jeremias; Lampe.

[59] Taylor, *JS*, pp. 124, 135; cf. also Higgins, pp. 49-54.

and the Last Day, it yet lacks something which will only be true at the end. Thus the tension that we have already found to be true of Christian piety is to be found here also. Christ is at once the present Lord and He Who is to come. The Christian's communion with Him is at once rich and expectant. The Church is both the dwelling-place of Christ and the community of the interval. The Eucharist is no exception to the general rules of Christian piety.[60]

While Christ cannot be said to have instituted the rest of the so-called Seven Sacraments, yet He used outward and visible signs in connexion with the blessings which He conferred and accepted outward expressions of devotion from others.[61] We know from the whole tenor of His teaching (e.g. Mt 23) that externals meant nothing to Him when unaccompanied by the devotion of the heart, but we may learn from these slight indications that, given faith, He was not opposed to outward signs.

He did not however expect the devotional life of His Church to be nourished solely by prayer and sacraments. In the religious life of the Jewish people the proclamations of the prophets had played a great, though necessarily somewhat irregular, part, right down to John the Baptist. Jesus Himself was a preacher, and His own example would be enough to commend preaching to His disciples. In the parable of the Sower, deliberately set at the beginning of the parables (Mk 4_{1-9}), He seems to be drawing on His experience as a preacher for the warning and encouragement of preachers. There are various 'commissioning' passages (e.g. Mt 10_7) in which the disciples are exhorted to preach; it is moreover said that the Gospel must be preached to the Gentiles (e.g. Mk 13_{9-18}), to which it is added that when they are on trial before councils, they are to say whatever is given them to say, 'for it is not ye that speak, but the Holy Spirit' (Mk 13_{11}).[62] If this saying is genuine, then the proclamation of the Gospel may in certain circumstances most certainly be a means of communion with God, if not of possession by God, for indeed if the words 'it is not ye that speak' were taken literally, it would suggest a supersession of the human faculties, a destruction of the I-thou relationship, and the use of the human speaker as a mere instrument of the divine.

[60] cf. Robinson, *In the End, God . . .*, pp. 61-2.

[61] e.g. Mk 1_{41}, 5_{25-34}, 10_{13-16}, Lk 24_{50-1}; Mk 14_{3-9}, Lk 7_{36-50}.

[62] cf. Mt 10_{20}, Lk 12_{12}; Barrett, pp. 130-2.

Fortunately, such a negative can be interpreted 'It is not *merely* ye that speak'. But whether the text be genuine or not, the preaching of the Word is surely not unrelated to personal communion with God. What the Old Testament prophets proclaimed was the Word of the Lord. The receiving of this Word was itself an experience of communion with God (using 'communion' as the generic word to cover both prophetic and mystical piety). The Christian preachers were to stand in the prophetic tradition. The content of their proclamation was indeed to be somewhat different; the Word entrusted to them was that the kingdom had come; and this coming of the kingdom was connected with the historic Jesus. Thus they would rather be expounding the significance of a past event than relating the Divine will to current events, which, rather than foretelling the future, was the task of the Old Testament prophets. Nevertheless we cannot doubt that they would receive inspiration from God in their task of proclamation.

We may conclude that Jesus contemplated the existence of a Church, in which the two sacraments would be observed and the Gospel would be preached; its members would also engage in private prayer. It was within this framework that its members would enjoy communion with God.

THE NATURE OF COMMUNION WITH GOD

Having now examined the synoptic material, we are now to ask under which of our three types of piety the piety here depicted falls; what is the right word to describe it; whether this communion is mediated, and, if so, by what media. We can best begin with the question, Was Jesus a mystic? Bultmann says 'All individualistic cultivation of the spirit, all mysticism, is excluded. Jesus calls to decision, not to the inner life'.[63] Evelyn Underhill, on the other hand, holds that Christ was a mystic, not merely in a broad sense of that word such as could hardly fail to make the statement true, but in a most precise and definite sense. 'The life of Jesus', she asserts, 'exhibits in absolute perfection . . . that psychological growth towards God, that movement and direction, which is found in varying degrees of perfection in the lives of the great mystics. All the characteristics of a Paul, a Suso, a Teresa, are found in a heightened form in the life of their Master.' Even

[63] Bultmann, p. 47; cf. 153. Contrast Kirk, p. 94 n.2.

in Mark, 'the least mystical of evangelists', the stages of the mystic life can be traced. The Baptism was the first great psychological crisis, though it differed from that of other mystics in that there was no sense of sin. The forty days in the wilderness then represent the *via purgativa*; then comes the *via illuminativa*, culminating in the Transfiguration, which was a mystic ecstasy. Then comes the Dark Night of the Soul, culminating in the Cry of Desolation. After the resurrection comes the *via unitiva* or the Deified life.[64] Within this framework many of the details of Christ's life are explained in a similar way. Some of the incidents here used, such as the Transfiguration and the Cry of Desolation, we have already considered, and we have not found it necessary to put this interpretation upon them. No doubt some of the incidents referred to have their parallels in many other religious lives, as for instance the period of withdrawal in the wilderness, but these parallels are found among religious people of all types, and are not confined to mystics, unless that word is taken in a very broad sense. We have, moreover, investigated the prayers and the teaching of Jesus, and everywhere we have found that they conform to the prophetic rather than to the mystical type.

We may now turn to the three types set out in the first chapter. The first type was mysticism *par excellence*, *unio-Mystik*, ἕνωσις, tending at least to speak of God (the Father) in the first person, blurring the I-thou relationship with notions of absorption. We can here state categorically that there is no trace of this in the synoptic Gospels. He who had, if we may put it so, the most right to be a mystic of this type showed no sign of being one. What went on in His inner consciousness, particularly at the Transfiguration, we cannot say; we can only judge by His recorded prayers, teaching, and acts. They show no trace of it. Even the most famous and intimate passage of a Johannine type speaks only of mutual knowledge (Mt $11_{27\text{ff.}}$). Those who deny that Christ was a mystic are presumably chiefly concerned to deny that He was a mystic of this type.

Turning to the other extreme, we may ask whether Christ's piety falls into the third of our classes, the type exemplified by Ritschl with his distrust even of the word *Verkehr*. Flew says of Ritschl,[65] 'The doctrine of prayer is altogether inadequate to the facts of Christian experience, and to the practice and teaching

[64] Underhill, pp. 76-7, 82, 89-154. [65] Flew, *Perfection*, p. 390.

of our Lord as recorded in the Synoptic Gospels'. The warm and confident tone of almost all Christ's recorded prayers, together with His teaching on prayer, are sufficient to dissociate Christ from this type of piety. It is true that Christ, like Ritschl, made much use of the concept of 'faith', but that word may be used with a rich connotation which includes rather than excludes communion with God. Certainly it does not exclude the richer types of prophetic piety.[66]

It follows that Christ's piety must fall into the second of our types; and in fact we find it does show just these characteristics. It is an I-thou relationship, with a strong sense of God as a Person, active in history, a real conversation with God, not a mere belief that He is. Avoiding the extremes of absorption in God the Father and of a chilly separation from Him, Jesus both practises and enjoins just this type of piety. The question remains whether within this second category, Jesus approaches more closely to the frontiers of the first or the third type. We may speak of this second type as having its mystical and prophetic sides; the mystical side of this type, together with all the first type, makes Heiler's 'mystical piety', whereas the prophetic side of the second type, together with all the third type, makes 'prophetic piety'. Heiler classifies Christ as the climax of the prophetic-Biblical type. In his account of the early contact of Christianity with mysticism, his first reference is to Paul. Jesus has the prophetic emphasis on faith. In common with the prophets and in contrast with the mystics, He had few visions and auditions. His attitude to ordinary social life is prophetic; there is no mystical asceticism; only a certain practical asceticism is demanded from His inner circle. 'A mystic would not have spoken words such as Matthew 5_{27-32}.'[67] These considerations confirm the results which we have already reached from a study of Christ's prayers and teaching on prayer; at every turn these show the marks of prophetic rather than mystical piety. In their brevity and simplicity, in their 'naïve' request for material as well as spiritual blessings, in their belief that prayer has a real effect upon God, in their persistent importunity, even in one instance of 'complaint', the prayers which Jesus makes and the type of prayer which Jesus commends are characteristically prophetic. The avoidance of the word 'see' tells in the same direction. Nor, apart from the rather doubtful

[66] cf. Heiler, pp. 143-4. [67] Heiler, pp. 117-18, 144-5; *Das Gebet*, 279.

logion in Matthew 18_{20}, is there much use of the idea of indwelling and the like. The affectionate use of 'Abba' speaks of a warm intimacy, but the intimacy of the synoptists is always sober and restrained, as we can see by contrast with Pauline piety. Of course the synoptic writers were not speaking of their own experiences after the resurrection of Christ. Even if it be asserted that Heiler has defined his types too sharply or indeed quite erroneously, it can hardly be denied that the type of piety set before us in the synoptic Gospels is one which is warm and intimate, but which never loses sight of the distinction between the person who prays and the God who hears and even carries that distinction in a crisis to a quite conscious separation. Prayer is a direct, vigorous speaking to God; its content is mostly petition and intercession, which God hears; but he who prays does not see God, still less is he absorbed in Him or united with Him. In the categories which we adopted earlier, this is prayer of the second type, and of that part of it which stands nearest to the third type. One qualification must, however, be made. The element of separation which characterizes other men of prophetic prayer, such as the Old Testament prophets themselves, is due largely to their sin. The element of separation which Jesus felt may have been due to His vicarious bearing of our sin, and that not only in the Cry of Dereliction; but it cannot have been due to any actual sin on His part. In that respect, He stood on a different basis from all others whose piety has been of this type.

This is in harmony with the decision which we had already provisionally reached about the choice of words. There is nothing in what we have found to support the idea of 'union', and of the other words 'communion' is best suited to describe piety of the second type.

THE MEDIATION OF COMMUNION WITH GOD

There remains the question of mediation. It is often said that the New Testament always conceives of communion with God as mediated through Christ; but of course this cannot apply to the communion of Christ Himself with the Father, which has been the chief topic of our investigation so far. There are indeed hints in His teaching that in future the disciples will have communion with Himself, and that communion with God will be mediated through Himself.[68] But we are not investigating these Christological questions here. We must approach the question from another angle. We must also note that this is not the same question as the question whether Jesus was a mystic, for though mysticism is often defined by reference to its immediacy, that is not a definition which commends itself to us. The question of the means whereby we have communion with God may be put in this way. Does nature or prayer or sacrament provide the right approach to God? In what activity should a man be engaged in order that thereby communion with God may be mediated to him; or does God encounter him without the mediation of any such activity?

There is not much in the teaching of Jesus to the effect that we may 'find God' (as we often say) in the 'secular' activities of life. We know, of course, that He Himself engaged in them as a young man,[69] and that His parables constantly refer to them in a way which suggests that they may be compared with the activities of God. He did indeed make ascetic demands, but they were qualified and limited, and it is difficult to see in the teaching of Jesus any warrant for those kinds of rigorist asceticism which have often been regarded as the ideal of Christian piety. Nevertheless the one saying that most clearly suggests 'finding God' in secular employment is an agraphon, namely, 'Raise the stone, and there thou shalt find me; cleave the wood, and I am there'. It is not entirely clear whether the words 'raise' and 'cleave' refer to human labour as the means of finding God, or whether they are simply a pantheist expression meaning that man can find God in nature wherever he looks. Jesus did not engage after the beginning of His ministry in 'secular' business.[70] He called the disciples away from their 'secular' pursuits to 'catch men'. Of course, that which He enjoined on the twelve disciples was not necessarily intended as the way of life for all His followers; yet the fact remains that we miss any unequivocal statement that 'secular' employment is also a means of communion with God. There is nothing that might be set beside the famous saying of a later Christian that he found God as near among the pots and pans of the kitchen as at the Holy Communion.

The same is true about nature. The praise of God for His glory

[68] e.g. Mt 18_{20} (if genuine), 11_{27ff}.
[69] Mk 6_{3}, softened in Mt 13_{55}.
[70] 'My Father's business' is religious discussion, if that is the right translation, in Lk 2_{49}; but a more likely translation is 'my Father's house'.

in nature was one element in Hebrew piety (Ps 19, 104), though it was not strongly characteristic of it. Christ's references to nature in the parables show great interest in it and feeling for it, far greater than is to be found in any other part of the New Testament; the agraphon cited above may be applied to nature as to work; and there is one striking example of an aesthetic judgement, 'But I say unto you that even Solomon in all his glory was not arrayed like one of these' (Mt 6_{29}, Lk 12_{27}). The reference is, of course, to lilies, which men are bidden to consider, not indeed explicitly that they may have communion with God, but that they may learn the ways of God. It is an interesting question how far the alleged resemblance to each other of goodness, truth, and beauty as three 'values' implies that Jesus must have had the same mastery in the aesthetic sphere as he had in the ethical, or indeed how far in any case His Deity would make His aesthetic judgements necessarily right; this further involves the question of kenosis. There is, of course, no record of achievement in the aesthetic sphere to match the sinless perfection of His life in the ethical; but we may say that this single judgement, so far as it goes (if it be not impertinent to appraise it) is both original and attractive. But there is no statement (apart from the agraphon) that in nature we may 'find God'. Jesus is true to the tradition of prophetic piety which here also preserves a certain distance from God. There is no pantheism, no union with God in nature; the natural world is the handiwork of God, not God Himself. There is no nature-mysticism of the type of which Wordsworth is the best-known example.

Nor do we find much about communion with God mediated through personal relationships. It is curious that no substantial school of piety has followed this path, especially as human relationships have often been used, as we have seen, to describe analogously our relationship to God. It is common to call God Father; comparatively rare to say that one sees God in a human father. Indeed the most striking metaphors drawn from human relationships, those of erotic or nuptial mysticism, have been most frequently employed by those who have never experienced the corresponding human relationships. Probably men have been deterred from regarding other men as a means of communion with God by the reflection that, whereas nature, even if not pantheistically conceived, is at least God's handiwork, man, though made in the image of God, is corrupted by sin. The assertion that nature groans in pain (Ro 8_{22}) and is also corrupt has not always been taken very seriously, but the sin of man has been too glaring to be overlooked. But is not man redeemed by grace far more expressive of God than nature is, seeing that he reveals God's redemptive as well as His creative power? Some elements in Christian doctrine, notably the stress on the fellowship of the Church, approach this truth; yet it is hard to think of any unambiguous statement that communion with God is mediated through our communion with our fellows. Christians have felt that such statements were dangerous. Nature cannot pride itself on being a means of communion with God, for it is incapable of such reflection; but a man, while ostensibly asserting that it is possible for him to have communion with God through other men, might be actually priding himself on the fact that it is possible for other men to have communion with God through him. At any rate, Jesus says nothing along these lines. Nor is it likely that He Himself enjoyed much communion with God through this medium, if indeed it is possible to speak of media in His case at all. In His lifetime the disciples were very imperfectly redeemed by grace; He was hampered by their stupidity and sometimes their disloyalty, as also by misunderstanding on the part of His own family. He cannot have known much of His Father through human intercourse.

Another possible means of communion with God is the service of those in need. Exhortations to love our neighbour, and to perform deeds of kindness, as for instance to cast out unclean spirits, are a commonplace of Christian ethics, and it might be supposed that obedience to this command would bring men close to God; the nearest approach to this idea is found in the Similitude of the Sheep and the Goats (Mt 25_{31-46}). The interpretation of this is a matter of some difficulty. The crucial verse is 'Verily I say to you, inasmuch as you did it to one of these my brethren, these least, you did it to me'. This is usually taken to mean that Christ, the Son of Man, identifies Himself with all sufferers, so that he who performs any act of kindness to anyone really encounters Christ, though he knows it not. This has occasioned some embarrassment to theologians, despite the beauty of the conception, because it seems to come perilously near to justification by works. But the word 'brethren', usually kept in the New

Testament for Christians, suggests another interpretation, as also does the word 'these', with its possible implication that they are standing near to Christ. Manson goes much further.[71] In accordance with his well-known view of the Son of Man, he takes the Son of Man here to be the body comprising the King (Christ) and His brethren. This corporate body exercises the judgement, the King acting as its spokesman. As all the Christians are included in this body, those who are judged are only the non-Christians, and they are judged, not by their acts of charity in general, but by their attitude to the messengers of Christ. The question is 'how he stood towards the Kingdom of God: was he on the side of the Kingdom or against it?' 'The good deeds done were deeds done to help the cause of God. They were an acknowledgement of God's sovereignty as manifested in His representative Jesus Christ.'[72] One objection to Manson's theory is that this is a picture of the judgement of 'all the nations (or Gentiles)' (verse 32), but not all of these will have had the opportunity of welcoming or rejecting the representatives of Christ, whereas all will have had the opportunity of being kind to their fellows in general. But whether the 'brethren' are any sufferers or only Christians, whether what is commended is kindness or the acknowledgement of God's sovereignty, there is a suggestion, though not a very explicit one, that those who serve others who are in need have, in some cases, at least, communion with Christ; on the somewhat doubtful theory here set out, the promise is to non-Christians, but it would apply *a fortiori* to Christians, who indeed enjoy the much closer link of being a part of the Son of Man.

Thus through these four media, the doing of daily work, the contemplation of nature, the love of friends, and even the service of others, Jesus does not seem to have found communion with God as much as might have been expected. Yet we must not argue too much from silence. In so far as He spent His time in these ways, or allowed others to do so, we may suppose that He was not merely doing something permitted by God, but also to some extent enjoying communion with God, or expecting others to do so. But the main mode of communion with God does not seem to have been any of these.

For Him communion with God seems to have consisted chiefly

[71] Manson, *Sayings*, pp. 249-52.

[72] cf. Mk $9_{37, 41}$, Lk 10_{16}, Mt 10_{40-2}; *supra*, p. 84.

in prayer, indeed in private prayer. We have already considered His own habits of devotion. On the whole there is more stress on private prayer than on corporate devotion, though that is not neglected. If all that we knew about Jesus were that He spent long periods in solitary prayer, we might be reminded of the mystical 'flight of the alone to the Alone', but long periods of prayer are equally compatible with prophetic piety, and that is the stamp, as we have seen, which the recorded prayers of Jesus plainly bear. Now private prayer is the most immediate of all the modes of approach to God. It is not indeed immediate in the sense in which mystical union is immediate, wherein there is nothing between God and man (or so the mystic imagines[73]) to prevent absorption. There are media in the sense that the intellectual concepts of the person praying play some part, though not the sole part, for prayer is an emotional and volitional experience as well.[74] It may be that prophetic prayer is more 'vocal' and less 'mental' than mystical prayer. But it is entirely immediate in that it dispenses with duty, nature, men, words spoken[75] or read, symbols and sacraments, at any rate during the period of private prayer, however great a part some of these may have played in preparation for it. 'Immediate' is indeed a somewhat ambiguous word, as is shown by John Baillie's phrase 'a mediated immediacy'.[76] But in an important sense immediacy is a prominent characteristic of Christ's mode of piety.

The question sometimes arises for us how we are to reconcile the claims made on our time by direct or immediate communion with God in prayer and those made by the indirect or mediated communion of personal contacts and daily living. Not merely is the problem actually difficult for individuals, but it is difficult to find by what criterion the two claims should be judged, though this theoretical problem is less often discussed. Different ways of viewing this might perhaps be compared with intuitionism and utilitarianism in ethics. Are these two uses of time for

[73] We must not assume because mystics speak of absorption into the Deity and the like that this really occurs. If our view of Christ's teaching is correct, then it does not rightly occur; probably it does not occur at all, but if it does occur, then men may perhaps be conceived as being absorbed into the Deity, so to speak, to their own damnation, like moths who come too close to a flame which is in itself good.

[74] Even in mysticism it is not clear that it is possible for the intellectual element to disappear completely; cf. Pratt, pp. 424-9.

[75] At least, spoken to others. Probably Jesus' private prayers were often uttered aloud, though not often overheard.

[76] J. Baillie, p. 181.

communion with God simply obligations related only by the fact that God commands them? If so, then how are we to judge how much of each He commands? Or are they to be judged by their utility to some further end? If this is the glory of God or the like, how does this differ from the first view? But if it is the salvation of men or the like, then is not communion with God being degraded to a mere means? These problems seem never to have been present to Jesus. He had a conflict between healing and teaching, which recurs throughout His ministry. But He seems to have solved the conflict between 'activity' and prayer by praying at night while others slept. In Gethsemane the contrast between His prayer and the sleep of the disciples is explicit (Mk 14_{32-42}). He met this issue in the lives of Mary and Martha; and though many sermons have been preached to the effect that Christ needs both Mary and Martha in His service, the actual words of Jesus are an unambiguous commendation of the contemplative Mary (Lk 10_{38-42}).

CONCLUSION

Our study of the teaching and piety of Jesus is now concluded. It remains to consider the subsequent developments in the life of the Church. The piety of Jesus Himself was of a certain marked type, for which we have approved the word 'prophetic'. Little was said to indicate that the piety of Jesus' followers should be of a different kind; only a handful of passages, doubtful in any case, hint at a richer and more christocentric and more ecclesiastical communion to be enjoyed by the disciples in the future. Yet Church, ministry, and sacraments were not founded for nothing. Christ's own communion with the old Israel, if we may put it so, was strained to breaking-point. 'Israel after the flesh' crucified Him; or, to use these categories in another way, He alone was at the moment of His death the true Israel, the Righteous Remnant. The religious observances of the old Israel, which in their main outline He faithfully observed, were the background rather than the medium for His communion with God. But the disciples were to live the Christian life in the setting of a fellowship, the fellowship of the new Israel, of which Christ was the Head, but from which in His lonely human life He could derive no fellowship. Moreover this community was to be reconstituted not only by the coming of Christ, but by His death and resurrection and ascension, and by the coming of the Holy Spirit; all this was bound to enrich the conception of communion with God; we must look to see whether the development is a natural one, such as could properly arise out of the teaching of Jesus. We must not indeed say that the early Church enjoyed a communion with God richer than that which Jesus, particularly in the unrecorded moments of solitary prayer, had with the Father; but it is reasonable to expect that the *conception* of communion with God, as set out in words will be richer than in the teaching of Jesus it could possibly be. The Cross and the resurrection effect a similar development of many other doctrines.

Before, however, we leave the synoptic Gospels, we may take another look at Christ as a Man of prayer. Christian thought to-day is often more concerned with the teaching of Jesus than with His devotional life; and indeed popular thought is often more concerned with His ethical teaching than with His teaching on theological and devotional subjects. But he is indeed blind who does not see that all His teaching is bound up with His teaching about God and man's communion with Him, that all His teaching springs from His life and character, and that the mainspring of His life, as of the life which He advocated, was communion with God. Only an academic systematizer could concentrate on the teaching of Jesus to the exclusion of that. We think of Him now as the Recipient of our prayers, our great High-priest, our Mediator, Advocate, and Intercessor, the Second Person of the Blessed Trinity, but we must not forget that He was a Man of Prayer. In the words of Isaac Watts,

> He in the days of feeble flesh
>   Poured out His cries and tears;
> And, though exalted, feels afresh
>   What every member bears.

The Son of God prayed: shall not we pray?

CHAPTER FIVE

THE PRIMITIVE CHURCH

SOURCES

WHEN we turn to the early Church before the activity of Paul as a Christian begins, we come to a period about which there is considerable uncertainty. The Acts is a convenient source, but there are varying views of its reliability. We take the view that the speeches ascribed to Peter (the most important item for our purpose) represent substantially the preaching of the Aramaic-speaking Church.[1] An earlier source is the Pauline Epistles, which throw a certain indirect light on the pre-Pauline Church. A third source is the synoptic Gospels, and if we were to accept the contention of the more extreme form-critics that many of the sayings ascribed to Christ have their real origin in some actual situation in the life of the early Church, in some problem which they were invited to solve, then they would be valuable evidence for this period; but if we take a more moderate view, and regard most of the sayings as genuine, even though the liturgical, catechetical, doctrinal, kerygmatic, and apologetic needs of the Church may have secured their survival, then their value for this period is correspondingly diminished.

THE THEOLOGY OF THE EARLY CHURCH

Four stages can be distinguished in the life of the early Church. We have first the Aramaic-speaking Church in Palestine; second, the Greek-speaking Church among Jews of the Diaspora, whether settled again in Palestine, or still dispersed in Greek-speaking lands; third, the Greek-speaking Church among the Gentiles before Paul; and fourth, the Gentile Churches under the influence of Paul, whose pre-eminence as the Apostle of the Gentiles must not blind us to the fact that there was a Gentile Church before him. The recent synthetic tendency to stress the unity of the New Testament, as represented by such writers as Dodd, Hunter, Flew,

[1] cf. Dodd, *Preaching*, pp. 19-20.

and Taylor, shows that there is not so great a gap as had once been supposed even between the first and last of these stages.

The important distinction suggested by Bousset in the title of his famous book *Kyrios Christos* needs some consideration, particularly in connexion with communion with God. The suggestion is that to the Jewish Church Jesus was Christos, Messiah; to the Gentile Church, He was Kyrios, Lord. There is clearly a great difference between the type of communion with God enjoyed by those who expect a coming Messiah and the type enjoyed by those who worship a present Lord whom they regard as God. We are faced here with a conflict between eschatological and non-eschatological conceptions such as met us at the beginning of our study of the synoptic Gospels in connexion with the concept of the kingdom. The criticisms of Bousset's theory are well-known.[2] Moreover, the contrast which he draws between the eschatological expectations of the Jewish Church and the worship offered to the Lord in the Gentile Church can be criticized on other grounds also. Whether or not we support fully Dodd's 'realized eschatology', we can hardly deny his statement that 'the apostolic Preaching as recorded in Acts does not (contrary to a commonly held opinion) lay the greatest stress upon the expectation of a second advent of the Lord'.[3] Moreover, as regards the Greek side of this contrast, quite apart from the particular argument about the word Kyrios, we may doubt whether the Hellenistic environment had as great an influence on the Christian communities as is often supposed. It is not now believed that Paul adapted the Gospel extensively to suit his environment, a theory once held in the form that he borrowed freely from the mystery-religions; and if Paul, who was by temperament a bold innovator, did not do so, then *a fortiori* we should not expect to find a great measure of adaptation to environment in the pre-Pauline Gentile Church. Nevertheless, the Gentile environment must have exerted a certain modifying influence on the meaning of the term Kyrios, even though it was taken over from the Jewish Church. There is a certain general truth in Bousset's contention, and we must examine the history of the concept of communion with God to see whether there is a certain shift of emphasis from eschatological expectation to worship of a present Lord.

[2] cf. Burkitt, pp. 49-52; Rawlinson, *The New Testament Doctrine of the Christ*, pp. 231-7; Dodd, *Preaching*, p. 15; but see Bultmann, *Theology*, pp. 51-3.

[3] Dodd, *Preaching*, p. 33.

Freed, however, from this theory in its more tyrannical form, we may proceed to examine the kerygma of the early Palestinian community for traces of its conception of communion with God. We may take Dodd's summary of it.[4]

'First, the age of fulfilment has dawned. . . . Secondly, this has taken place through the ministry, death, and resurrection of Jesus. . . . Thirdly, by virtue of the resurrection, Jesus has been exalted at the right hand of God, as Messianic head of the new Israel. . . . Fourthly, the Holy Spirit in the Church is the sign of Christ's present power and glory. . . . Fifthly, the Messianic Age will shortly reach its consummation in the return of Christ. . . . Finally, the *kerygma* closes with an appeal for repentance, the offer of forgiveness and of the Holy Spirit, and the promise of "salvation", that is, of the "life of the Age to Come", to those who enter the elect community.'

There is no explicit reference to communion with God; indeed there is only one explicit reference to God at all. But the theme of communion with God is indirectly involved in this in a number of ways. First, the 'age of fulfilment' might reasonably be expected to bring men into closer communion with God than they had enjoyed in the age of expectation. This part of the kerygma is reminiscent of the proclamation of Jesus Himself that the kingdom had come; and here as there a realized eschatology harmonizes better with an intimate communion with God than does a futurist one. Second, though the kingdom had in one sense come in the life-time of Jesus, the death, resurrection, ascension, and heavenly session of Christ had not been without significance. The kingdom was, as it were, more fully constituted; and communion with God might be expected to be more intimate, not indeed than that which Jesus had enjoyed, or than that of which He had spoken, but more intimate than that which the disciples had hitherto enjoyed. The resemblance of the message of Jesus Himself to the apostolic preaching, when they are both brought under the category of realized eschatology, rightly frees our minds from the old contrasts between the religion of Jesus and the religion about Jesus, from the idea that the early Church distorted the simple teaching of the Galilean Carpenter or that Paul was the second founder of Christianity; but it must not be allowed to disguise or obscure the fact that the death and resurrection constitute a tremendous watershed. Third, the various references to a

[4] Dodd, *Preaching*, pp. 21-3.

new community, whether it is called the New Israel, the Church, or the elect community (terms not actually explicit in the usual form of the kerygma) show us the context in which communion with God is to be enjoyed, and the fact that it is a *new* community suggests a new quality of communion. Fourth, the references to salvation, the life of the Age to come, and the Holy Spirit give some indication of the nature of this new communion. But, on the other hand, fifth, the reference to the imminent consummation of the Messianic Age in the return of Christ is a piece of futurist eschatology, and suggests that piety will take the form of 'prophetic' petitions for speedy consummation rather than that of intimate communion. But, as we have already noted, this is the least prominent feature of the prophetic kerygma, being much less prominent than is popularly supposed.[5] If therefore we may trust the perspective suggested by Acts, we need not expect this to have a very great influence on piety; we cannot, however, ignore it absolutely.

THE HOLY SPIRIT

When we turn to consider the kind of devotional life which the members of the early Church are actually recorded in the Acts as having lived, our first impression is that of the prominence of the Holy Spirit. This phrase, so little found in the synoptic Gospels, is exceedingly common in the Acts;[6] and we are precluded from thinking that this is a mere peculiarity of Acts, by the fact that it is equally common in the rest of the New Testament (apart from the synoptic Gospels), especially Paul. The Holy Spirit, promised in Acts 1_{8}, was poured out on the Day of Pentecost, not on the Eleven (or Twelve) only, or as such, but on the whole company of the believers (Ac 2_{1-11})[7] and subsequently renewed. Its more ecstatic accompaniments, such as glossolaly, were not its essence, as Paul afterwards perceived, nor were they always repeated (1 Co 12-14). The whole life of the young Church was indeed the creation of the Spirit and the best commentary on Pentecost. The Spirit is not so much a means of having communion with God as the very essence of God's communication of

[5] Ac 3_{21}, 10_{42}; Dodd, *Preaching*, pp. 33-5; Cadoux, pp. 292-8.

[6] cf. Taylor, *HS*, pp. 50-60; Flew, *Church*, pp. 66-72; Barrett, pp. 141-3; but see also pp. 140-62.

[7] cf. Flew, *Church*, pp. 147-8. This has an important bearing on the doctrine of the ministry. cf. Swete, p. 100.

Himself to men. It was this fact, of course, which started those processes of reflection which led to the formulation of the doctrine of the Trinity.

The phrase 'Holy Spirit' or 'Spirit' is used, then, in a bewildering variety of ways. A prominent expression is that men were filled with the Spirit, some apparently more than others (Ac 6_3); and it was possible for those who already had the Spirit to be filled again, presumably in fuller measure (Ac 4_{31}). Sometimes the expression is almost a synonym for 'God' (compare Ac 5_3 with 5_4): yet a phrase such as 'full of faith and Holy Spirit' (Ac 6_5) suggests a somewhat incongruous juxtaposition and irreverent order of words, if the Holy Spirit is conceived as personal and as God. There can be no doubt that the doctrine of the Spirit began with a very primitive stage.

The Spirit is also a notable source of guidance. Sometimes it seems a mere literary variation that some communications are ascribed to an angel and some to the Spirit, though there is a tendency to keep the Spirit for the climax (Ac $8_{26, 29, 39}$, 10, esp. 10_{19}). The most notable instance of guidance was in the famous phrase 'It seemed good to the Holy Spirit and to us' (Ac 15_{28}). A somewhat similar gift was prophecy (Ac 11_{27-8}).

A confusing group of passages relates the Spirit to the rites of the Church. Was the Spirit conferred at Baptism or some further rite roughly corresponding to confirmation?[8] But the main fact is clear that the possession of the Spirit is an essential part of the full equipment of a Christian.

One other passage on the Spirit raises interesting questions. In Acts 9_{31} (where we may leave out the problems of punctuation), we read the phrase τῇ παρακλήσει τοῦ Ἁγίου Πνεύματος. There are two possibilities. The first, suggested by Hort,[9] is to translate 'the invocation of the Holy Spirit', which he explains 'probably the invoking His guidance as Paraclete to the Ecclesia'. This means taking the genitive as objective, and giving to παράκλησις a meaning similar to that of ἐπίκλησις, though with some overtones derived from the meaning of Παράκλητος which afterwards found expression in the Fourth Gospel. This would be an important conclusion for the study of piety, for it would suggest

[8] cf. Flemington, pp. 44 n.1, 148-52; Cullmann, *Baptism in the New Testament*, pp. 11-12; Lampe.

[9] Hort, p. 55.

that the devotional attitude of the early Church, indeed the actual content of its prayers, included the Invocation of the Holy Spirit. Indeed, as much of their praying was done at the Eucharist, we might well think that the rite at this early date already contained an Epiclesis, though this would be no evidence that the Spirit was invoked on the elements. But it is doubtful whether the word παράκλησις can bear this meaning, and thus we come to the second possibility, that it means the 'comfort' or 'encouragement' which the Holy Spirit supplies, the genitive being subjective. The comment with which Swete[10] supports this conclusion is noteworthy.

'The attitude of the primitive Church towards the Spirit was rather one of joyful welcome than of invocation; the cry *Veni, Creator Spiritus* belongs to a later age, when the Spirit was sought and perhaps expected, but not regarded as a Guest Who had already come, and come to abide.'

We might perhaps say that the eschatology of the Spirit has now been realized. This seems to be true, and together with the silence of our records about prayers for the Spirit (except on the first interpretation of this passage), suggests that our common practice of invoking the Spirit[11] in hymn and prayer is perhaps a mistake, except presumably that the Spirit may be invoked at the entry into the Christian life, namely Baptism, to which some would add confirmation. On the other hand, we have already seen that those who had already received the Spirit might be said on a subsequent occasion to be filled with the Spirit (Ac 4_{31}), presumably in a fuller measure; and this might be held to justify prayer for the Holy Spirit. There is no evidence how far this might cover also ordination. All these passages, taken together, lead us to conclude that the gift of the Spirit gave a new warmth and intimacy to the communion with God which the early Church enjoyed. They were, so to speak, in touch with God in a new way.

OTHER ASPECTS OF PIETY

We turn from these references to the Holy Spirit to other indications of the type of piety practised in the early Church, and even

[10] Swete, p. 96 n.2.

[11] Most modern Eucharistic rites include the Epiclesis, which has never been omitted in the East. But the Roman, Anglican (1662), and Methodist rites lack it.

when we allow for the fact that Luke was specially interested in prayer, it is clear that prayer had a conspicuous place in the life of the early Church.[12] No book in the New Testament (save Luke) shows such a frequent use of προσεύχομαι, though γρηγορέω, its companion in the synoptics, occurs only once (Ac 20_{31}). These prayers were mostly of petition or intercession, sometimes in connexion with ecclesiastical acts such as healing, ordination, and what would later be called confirmation. Indeed the frequent connexion between prayer and the imposition of hands suggests that the gifts were not magically conferred by those who laid on hands, but rather that these had authority to ask for the gifts to be given. Sometimes these prayers were offered in special circumstances such as the imprisonment of Christians. Even when the occasion is a release from prison, intercession prevails over thanksgiving (Ac 4_{24-30}), unless the prayer is a later composition. It is true that a historical narrative would be more likely to refer to such prayers than to prayers of adoration, which may have gone on regularly all the time;[13] yet there is no evidence that the prayers departed from the customary 'prophetic' style.

The death of Stephen has two interesting features in this connexion. His prayers 'Lord Jesus, receive my spirit' and 'Lord, lay not this sin to their charge' (Ac 7_{59-60})[14] are the first recorded prayers offered to Jesus. The first is explicitly so offered, and the context suggests that the second must have been. The words are thus important for Christology but also for the study of piety. It was later laid down that prayers should be offered *to* the Father *through* the Son; but there have been many exceptions. Some of these have been very sentimental, but the first of them, which we find here, seems entirely natural and fitting. His example was not much followed, so far as we can judge, in the New Testament period. The content of the prayer is 'prophetic'; there is nothing in it of 'Christ-mysticism'. The other remarkable feature of the death of the first martyr is that he had a vision of the glory of God, and of Jesus (Ac 7_{55-6}), and vision is characteristic of 'mystical' rather than 'prophetic' experience. But the 'prophetic' experience

[12] e.g. Ac 1_{24-5}, 4_{24-30}, 6_{6}, 8_{15}, $9_{10-16, 40}$, 10_{9}, 11_{5}, 12_{12}, 13_{3}, 14_{23}, 16_{25}, 20_{36}, 21_{5}, 22_{17}, 28_{8}. Cornelius is described as praying at a time when he was not a member of the Church. The Christians attended the Temple and Synagogue for a time (e.g. Ac 3_{1}, 18_{4}, 21_{26}).

[13] Ac 16_{25} is a reference to praise in an emergency.

[14] cf Lk 23_{34}. For references to praying to Jesus, see Ac 9_{14}, 22_{16}.

is not wholly devoid of vision. No one could call Stephen a mystic on this ground.

This author is indeed fond, both here and in his Gospel, of mentioning visions, ecstasies, and angels.[15] If we leave out the appearances of the Risen Christ, which were presumably more than visions, and defer the experiences of Paul, we find that the visions in Acts are mostly of angelic figures, men at a distance, or objects to which a special significance is attached (e.g. Ac 1_{10}, 9_{12}, 10_{11}), rather than of God, though there is a colloquy with Christ (Ac 9_{10-16}). They are thus not of major importance for our purpose, but as they show a tendency to write freely about visions, they make the account of Stephen's vision less significant. The angels are part of a tradition going back to the Old Testament, in which their appearance as mediators is due to motives of reverence, in order to exalt the divine transcendence. They are among those mediating ideas, like Word, and Wisdom, which prepared the way for the understanding of the Incarnation. After the Incarnation, they play a different role; but they are still often a necessary part of the mechanism of the story, for it would not be possible to speak of God Himself appearing. Even the angels are often only *heard*. There are indeed other ways (such as Ac 16_6) of speaking of the divine guidance; but this is one possible way of introducing a speech in direct speech. We may believe in the existence of non-human intelligent beings in the universe without thinking that we have here anything more than a conventional mode of speech, which throws no real light on the kind of communion with God enjoyed in the early Church.

The word 'ecstasy' tends to suggest mysticism, but we have seen that it is rather the culmination of either type of religious experience, mystical or prophetic. We must judge from its description in each case to which experience it refers. The word ἔκστασις is used once in Acts (Ac 3_{10}), as it is used in the Gospels, in a purely secular sense, where it can be translated 'amazement'. There are three religious instances in Acts. Two (Ac 10_{10}, 11_5) refer to an ecstasy of Peter; this is no mystical ecstasy, for there is no vision of God or sense of mystical union, nor has the experience that ineffability which is a characteristic mark of mystical experience. On the contrary, visual and auditory phenomena are used to convey a certain definite message from God, which is a

[15] Michaelis, *KTW*, V.351-2.

clear sign of prophetic ecstasy. The same is generally true of Acts 22_{17}, though here the vision was of the Lord, and not merely of a material object.

Acts shows several ecstatic features where the word 'ecstasy' is not used, notably the Pentecostal outpouring (Ac 2), and in particular the glossolaly. We notice also an instance of sobriety and disapproval of mere ecstasy divorced from morality and love (Ac $8_{9ff.}$).[16]

FELLOWSHIP

One major passage remains, and introduces an important linguistic question. The concluding verses of Acts 2, containing the first account of the life of the new community, are in their way as important as the first part of the chapter containing the descent of the Holy Spirit and the central verses containing the first preaching of the kerygma. The description of the early Church has a somewhat stylized appearance; but its main features may well be accurate. We notice the importance of Baptism and the fact that the existence of the community is simply taken for granted by the phrase 'there were added', used absolutely (Ac 2_{41}). The most important verse is:

Ac 2_{42}. ἦσαν δὲ προσκαρτεροῦντες τῇ διδαχῇ τῶν ἀποστόλων καὶ τῇ κοινωνίᾳ, τῇ κλάσει τοῦ ἄρτου καὶ ταῖς προσευχαῖς.

And they continued stedfastly in the apostles' teaching and fellowship, in the breaking of bread and the prayers.

We have given the RV translation, the defect of which is that it omits some of the definite articles; every noun in the Greek sentence has the article. It is true that the English idiom does not always require the article where the Greek has one (as, for instance with a proper name); nevertheless, though RV is greatly to be preferred to AV, which omits all but one of these articles, it would have been better if RV had inserted the articles which it omits, those, namely, before 'fellowship' and 'bread'. Next, how are the phrases to be grouped? RV, with its only comma after 'fellowship', is surely right in making two groups, as against AV, which has a comma also after 'bread', thus making three groups.

[16] cf. Behm, *KTW*, I.725; Oepke, *KTW*, II.455.

The omission of a καί before τῇ κλάσει seems clearly to indicate two groups. This tells clearly against the Vulgate *in doctrina Apostolorum, et communicatione fractionis panis, et orationibus.*

Within the first group, is the genitive τῶν ἀποστόλων to be taken with both datives or only with the first? The analogy of the second group and the general rhythm would suggest that it should be taken with τῇ διδαχῇ only. This is presumably what RV mg. means to suggest by 'in fellowship', though it might have done so more clearly by the insertion of the article also. What is the general relation of the second group to the first group? Is it co-ordinate with it, or is it in apposition to τῇ κοινωνίᾳ so that 'the breaking of the bread and the prayers' (without our going as far as the Vulgate), would further define the nature of the κοινωνία? From a strictly grammatical point of view, the second group is probably co-ordinate; yet it concerns itself with the outward manifestations of that which is described in the first group. There is thus a certain general appropriateness in the rhythm of Moffatt's translation, despite its omission of some articles, 'They devoted themselves to the instruction given by the apostles and to fellowship, breaking bread and praying together'.[17]

The chief problem remains, what are we to understand here by κοινωνία? We thus arrive for the first time at the word of which the translation forms the operative word in our title, though of course this is not its earliest occurrence in the New Testament. But our subject is broader than the investigation of this word; we use it generically to cover a number of other expressions. It will suffice therefore to give here a brief summary of the state of investigation upon this subject. The researches of Heinrich Seesemann in *Der Begriff* KOINΩNIA *im Neuen Testament* constitute the most thorough work on this subject, and were of course used by Friedrich Hauck in his article on κοινός and its cognates.[18]

The grammatical use in general literature is as follows. κοινωνέω means to share in something (genitive) with someone (dative); either of these may be replaced by prepositions; and there are other constructions; but this is the most characteristic. Very rarely it means 'to give a share in'.[19] κοινωνία means 'having a

[17] cf. Thornton, p. 72.

[18] Hauck, *KTW*, III.789-810. A list of authorities in chronological order is given in the Bibliography, section D (*supra*, pp. xix-xx).

[19] So Seesemann, pp. 4-9, against Campbell, pp. 367-70, 378.

share in' or (corresponding to the most characteristic construction of κοινωνέω) 'having a share in something with someone': thus it is commonly used with genitive of the thing shared. Secondly, very occasionally, it is used actively, of 'willingness to give a share, generosity'. Thirdly, out of the first use arises the meaning 'sharing' or 'fellowship (which arises out of the common sharing of something)'. κοινωνός means 'participant' in something with somebody. The important thing is that these words refer primarily, though not invariably, to participation in something rather than to association with others: and there is often a genitive to indicate that in which one participates or shares.

In accordance with all this, the New Testament passages where κοινων- words occur may be divided into three classes, according to whether the predominant idea is 'having a share', 'giving a share', or 'sharing'. Thus κοινωνία has the three meanings already indicated. The word 'fellowship', so common in this connexion, could be avoided altogether. Even the third meaning 'sharing', though that bald word would not suffice in (say) Galatians 2_9, might be rendered 'partnership in a common enterprise'. Yet in these cases 'fellowship' is the obvious rendering. It could be used in some of the other cases: thus 'having a share in' might be rendered 'fellowship' when the following genitive is a person, (e.g. 1 Co 1_9). The use of 'fellowship' in an English version is thus not a reliable guide to the understanding of the Greek construction. Passages with the third meaning 'sharing' or 'fellowship' use κοινωνία absolutely or with μετά. There are perhaps only three in the New Testament (Ac 2_{42}, Gal 2_9, 1 Jn $1_{3ff.}$).

Greek thought made extensive use of the word κοινωνία. It could mean friendship, partnership, or marriage. A cosmic function is ascribed to it by Plato,[20] who says that an evil man cannot be dear to man or god:

'for he is incapable of having fellowship (κοινωνεῖν); but with one in whom there is no fellowship (κοινωνία), friendship is impossible. And, Callicles, the wise say that heaven and earth, and gods and men are kept together by fellowship (κοινωνία), friendship, orderliness, temperance, and justice, and that is why they call this whole "cosmos" (κόσμος).'

[20] Plato, *Gorgias*, 507e-508a.

The word κοινωνία was also used to mean sharing with gods in a common meal.[21] Though the Greek mystery-religions characteristically prefer to speak of 'union', yet in Greek contexts it is quite possible to speak of fellowship (κοινωνία) with a god.[22]

The usage of the Old Testament is quite different. κοινωνία in LXX only once translates a Hebrew word. At Leviticus 6_2 (He 5_{21}) it translates an expression which is itself an obscure hapax legomenon: κοινωνία is also found[23] at Wisdom 8_{18}, 3 Maccabees 4_6. The other κοινων- words are a little more frequent, and the root which they represent (which is also translated by other Greek words) is חבר, *chabar*, which contains the notion of 'unite', 'join', 'bind together'. Words from this root refer to all kinds of partnership, including that between worshippers (Ps 119_{63}): it is also once used of being 'joined to idols' (Hos 4_{17}), and, of course, it gave rise to the word חֲבוּרָה, *Chaburah*, which was used in later Judaism to mean a religious society or association. The important point is that in all these cases (except for the reference to idols), even when the association is religious, the relationship referred to is that between man and man, never between man and God,[24] no doubt from motives of reverence. They did not lack the experience of fellowship with God, as for instance at sacrificial meals:[25] the Psalms and the Prophets also are full of such experiences. Yet such was their sense of inequality with God that they did not use words expressive of fellowship, but those expressive of inequality and distance, such as 'servant' and 'covenant'.

Against this background the use of κοινωνία in the New Testament is the more striking. Sometimes the κοινων- words were used in connexion with purely secular partnerships (e.g. Lk 5_{10}), and sometimes in connexion with religious associations, where the reference is to the relation between the partners, what we may call the 'horizontal' relationship. But we shall come to other

[21] See the excursus on cult-meals in Lietzmann, pp. 49-51. We must distinguish the view that gods and men have fellowship with each other by sharing the food of the sacrifice from the view, also found, that the worshippers partake of the god. Lietzmann quotes instances of both, though the instances of κοινωνία relate to the former. But see Jourdan, pp. 121-2.

[22] e.g. Epictetus, II.19. 27. τῆς πρὸς τὸν Δία κοινωνίας. Seesemann, p. 101 n.3 perhaps dismisses these parallels rather too lightly.

[23] Hauck, *KTW*, III.801, adds Wis 6_{23} (in some editions 6_{25}), but the word is κοινωνέω.

[24] Cranfield, *RTW*, p. 81, rightly notes Ps 94_{20} as a possible exception; this is חבר, but not κοινων-.

[25] This is usually assumed, but is questioned by Jourdan, p. 113 n.6.

passages where there is a reference to the relationship between man and some Person in the Trinity, what we may call the 'vertical' relationship: and clearly a root which means 'sharing in something with someone' is capable of referring to both these relationships at once.

In general the precise use of the word is fairly well-established: there is a continual train of development, broken only by C. A. Anderson Scott. His view that ἡ κοινωνία was a translation of *Chaburah* was, in our opinion, effectively dealt with by Wood in 1921, though Scott continued to maintain it in a series of works. Wood's views have been echoed by many others, including Seesemann and Hauck. The question also affects the translation of several Pauline passages, which are disputed from other angles also: and here Seesemann's conclusions have recently been assailed by Jourdan.

We now turn back to the passage with which we were dealing,[26] Acts 2_{42}. We may reject here the meanings 'almsgiving', 'generosity'.[27] The grouping of the phrases rules out a specific reference to the Holy Communion.[28] It might be a technical term for having all things common (κοινά), mentioned in verse 44[29]. But it is improbable that it could bear this specific meaning before this feature of the life of the early Church had been mentioned. We have already referred to the best-known of the interpretations of this verse: Scott maintained that ἡ κοινωνία here is a translation of *Chaburah*, and that the early Church would be known naturally as the *Chaburah* of Jesus. It may or may not be true that the disciples were commonly regarded as a *Chaburah*, and that this probably influenced the ritual of the Last Supper:[30] but it has been shown by Wood and others that it is very unlikely that κοινωνία by itself could bear this meaning. Nor is it likely that the word here should be taken closely with τῶν ἀποστόλων in the sense 'the fellowship of which the apostles were heads' (a sort of possessive genitive). Scott was speaking in a very unscriptural way when he wrote, [31] 'this Koinonia, called into being by the Holy Spirit, was prior to the organised Ecclesia'. It is an

[26] The fullest account is in Seesemann, pp. 87-92. Hauck, *KTW*, III.809-10, is very brief.

[27] But see Campbell, pp. 374-5.

[28] But see Dodd, *The Johannine Epistles*, p. 7; Nelson, p. 56.

[29] So Cranfield, *RTW*, p. 82.

[30] Dix, pp. 50-102.

[31] Scott, in (ed.) Streeter, *The Spirit*, p. 142.

equal error of many writers to regard κοινωνία as a synonym for ἐκκλησία. Similarly such expressions as 'to have a share in the new *koinonia*, the new communion',[32] are far from happy, as κοινωνία means primarily 'having a share'.

The remaining possibility is to take the word to mean 'fellowship' not as the designation of the group, but as the description of their inner harmony and unity, 'an interior spiritual reality, an activity of sharing or communion, constituting the interior bond of that brotherly concord which, in turn, is realized and expressed in the life of the community',[33] 'the inward bond which necessarily called for outward acts in which it could be expressed'.[34]

As in Galatians 2_9, the word is here used absolutely; but its lexical origin suggests that without saying that any genitive is grammatically 'understood', we ought to be prepared to say in what they had a share. And, apart from such lexical considerations, any fellowship must be based on something, on some common interest, activity, or possession. Often when a genitive does follow, it is hard to say whether it is subjective or objective; yet it is safe to say that the early Church shared in both Christ and the Spirit. In this context the gift of the Spirit seems chiefly to be in mind, so that without translating κοινωνία as 'participation' or adding any grammatical note 'sc. Πνεύματος', we may yet say that the 'fellowship' was constituted by a common participation in the Spirit, and manifested itself in the almsgiving, sharing of property, breaking of bread, and so forth, which have sometimes been suggested as the actual meaning of the word.

WORDS DESCRIBING COMMUNION WITH GOD

The other words relevant to this investigation are not much found in relevant senses in Acts: γινώσκω is used once with Jesus as the Object (Ac 19_{15}); but the unclean spirit who was the speaker is no model for Christian piety; ἐπιγινώσκω, though common, is not used in a theological sense: the corresponding nouns are not found. οἶδα is not used with God as the Object. ὁράω is used in the passive of visions of God (Ac 7_2), and of Christ, both in respect of resurrection-appearances (Ac 13_{31}) and of

[32] Aulén, p. 18.
[33] Thornton, p. 451.
[34] Flew, *Church*, p. 153; cf. Hauck, *KTW*, III.810, 'die *Gemeinschaft* des brüderlichen Zusammenhaltens, das sich im Gemeindeleben bewährt und auswirkt' (his italics).

the special appearances to Paul (Ac 9_{17}, 26_{16}), as well as of visions in general: θεάομαι is used of the ascension (Ac 1_{11}); εἶδον is a good deal used of visions including the appearances of Christ to Stephen and Paul (Ac 7_{55}, 9_{27}); but all this only emphasizes the complete failure of the writer to make any use of these words to describe the normal life of the Christian. No support for the use of the phrase 'vision of God' or even 'knowledge of God' can be found here.

THE CORPORATE ASPECT OF COMMUNION WITH GOD

As we said in dealing with the Gospels, we need only mention here the peripheral questions of Church, Ministry and Sacraments, which have been fully treated by other writers. It is clear, though we do not hear much of the word ἐκκλησία, that the Christian's communion with God is corporate. That follows from all that we have said about κοινωνία; as yet we know nothing of solitary Christians; the society is taken for granted as the context of the experience. Baptism,[35] even allowing for a certain stylization by Luke in an ecclesiastical interest, was clearly a common feature of the Church's life, and there are sufficient references to the Eucharist[36] to make it clear that this was common, though some of the references to the breaking of bread seem to suggest a rite something like that of the *Didache*, with little reference to the death of Christ, or even simply lovefeasts, not intended to be eucharistic. We may perhaps infer from Paul's use of παρέλαβον ('I received') (1 Co 11_{23}), even though the following words ἀπὸ τοῦ Κυρίου ('from the Lord') are obscure, that the Eucharist was celebrated in the pre-Pauline Church with the use of the Words of Institution. The Acts of the Apostles is naturally a fertile field for the student of the Christian ministry, but there is nothing here to suggest that communion with God is mediated through the ministry, except perhaps for the curious incident recorded in Acts $8_{14ff.}$ Peter and John laid their hands on those who had only been baptized and prayed that they might receive the Holy Spirit. It then seemed to Simon Magus that the Holy Spirit was given 'through the laying on of the hands of the apostles'; and though his offer of money that he might receive the same authority (ἐξουσία) was sternly condemned, his initial

[35] cf. Ac 2_{41}. [36] cf. Ac 2_{42}.

assumption was tacitly allowed. Here was a special authority which the Apostles possessed. But nothing clear can be gathered from the Acts or indeed from the rest of the New Testament as to the way (if any) in which this could be passed on to some other group within the Christian ministry: or (if so) which group that would be.

THE NATURE AND MEDIATION OF COMMUNION WITH GOD

We may now ask about the early Church the same questions which we asked about Christ Himself. First, what type of piety is to be found here? In so far as we must base our answer on Acts, we may say that it is one of the most prophetic books in the New Testament. It is not a cold book; the warm, vigorous activities of the Holy Spirit run through its pages: the devotional life of the early Church is keen and eager; every day they are worshipping together. The hallmark of their lives is κοινωνία; but there is nothing of union with God, of mystical ecstasy, or even explicitly, as far as Acts goes, of being 'in Christ', though that phrase is sometimes held to be pre-Pauline. Christian mysticism, in even the broadest sense of that term, has not begun. It is true that Acts is not the whole story, and is a comparatively late work; and that we should expect to find in it much the same tone that we find in Luke; but what little we can learn elsewhere about the Church before Paul does nothing to suggest another point of view. The piety of the early Church was of our second type, and of the prophetic sub-section of that type. It was the very type of piety which we associate with the teaching of Jesus; there is, however, this difference, that the eschatological watching is no longer so necessary (even though the Second Coming lay still in the future); they were more concerned, though in a non-mystical way, with a present experience.

When we ask what words are appropriate to describe man's intercourse with God, we find that words such as 'vision', 'union', and the like remain as inappropriate as ever; the word 'knowledge' makes no progress; but the word κοινωνία, to which we had already given a temporary and provisional approval, begins to come into its own.

Finally, is communion with God in the early Church mediated or unmediated? It remains true that we hear nothing of immediate communion with God in the mystical sense, and virtually nothing of those media, such as nature, which we are prone to stress to-day. The chief mode of communion with God lies in prayer and worship. We are not here considering Christological and Trinitarian questions, save to observe that as they now enjoyed communion with the risen Christ (as is shown, for instance, by Stephen's prayers to Him, Ac 7_{59-60}, though they did not formulate in so many words a doctrine of communion with Him), and as the Holy Spirit was now richly given to them, they enjoyed a far richer communion than they had done in the days of Christ's flesh, though not, of course, than that which Christ Himself had enjoyed. They thus had the materials for a richer *conception* of communion with God, for a fuller formulation of the doctrine, than Christ could possibly have put to them in the days of His flesh, for such a doctrine would have been unintelligible to them before the Cross and the resurrection and the coming of the Holy Spirit. But this formulation was largely the work of Paul.

CHAPTER SIX

ST PAUL

INTRODUCTION

ANY consideration of Paul[1] must hinge on the question: was his outlook predominantly Jewish or Hellenistic? The consideration of his conception of communion with God must itself afford part of the evidence on that question; yet a short preliminary survey of it is indispensable.[2] Ritschlianism gave a great impulse to the study of the history of dogma, and (in its later stages) to the comparative study of religion, and Harnack had drawn attention to the question of the hellenization of the original Gospel. It was above all Reitzenstein who encouraged the view that Paul had been deeply influenced by the Hellenistic mystery-religions. Bousset, whose thesis we have already mentioned, also stressed the Hellenistic character of Paul's thought; but he did not regard Paul as the hellenizer of Christianity; that work had begun in the pre-Pauline Gentile Church. The view that Paul's thought was predominantly Jewish was represented in this period (roughly from 1900 to 1914) by Wrede, who took the view that Paul was influenced by Jewish apocalyptic writers; but that he was thus influenced by a different strand in Judaism from that which influenced Christ, and so transformed the original Gospel that he may be called 'the second founder of Christianity.'[3] Meanwhile in the same period Deissmann, whose *Paulus* was first published in 1911, laid much emphasis on Paul's Christ-mysticism, taking the view that both Jewish and Hellenistic terms were used to give expression to an experience which could not be reduced to a system, which really derived all its content and richness from the initial experience on the Damascus road. In 1927 Anderson Scott[4] asserted clearly that 'The influence of Hellenistic

[1] We take all the Epistles commonly ascribed to him (not, of course, Hebrews) to be genuine, except the Pastorals. Anyone who rejects (say) Ephesians can tell from the references how far this would affect the argument.

[2] The history of it to 1929 is surveyed in Schweitzer, *Mysticism*, pp. 26-40.

[3] Wrede, p. 179.

[4] Scott, *Christianity according to St Paul*, p. vii.

thought upon St Paul's interpretation of Christianity was negligible'. In 1930 Schweitzer argued strongly that the Pauline 'Christ-mysticism' as he calls it, had its origin, not at all in Hellenistic thought-forms, but in Jewish eschatology; that is why Paul's message was not felt as strange or unintelligible in his own age, but was misunderstood, though ostensibly reverenced, in the next. Immediately after Paul, Ignatius and the Johannine school did at last hellenize the Gospel. In recent years the consensus of opinion has been strongly that Paul's forms of thought were strongly Jewish, and indeed the same is now said of the Johannine school, so that the date for the hellenization of the original Gospel must be further postponed. The motif-research conducted by Nygren has had the incidental effect of confirming this point; but the strongest blow struck in its defence was the work of Davies, in which it is maintained that he 'belonged to the main stream of first-century Judaism, and that elements in his thought, which are often labelled as Hellenistic, might well be derived from Judaism'.[5] It is true that Bultmann[6] is still substantially of Bousset's opinion, despite Schweitzer, but the position which Davies has done so much to commend now finds widespread support.

It is sometimes said that there are two distinct periods in Paul's thought. This view, which is somewhat reminiscent of the attempt to reconcile the ethical and eschatological elements of Christ's life by positing a sharp change at Caesarea Philippi, has various forms which are inconsistent with each other, though that is no reason why one of them should not be true. The turning point is what has been called his Romanes lecture at Athens. On one view, he turned thereafter to the simple Gospel of Jesus Christ and Him crucified, as we see in 1 Corinthians; on the other, he perceived the need for something more than a Gospel in Jewish eschatological categories, and turned to Hellenistic mysticism. The Epistles hardly bear out either contention.[7]

PAUL AS A MAN OF PRAYER

For some considerable time now stress has been laid, as for instance by Deissmann, on the need to consider the man Paul and

[5] Davies, p. 1. [6] Bultmann, *Theology*, esp. pp. 51-3, 187-9.

[7] J. Lowe, in *Journal of Theological Studies*, XLII.129-42.

not merely the Pauline system of theology. This has resulted in a certain healthy shift of attention from the forensic categories in which Pauline theology was often discussed to the relational categories which are more suited to the so-called Pauline Christ-mysticism and may perhaps even reflect more truly the meaning of the apparently forensic words like δικαιόω. But we are still in the realm of Paul's teaching rather than his personal experience. We do not have for our material recorded prayers of Paul as we have recorded prayers of Jesus. What we have is rather Pauline teaching on communion with God; anyone can readily see that this teaching comes from the heart as well as from the head, that Paul is not inventing unverified theories, but writing out of the depths of his personal experience. Thus, for instance, he who used so richly the phrase 'in Christ' surely knew himself what it was to live 'in Christ'. Nevertheless we must treat what he wrote on that subject as part of his teaching rather than as autobiography. He who would study Paul as a man of prayer must infer it from what we shall find below about Paul's teaching: the inference will not be difficult.

A further contrast will be found with our treatment of the synoptic Gospels. There the treatment of communion with God was largely contained in teaching on, and instances of, prayer. Words like κοινωνία, phrases like ἐν Χριστῷ, were not found; the outlook of Jesus on the more general aspects of communion with God had to be deduced from His own prayers, the Lord's Prayer, and His teaching on prayer. But in the Pauline Epistles prayer is a topic of secondary importance: the interest shifts to other aspects of communion. The very word προσεύχομαι occurs less frequently than in the synoptic Gospels.

When we consider the spiritual autobiography of Paul, in so far as it is recorded, and not simply inferred from his teaching, we naturally think first of his conversion-experience.[8]

As Paul is the outstanding example of 'evangelical conversion', by which later Christians have consciously or unconsciously been influenced, this dramatic change has naturally been much studied in the growing volume of literature on the psychology of conversion. Many of the accounts or 'explanations' thus given may be perfectly true at their own level, but they do not exhaust the subject, nor are they of particular relevance here. The important

[8] Ac 9_{1-19}, 22_{3-21}, 26_{9-20}, 1 Co 15_{8}, Gal 1_{15-16}.

question for us is how far this experience was typical of or normative for Pauline piety. His own comment (1 Co 15_8) makes it clear that he regarded it as a Christophany, in general similar to those which had been granted to the other Apostles: the words 'last of all, as to one untimely born' do indeed suggest that his case was somewhat different from theirs: but they equally suggest, that he was the last of the series, not only the last so far, but absolutely the last: it follows that the experience is not regarded as normative for future piety. The expressions used, in particular the verbs of 'seeing',[9] are not typical of Pauline piety. Deissmann may nevertheless be right in thinking that the experience deeply influenced Paul's subsequent choice of expression. He compares Paul's account of the conversion-experience 'was pleased to reveal his Son ἐν ἐμοί' (Gal 1_{16})[10] with the phrase used of his Christian life in general 'Christ lives ἐν ἐμοί' (Gal 2_{20}), and describes the Damascus-road experience as 'the basal mystical experience'. 'All that can be called Paul's Christ-mysticism is the reaction to this initial experience. Damascus is perhaps the clearest example of an initial impulse to reacting mysticism.'[11]

The other notable autobiographical passage in Paul (2 Co 12_{1-4}) reads like a mystical ecstasy: in particular the phrase 'unspeakable words, which it is not lawful for man to utter' is significant. Those who stand in the prophetic tradition of piety not only *can* but feel that they *must* give an account of what has been revealed to them: 'thus saith the Lord' is their characteristic utterance. But there is another tradition which stresses the ineffability of what has been experienced; and the very name 'mystic', with its ultimate derivation from μύω, 'I shut (whether the lips or the eye),' suggests that this ineffability is a mark of mystical rather than prophetic experience. Those who do not regard the Pauline so-called 'Christ-mysticism' as mysticism in the narrower sense of the word must admit that there is mysticism in that sense here. Nevertheless Michaelis[12] gives a somewhat minimizing account of the incident, and suggests that the genitive Κυρίου in 2 Corinthians 12_1 (like that, he says, in Gal 1_{12}) is not objective, but genitive of author. In any case it was an isolated experience. Despite the reference to 'visions' in the

[9] cf. 1 Co 9_1; Michaelis, *KTW*, V.357-62.
[10] But see Oepke, *KTW*, II.535.
[11] Deissmann, *Paul*, pp. 130-1. cf. his *Religion*, pp. 182-7.
[12] Michaelis, *KTW*, V.352-3, 357-8.

plural (2 Co 12_1), there are no more such visions, though there is a further 'revelation' (2 Co 12_9), which takes the form of a spoken word.

There is some slight evidence of other ecstatic experiences of a general kind. The word 'ecstasy' is explicitly used of Paul once (Ac 22_{17})[13]: there is also his claim to speak with tongues, but the same passage shows how little importance he himself attached to this.[14] There are also instances of special guidance such as Acts 16_6, and of visions such as Acts 16_9, 18_{9-10}, 27_{23}: but we do not know how far these have been touched up by the author, and we cannot attach the same importance to them that we do to expressions in the Pauline Epistles. The Damascus-road experience is a Christophany rather than an ecstasy.

The Epistles bear ample testimony that quite apart from these special experiences Paul was a man of prayer. The Epistles usually begin with a thanksgiving for the faith of the recipients and a prayer for them (e.g. Ro 1_{8-9}). Such sentences, though undoubtedly sincere, are not actual overheard prayers of Paul in the sense that we have actual prayers of Jesus: he is describing to them his prayers, not actually praying. Ephesians 3_{14-21} is sometimes regarded as an 'actual' prayer of Paul. We have also salutations and benedictions, and doxologies (e.g. 2 Co 1_2, 13_{13}, Ro 11_{36}). The Epistles often end, as they begin, with references to his prayers: and it is clear that, fully in the prophetic tradition, he gave much time to intercession, including intercession for individuals. He prays for the Jews (Ro 10_1): we do not read of prayers for the unconverted Gentiles, but they are implied by his zeal for the spread of the Gospel. There is also one poignant autobiographical description of his petition for himself, the triple prayer for the removal of the thorn in the flesh (2 Co 12_{8-9}).[15] This is the classic instance in the New Testament of unanswered prayer, or rather of prayer which was not answered as the petitioner had hoped. The real answer lay in the strength that was given to him in his weakness: and his acceptance of this was tantamount to Christ's 'Not what I will, but what thou wilt'. Petition is justified when it is offered in that spirit.

One great autobiographical passage remains, Galatians 2_{20}.

[13] We can hardly count 2 Co 5_{13} as evidence.

[14] cf. Behm, *KTW*, I.723; Oepke, *KTW*, II.455.

[15] cf. also petition for a particular 'non-spiritual' good in Ro 1_{10}.

Though Paul, when using the first person plural, is no doubt drawing on his personal experience, yet the use of the first person *singular* here marks the passage as autobiographical in a special sense. But it is so bound up with his *teaching* on these subjects that we are bound to defer its consideration.

PAUL'S TEACHING ON PRAYER

The most striking feature of Paul's teaching on prayer is his reference to the intercession of the Holy Spirit in Romans 8_{26-7}, which, like so much else in his teaching, is clearly a reflection of his own experience.

We do not know how to pray as we ought, but the Spirit himself intercedes[16] *for us with sighs too deep for words.*

We know in general terms the will of God, but if we wish to make our intercessions concrete, we are often, through our ignorance, in danger of asking for something contrary to His will. This is the constant problem that besets intercession and petition, and we have already considered it in connexion with Christ's prayer in Gethsemane. The mystic gives this difficulty as a reason for abandoning intercession altogether. Paul's phrase 'sighs too deep for words' is probably not a reference to glossolaly, but an apt psychological description of those inarticulate longings which the Christian feels in such circumstances, when he must intercede, but he does not know how. Paul with profound spiritual insight transfers the whole problem; when he says that the Spirit intercedes with sighs too deep for words, he does not mean that the Spirit is as inarticulate and baffled as we are; but that the Spirit takes those sighs and longings and makes them His own. This aspiration is thus itself the work of the Spirit; He is able to present it to God.[17] He goes on:

And he who searches the hearts [*i.e. God the Father*] *knows what is the mind of the Spirit, because he* [*i.e. the Spirit*] *intercedes*[18] *for the saints according to the will of God.*

That is to say, though we may not understand what we mean, yet God the Father knows: even the Spirit's intercession takes place,

[16] ὑπερεντυγχάνει, only here in N.T. [17] cf. McEwen, *RTW*, p. 171.
[18] ἐντυγχάνει: also in Ac 25_{24}, Ro 11_2; and in Ro 8_{34}, He 7_{25}, which are about to be mentioned.

apparently, within the human heart, but God understands the Spirit, for the Spirit is able to intercede in accordance with God's will, if that is the meaning of the somewhat ambiguous phrase κατὰ Θεόν. All this is 'of a piece with Paul's whole conception of the Christian life as one in which the divine initiative is displayed at every point'.[19] It is a striking enrichment of the doctrine of prayer by means of the doctrine of the Trinity, and fittingly supplements the answer to the problem given in Gethsemane. It is no mere doctrine of immanence: the Spirit prays within us: but there is also a God above us who hears. Rich as is the concept of communion with God which this implies, it is yet still in harmony with the prophetic tradition.[20] Indeed the Old Testament has the idea that the prophets by virtue of their possession of the Spirit of God had special power in intercession:[21] and thus the very idea which we find here in Romans is prepared for in the prophetic tradition. Before leaving this passage we must notice that the object of this intercession is 'the saints', i.e. the Christians, as in John 17, not mankind in general: yet he prays for the spread of the Gospel.

Two other passages in the same chapter bear on various points in these verses. The reference to the intercession of the Spirit recalls Romans 8_{15}, 'you have received the spirit of adoption, in whom (ἐν ᾧ) we cry Abba Father'.[22] Here, as also in Galatians 4_{6}, the Spirit takes the initiative in prayer. The other passage of which Romans 8_{26-7} reminds us is Romans 8_{34}, where it is Christ who is referred to in the phrase 'who also makes intercession for us'. The same Greek word ἐντυγχάνειν is used in Hebrews 7_{25}; and indeed Hebrews is much concerned with the kindred thought of the priesthood of Christ; we meet the same idea in 1 John 2_{1}. There is no inconsistency here: our prayers to the Father are supported by the exalted Christ and by the indwelling Spirit, if indeed the Spirit should not be described rather as initiating than supporting them.

[19] Dodd, *Romans*, ad loc.

[20] Dodd, loc. cit., is one of the few who puts inverted commas on to 'mysticism' and adds the phrase 'if we are to call it so'. On the relation of the Holy Spirit to prayers, cf. Hodgson, pp. 179-81.

[21] McEwen, *RTW*, p. 170-1.

[22] The punctuation is doubtful and perhaps a sentence ends at 'adoption': then ἐν ᾧ should be translated 'when', introducing the next sentence. But a somewhat similar sense results; indeed we are spared the difficult question of the relation of the 'spirit of adoption' to the Holy Spirit.

The idea that prayer is difficult is further supported by his use of the idea of a 'contest' (ἀγών) in connexion with prayer (Ro 15_{30}, Col 4_{12}; cf. Col 2_1).

The rest of Paul's teaching on prayer consists largely of exhortations to it;[23] and though indeed the word is not extremely common, yet it is clear that Paul attached considerable importance to the mutual intercession of himself and his converts as a bond between them. We have also in Paul instruction on worship and the place of prayer in worship, which form a large part of the theme of 1 Corinthians (also Eph $5_{19\text{-}20}$, Col $3_{16\text{-}17}$). These passages do not bear closely on our theme: but the great emphasis on order and sobriety in public worship tells strongly against any stress on ecstasy, and might be thought to favour prophetic rather than mystical piety. His emphasis on prophecy rather than speaking with tongues (1 Co 14) and the need for the interpretation of tongues tells in the same direction: for though we must distinguish the ineffable words of the mystic from ecstatic glossolaly, yet it is clear that Paul would have little use for an absorption in God which did not assist the edification of others; Paul was ever an evangelist, and it is the prophet rather than the mystic who is eager to communicate his experience to others.

'IN CHRIST' AND 'IN THE SPIRIT'

But Paul's teaching on prayer is, as we have said, only a part of his teaching on communion with God. When we turn to these other categories, we see at once that he speaks of communion with Christ in a way quite foreign to (say) Acts. The phrase that catches the eye, though by no means the only phrase, is 'in Christ'. Deissmann[24] counted 164 instances of this or of 'in the Lord' in those Epistles which he reckoned genuine.

We shall deal here with two authors who minimize or altogether deny the so-called 'mystical' sense of these passages, deferring to a later point (when we have considered certain similar formulae) the consideration of their origin. The matter is con-

[23] Ro 12_{12}, 15_{30}, 2 Co 1_{11}, Eph 6_{18}, Col $4_{2\text{-}3}$, Ph 4_6, 1 Th $5_{17, 25}$, 2 Th 3_1, Philem 22.

[24] Deissmann first drew attention to this in 1892; and his *Paul*, pp. 140-1, provides a bibliography down to 1924: see also his *Religion*; Rawlinson, *The New Testament Doctrine of the Christ*, pp. 155-60; Schmauch; Oepke, *KTW*, II.534-9, which brings the literature to 1933, and has a long list of instances; Taylor, *FR*, pp. 113-16; Bultmann, *Theology*, pp. 311-12, 327-9.

fused by the ambiguity of the term 'mystical', which we should prefer not to use at all in this connexion. Nevertheless, it is the term most frequently used in this discussion, and is used customarily as a synonym for such expressions as 'related to communion with Christ' or 'related to union with Christ', which are themselves confused with each other.

The first attack comes from Weiss:[25] no doubt he attacks the 'mystical' meaning in too many passages, and Deissmann defends it in too many. The main point, however, lies not in the consideration of particular passages, but in Weiss's argument that the formula 'occurs frequently simply as an expression denoting to be a Christian, without any accompanying expression showing deep religious feeling'. He instances Romans 16_{1-16}. He thinks it originated in a mystical circle of thought, but became like a coin thinned by handling, 'an expression for the connexion (*Verbundenheit*) with Christ'. It is not the dominant note of Pauline religion.

Deissmann had admitted in answer to earlier attacks by Weiss that 'the Christ-intimacy of the Apostle itself had . . . its differing degrees of elevation'.[26] The great mistake of Weiss is to suppose that the expression cannot have any very profound meaning when it is not accompanied by expressions of deep feeling. In fact, a good deal of deep feeling may have underlain such a chapter as Romans 16; but the glory of the Pauline conception lies just in this, that the normal Christian in his normal life is 'in Christ'. To be 'in Christ' is not confined to a few people in moments of peculiar exaltation; it is ordinary Christian experience. Christianity transforms the ordinary. However freely the phrase is used, the reality to which it so succinctly refers is communion with Christ. Weiss does indeed allow that the passages refer to 'connexion' with Christ; and if he had left it there, we might have regarded that phrase as equivalent to 'communion' with Christ: but by allowing to other passages the 'full mystical sense' of 'union with Christ', he depreciates the word 'connexion'; 'union' goes too far, farther indeed than Deissmann, who distinguished it from 'communion' and used only the latter of the Bible; 'connexion' does not go far enough. But the cardinal error is to distinguish two types of experience, one more exalted, the other that of the ordinary Christian.

A more serious difficulty is raised by Schmauch. He reminds

[25] Weiss, pp. 468-9. [26] Deissmann, *Paul*, pp. 140-2.

us of what we often forget, that the phrase 'in Christ' is never found with the infinitive 'to be', though 'with Christ' in one of its relatively fewer occurrences is so found (Ph 1_{23}). It is true that 'in Christ' and 'in Christ Jesus' are found in sentences in which other parts of the verb 'to be' occur, but in all these sentences the main emphasis falls elsewhere, and is not simply that the people are in Christ,[27] though the main emphasis falls on 'in God' in Acts 17_{28}. The emphasis does once fall to some extent on 'in the Lord' (Ro 16_{11}). He then distinguishes between various phrases: 'in Christ Jesus', which is never used of an individual believer, and is often (e.g. Ro 3_{24}) used of a thing rather than a person; 'in Christ', which is never defined by the believing 'I'; 'in the Lord', which is more concerned with the activity of the human subject and 'in Christ Jesus our Lord', which combines these various notions, which are much more fully defined than in this brief summary. They are then contrasted with 'in the law', a Jewish phrase, and their origin is thought to lie in this contrast.[28] Whether or not we accept all this, we receive a salutary warning against supposing that every occurrence of these formulae speaks simply of a believer being 'in Christ': that is rather a phrase which can be used to qualify or characterize the most diverse nouns and verbs.

We need only mention the unusual use of 'in' with God the Father (1 Th 1_1, 2 Th 1_1), but it is important to refer to the not infrequent use of 'in the Spirit' or the like.[29] Prominent as Christ is in the thought of Paul, there is no diminution of the emphasis on the Spirit which marked the life of the pre-Pauline Church. There are nearly 120 references to the Spirit in the Pauline writings,[30] one or two of which will concern us later in connexion with κοινωνία. It would be disproportionate to summarize the rest of the Pauline references here; and for two reasons this is unnecessary. First, Paul connects the Spirit with almost every aspect of the Christian life; there is no need to ask what were the peculiar functions of the Spirit; the whole Christian life was lived 'in the Spirit' as it was 'in Christ'. Deissmann indeed argues, very questionably, from the fact that the two phrases are used in connexion with the same fundamental ideas that Christ and the Spirit are to be

27 Ro 12_5, 1 Co 1_{30}, 2 Co 5_{19}, Gal $3_{26, 28}$, Col 2_{10}; Schmauch, pp. 18-20.
28 Schmauch, pp. 41, 81, 130, 158, 164-8.
29 Typical instances of this and of 'in Christ' are in Taylor, *FR*, p. 114.
30 cf. Taylor, *HS*, p. 43.

identified.[31] Not that 'in the Spirit' is the only phrase used; 'the Spirit' is also subject of many verbs. Second, the functions already ascribed to the Spirit in the pre-Pauline Church, as recorded in Acts, are for the most part continued in Paul and the other strands of the New Testament. There they were mentioned, because they were a new feature in comparison with the synoptic Gospels: Pentecost had changed the whole situation; but in subsequent strands they may be taken for granted. Prominent as the concept of the Spirit is in Paul, it is not the most distinctive feature of his teaching on piety; that place must be given to the phrase 'in Christ' and those ideas of communion with Christ that are bound up with it. There are, however, certain special features of the Pauline concept as compared with that found in Acts. We have already considered the relation of the Holy Spirit to prayer. In such passages as Romans 8, a contrast is drawn between the spirit and the flesh. Here and in some other passages the word must refer to the human spirit, for example, in such a phrase as 'spirit of meekness' (1 Co 4_{21}). It is a perpetual problem when to spell it with a capital letter. But the human spirit thus referred to is not an endowment of the 'natural' man. Man has spirit only as he is indwelt by the Holy Spirit, though of course the Holy Spirit in this sense was active before Pentecost, as the Old Testament usage shows. Paul has an important passage on the 'grace-gifts' (χαρίσματα) of the Spirit (1 Co 12-14); the word is in the New Testament distinctively Pauline apart from the instances in the Pastoral Epistles and 1 Peter 4_{10}. He shows a marked wariness in connexion with the more ecstatic and dramatic gifts of the Spirit: and that 'love' which he preferred is part of the 'fruit of the Spirit' (Gal 5_{22}), so that it is not too much to say that he laid a greater stress than had previously been laid on the ethical aspect of the Spirit.

'WITH CHRIST'

As has been widely recognized, we cannot consider 'in Christ' without considering also 'with Christ', and particularly the numerous compounds of σύν which occur in Paul, especially as it is the word from which κοινός and thus indirectly κοινωνία are derived.[32] In these compounds three sets of experiences are

[31] Deissmann, *Paul*, pp. 138-40.

[32] For lists, see Hauck, *KTW*, III.806; Taylor, *FR*, p. 117; Cranfield, *RTW*, p. 82; and in general, see Lohmeyer; Schneider; Hahn; Robinson, *The Body*.

described and linked together: first, the suffering, crucifixion, death, burial, resurrection, and glorification of Christ; second, the descent of the Christian into the water at Baptism, and his re-emergence; and, third, the inner experience of the Christian, whereby he 'dies' to sin, and enters on a new experience comparable with the risen life of Christ. Usually the Christian ('we' or 'you') is the subject, and the third set of experiences is described by the verb; the συν- compounded into the verb is connected with Χριστῷ in the dative.[33] The references to Baptism are not always explicit, but they are often found. The most typical of all these passages is Romans 6_{1-11}, which also contains an adjective compounded with συν-, viz. σύμφυτος.[34] We may compare with it Colossians 3_{1-4}, which the Church soon saw to be the appropriate Epistle for the baptismal Eucharist which was also the first Eucharist of Easter. These verbs are often used in pairs: to share Christ's sufferings gives us the assurance that we shall share His glory (Ro $6_{4ff.}$, 8_{17}; cf. 1 P 4_{13}).

The tenses of these verbs raise an important question. Those which refer to definite occurrences are for the most part in the aorist or perfect tenses, viz. the references to crucifixion (Ro 6_6, Gal 2_{19}), death,[35] burial (Ro 6_4, Col 2_{12}), giving life (Eph 2_5, Col 2_{13}), and setting down in the heavenly places (Eph 2_6, all compounded with συν-. Raising from the dead is more diverse; the compound verb is used of the past (Col 2_{12}, 3_1, Eph 2_6), but σὺν Ἰησοῦ ἐγείρειν (2 Co 4_{14}) and ἐξεγείρειν (1 Co 6_{14}) are used in the future; and sharing in the resurrection is future (Ro 6_5).[36] The present state is that of being a joint heir (Ro 8_{17}): the future tense is not much used, apart from the references we have already made to resurrection, but it is once used of living with Christ (Ro 6_8),[37] and, virtually, of being glorified (Ro 8_{17}).[38]

[33] But often the verb is uncompounded, and the sentence has σὺν Χριστῷ: e.g. Ro 6_8, where both methods are virtually used.

[34] Does σύμφυτοι go directly with τῷ ὁμοιώματι, or is Χριστῷ to be supplied, τῷ ὁμοιώματι being dative of respect? cf. Flemington, pp. 59-61.

[35] 2 Ti 2_{11} is hardly Pauline, but the same verb occurs uncompounded in a sentence which has σὺν Χριστῷ in Col 2_{20}. 2 Co 7_3 is no exception; the aorist *infinitive* indicates instantaneity rather than pastness; yet this instantaneous occurrence must presumably have been in the past.

[36] cf. Dodd, *Romans*, ad loc.: note also the subjunctive in Ro 6_4 for 'walk in newness of life'.

[37] 'living' is a doubtful case, which must be further considered.

[38] It is in the subjunctive in a final clause, but the reference is future, not merely future relatively to the suffering, but eschatological, a reference to the future life; cf. Kittel, *KTW*, II.253. To these future instances we may add from the Pastorals 'reigning' (2 Ti 2_{12}).

This impressive list of past tenses suggests that the Christian has already passed through all the experiences which have befallen Christ, right up to the heavenly session, but the occasional use of the future hints that some of the experiences which have already befallen Christ have *not yet* befallen the Christian, and this is strongly reinforced by the fact that suffering also[39] (Ro 8_{17}, in the protasis of a conditional sentence) is spoken of (for the believer) as being in the present. We may compare with this the bold expressions in Philippians 3_{10} and Colossians 1_{24}.[40] Here is another way in which the Christian now differs from Christ. We do indeed sometimes say that our sins keep Christ nailed to the Cross, but that is not a Biblical conception. A philosopher might say that Christ's reign is timeless, but the Bible is more naïve; and we must think of Christ as *now* primarily triumphant: for Him suffering is past, whereas for the Christian, despite the fact that he has been raised and quickened, suffering is a present reality. In so far as he has not yet reached glory, the Christian has not travelled so far through these experiences as Christ; and, in so far as the Christian is still suffering, he is not going through them in the same order. This conclusion is based largely on the actual compounds. The tenses of the uncompounded verbs describing the Christian life are even more varied.

The problem raised by these tenses, and particularly the discrepancy which can be observed between Romans 6 and Colossians 2, was carefully investigated by Hahn, who points out that Paul is presenting two sides of a unity. The new life is given as a whole; both death and renewal are daily, continuing, present experiences, as is clear from the use of the uncompounded verbs (1 Co 15_{31}, 2 Co 4_{16}); but not till the Parousia will that which is already given be a final and undisputed possession.[41] Nevertheless, when the verbs refer to a definite point of time, the reference is to Baptism.[42] Hahn proceeds to emphasize that that with which the Christian is thus connected is a historical event; he accuses Deissmann, among others, of forgetting this, with the result that the interest shifts to the psychological experience of the Christian. That a man in his place in history can thus be connected with

[39] The word occurs also at 1 Co 12_{26}.

[40] cf. Lightfoot, ad loc. Schneider, pp. 54-7, and Robinson, *The Body*, pp. 70-1, give an exegesis which avoids the idea that anything is lacking in Christ. cf. 1 Co 15_{31}, 2 Co 1_{4-7}, 4_{10}, Gal 6_{17}.

[41] Hahn, pp. 31-45, esp. 43, 45.

[42] cf. Schneider, p. 68.

another historical event is sheer miracle, but in the Christ-event the category of time is abolished.[43] We have of course here a paradox similar to that connected with the kingdom; and also, in so far as we are speaking of the Christian as at once suffering and triumphant, we are reminded of the problem connected with the Cry of Dereliction.

All this is perhaps possible only because, as both Schneider and Robinson stress, the Christian has these experiences as a member of the Body of Christ, a phrase which Robinson goes to great lengths in taking literally. 'It is almost impossible', he says, 'to exaggerate the materialism and crudity of Paul's doctrine of the Church as literally now the resurrection *body* of Christ.'[44] But if the theory is admittedly so dependent on a 'crude' doctrine, it is exposed to objections from mere considerations of time which might themselves appear crude in other spiritual contexts. He faces however the difficulty that we are still suffering while Christ is reigning. Thus he admits 'In the most obvious sense it is only in "the likeness of his death" that we are at present united with Him: "the likeness of his resurrection" lies in the future (Ro 6_5) . . . And yet the "newness of life" is ours, already in this age (Ro 6_4).' He refers also to 'the tension between both these facts of Christian existence—the present possession alike of suffering and of resurrection'. He attributes this paradox to the fact that the resurrection body of Christ to which we are joined 'is the body of His death, bearing the imprint of the nails'.[45] This mitigates but hardly removes the difficulty.

Schneider[46] in the same context refers to the objective character of the Pauline 'mysticism' (as he calls it), which he asserts is not primarily psychological. He is quite right in saying that Paul's emphasis lies not on the experience, but on the facts: it is not simply a matter of *Vergegenwärtigung*, our making things present to the mind. Schneider goes on to attack Brunner, who connects mysticism with religious experience, and faith with the living God. We may readily agree with Schneider that these two can be, and in Paul are, combined, though it is another and subordinate question whether that combination is best known by the name of 'mysticism'.[47] But though we may agree that we are dealing here

[43] Hahn, pp. 23, 88-9, 175. [44] Robinson, *The Body*, p. 51.
[45] Robinson, *The Body*, pp. 74-5. [46] Schneider, pp. 69-74.
[47] Of course, it gave rise to a good deal of undoubted 'passion-mysticism'. cf. Schneider, pp. 118-82.

with far more than psychological experiences, there are surely limits to the degree in which these expressions can be taken quite literally. They are rightly understood to indicate a far closer intimacy with Christ in His various experiences than the non-Christian can ever conceive; yet the difficulties to which we have called attention serve to remind us that in this life the closest intimacy is not yet attained.

We must consider not only the συν- compounds, but also the concept 'with Christ'.[48] Sometimes (e.g. Ro 6_{8a}, cf. Col $2_{13, 20}$, 2 Co 4_{14}) the phrase is such that the σύν might just as well have been compounded into the verb. We have already treated these cases. 'Live' is a doubtful case. The compound συνζῆν is used in the future (Ro 6_{8b}: cf. 2 Ti 2_{11}), but also in the present infinitive (2 Co 7_{3}), where it is not entirely clear to what time it refers. But the uncompounded verb appears with σὺν αὐτῷ (1 Th 5_{10}); here 'together' (ἅμα) strengthens the expression, and the reference is future, as the waking and sleeping referred to in the context are to be understood eschatologically. The same is true of the remarkable sentence 'We are weak in him, but we shall live with him' (2 Co 13_{4}); 'live', as usual, refers to the future, and there is in some MSS. a distinction between ἐν[49] and σύν. Paul may have thought 'with', not 'in', suitable to all references to future glory. The uncompounded verb 'live' unaccompanied by 'with' is used in the present, both absolutely (1 Th 3_{8}), and with other datives, e.g. 'to God' (Ro 6_{10}), 'to the Lord' (Ro 14_{8}), and so on (cf. 2 Co 4_{10}).

This use of σύν in future contexts prepares us for the use of 'with Christ' with the verb 'to be', which quite clearly refers to the future glory in the phrase 'to depart and be with Christ' (Ph 1_{23}),[50] the only Pauline use of this phrase. Indeed, except in Colossians, he does not make much use of σύν, which was being replaced by μετά.[51] (μετά is not, however, used by Paul with any

[48] Lohmeyer, pp. 218-57, the standard work, gives these twelve instances (see p. 218 n.2): Ro 6_{8}, 8_{32}, 2 Co 4_{14}, 13_{4}, Ph 1_{23}, Col $2_{13, 20}$, $3_{3, 4}$, 1 Th $4_{14, 17}$, 5_{10}. 'Christ with (σύν) us' does not occur. There are no corresponding expressions about God in LXX (Lohmeyer, p. 224). But Lohmeyer thinks that the idea is found in the Jewish apocalyptic tradition in other forms, and in the Johannine Apocalypse; cf. also Lk 23_{43}, Mk 10_{35-45}, 14_{25}. It has nothing to do with Hellenistic mysticism.

[49] ἐν most MSS., inc. B D: σὺν ℵ and some others, which spoils the distinction.

[50] cf. 'with the Lord' (1 Th 4_{17}). A difficulty arises from the fact that in Ph 1_{23} Paul seems to expect this state to begin at death: elsewhere he speaks of waiting for the Parousia.

[51] Moulton and Milligan, pp. 599-600.

Person of the Godhead in the dependent genitive.) We note, however, two passages, both plainly eschatological: 2 Corinthians 4_{14}, 1 Thessalonians 4_{14}.[52] The only other relevant passage is Colossians 3_{3-4}. Here the second σύν is clearly eschatological. Here we read 'Your (or possibly 'our') life is hid with Christ (σὺν τῷ Χριστῷ) in God'.[53] The reference to 'hiding', coming immediately after the reference to 'dying', may contain some thought of the burial of Christ, to which Paul refers elsewhere. There is no warrant for supposing that the words refer to an extreme type of mysticism. The thought is rather that 'through Christ his life is one of abiding fellowship with God'.[54]

We may thus conclude as follows about σύν: certain experiences in the past, notably 'dying', are experienced 'with Christ', though the phrase is more commonly used in connexion with the Parousia and the future glory, but the actual state of *being* 'with Christ' or 'with the Lord', though only mentioned twice, is described as a future experience. Thus there is some ground for saying that the Christian *is* now 'in Christ', but *will be* hereafter 'with Christ'; and this means that some limit must be put on the 'mystical' or 'ontological' interpretations of 'in Christ'.[55]

Before we leave this, we must notice that a large number of the συν- compounds indicate the relations of Christians to each other. Cranfield well says 'The fact that many of these syn- compounds first occur in the N.T. indicates the newness and uniqueness of the Christian fellowship'.[56] Sometimes the σύν relating horizontally to fellow-Christians is compounded into a word which refers vertically to participation in something else, e.g. συνμέτοχος (Eph 3_6; but see 5_7); so also the συνκοινων- words.

THE CHIEF INSTANCE OF 'CHRIST-MYSTICISM'

Another check on exaggerated conclusions is supplied by Paul himself in a passage often discussed in this connexion:

[52] Ro 8_{32} is not relevant, if it means 'in addition to him', but there may be an eschatological reference, if it means 'when we are with him'. But this is unlikely. cf. Lohmeyer, p. 219 n.4.

[53] cf. Flemington, p. 74, for the relation to Baptism.

[54] Taylor, *FR*, p. 124, who compares Ph 3_{20}; cf. Cullmann, pp. 218-19.

[55] cf. Seesemann, pp. 49-50; Robinson, *The Body*, p. 62; but Robinson does not make the point that 'with' really brings out the limitations of 'in'.

[56] Cranfield, *RTW*, p. 82.

Χριστῷ συνεσταύρωμαι· ζῶ δὲ οὐκέτι ἐγώ, ζῇ δὲ ἐν ἐμοὶ Χριστός· ὃ δὲ νῦν ζῶ ἐν σαρκί, ἐν πίστει ζῶ τῇ τοῦ υἱοῦ τοῦ Θεοῦ τοῦ ἀγαπήσαντός με καὶ παραδόντος ἑαυτὸν ὑπὲρ ἐμοῦ.

I have been crucified with Christ; yet I live; and yet no longer I, but Christ liveth in me: and that life which I now live in the flesh I live in faith, the faith which is in the Son of God, who loved me, and gave himself up for me. Gal 2_{19b-20}.

At first sight the passage speaks strongly not merely for mysticism in a general way, but for absorption-mysticism. The words ζῶ δὲ οὐκέτι ἐγώ[57] seem clearly to state that his ego no longer lives; apparently it is absorbed in the divine. The whole passage indeed is the *locus classicus* of what is called Christ-mysticism.[58] But we notice, first, that verse 19, though it contains an expression of 'Christ-mysticism' ('I have been crucified with Christ'), also contains in its first half the expression (in a purpose clause, but the purpose has presumably been realized) 'live unto God' (ἵνα Θεῷ ζήσω), and this, though it has no 'mystical ἐν' suggests that if we must use these categories, 'God-mysticism' must be set beside 'Christ-mysticism', and that, when 'to God' and 'in Christ' are used interchangeably, we must not press them too far. Secondly, Paul immediately goes on to speak of his ego as living: ὃ δὲ νῦν ζῶ ἐν σαρκί: it is true that there is no ἐγώ, but, of course, 'I' is the subject. Both the 'now' and the 'in the flesh' confine the application of the rest of the sentence to this present world. This does not mean that there will be absorption in heaven, but that life will be lived there not in faith, but in sight. But for the moment the point is that the ego still lives. Thirdly, this present life (and here again he says 'I live'; ζῶ) is lived in faith. The use of 'faith', rather than 'sight', with which it is often contrasted, is a reminder of limitation; and the word itself breathes a very different atmosphere from that of 'mysticism'; it is the very key word of prophetic piety. Weiss goes so far as to say,[59] 'It will

[57] The usual English translation 'I live etc.' slightly alters the emphasis. More literally it would be 'there lives—no longer I'; but neither translation is perfect. To put a comma after δέ makes no great difference.

[58] The passage is also the *locus classicus* in Paul of the corresponding phrase 'Christ in me'. (Ro 8_{10}: cf. Col 1_{27}, Gal 4_{19}). The stress on *mutual* indwelling is commoner in the Johannine writings. cf. Ro 8_{9-10} for a similar corresponding pair of expressions about the Spirit and also the expression 'Christ in you'. cf. Oepke, *KTW*, II.538-9 On the relation between 'Christ in us' and 'the Spirit in us', see Oulton, pp. 54-6.

[59] Weiss, p. 470.

always remain suggestive that the most impressive mystical statement upon which, as a matter of fact, all our knowledge of his mysticism is based (Gal 2_{20}), is at once interpreted or qualified by a confession entirely in the spirit of the I-and-thou-religion'. It is a gross exaggeration to say that all our knowledge of his mysticism is based on this passage, though it might be asserted that the qualifications which this passage suggests may be read into all the others; but the qualifications are clear, and the concluding words of the sentence derive an added significance from the popularization of the expression 'I and thou' by Martin Buber. Weiss prefers the conception of a servant's devotion, and refers to the 'Christ-mysticism' as 'perhaps a completely strange element'. But surely the passages on dying and rising with Christ are fundamental to Paul's thought, and the formula 'in Christ' is a kind of shorthand expression for the whole experience.[60] Though not to be taken with an exaggerated literalness, it is the fundamental feature of his thought.

OTHER EXPRESSIONS RELATED TO 'IN CHRIST'

These uses of 'in' and 'with' are the chief evidence for the so-called Christ-mysticism; but intimate relations with Christ are also indicated by 'through' (διά) (e.g. Gal 6_{14}; cf. Ro 7_4),[61] by 'into' (e.g. Ro 6_3, Gal 3_{27}, Eph 4_{15}), or by the genitive (Gal 5_{24}), 'a natural way of describing those who elsewhere are said to have been baptized "into Christ Jesus" (Ro 6_3) or "into Christ" (Gal 3_{27})'.[62] Another striking metaphor is 'to put on Christ' (Gal 3_{27}, Ro 13_{14}); this verb is a favourite with Paul in other connexions also.[63] Many of these are in contexts which refer, directly or indirectly, to Baptism. We note also 'For me to live is Christ' (Ph 1_{21}).

Paul is by no means confined to these more intimate modes of expression. We find also ἔμπροσθεν (e.g. 1 Th 3_9), ἐνώπιον (Gal 1_{20}) and παρά (e.g. Gal 3_{11}). We know the things of God (1 Co 2_{11}), have the mind of Christ (1 Co 2_{16}). We give thanks to

[60] Weiss, pp. 470-1; a better view is in Taylor, *FR*, pp. 118-19.
[61] On διά, see Oepke, *KTW*, II.66.
[62] Flemington, p. 60.
[63] Flemington, pp. 57-8, has produced O.T. parallels which dispose of the idea that this must refer to the mystery-religions. Robinson, *The Body*, pp. 63-4, suggests that the 'new man' which follows this verb in Eph 4_{24}, Col 3_{10}, is also Christ. cf. Oepke, *KTW*, II.320-1.

(e.g. 1 Th 1_2), worship (1 Co 14_{26}), pray to (e.g. 1 Co 11_{13}), and of course love God (e.g. 1 Co 8_3). We have faith in (Gal 2_{16}), swear by (1 Th 5_{27}), imitate (e.g. 1 Th 1_6), seek to please (1 Co 7_{32}) and are the slaves of (e.g. Ro 14_{18}) the Lord Jesus Christ.

THE ORIGIN OF PAUL'S CONCEPTION OF BEING 'IN CHRIST'

Having considered the chief passages in which the so-called 'Christ-mysticism' appears, we must consider the origin of this strand of Paul's thought, both Hellenistic and Jewish theories, and also the propriety of this name for it.

Deissmann believed that the identification of the exalted Christ with the Spirit (2 Co 3_{17}) makes it possible to conceive of Christ as an Atmosphere in which we live. Just as we live in air, and at the same time air is in us, so we can speak both of 'Christ in us' and of ourselves as being 'in Christ'.[64] In all this he saw some Hellenistic influence; indeed the idea was at one time widespread that Paul was deeply influenced by the mystery-religions. But we have already seen that there are limitations in the use of this language. Warm and intimate as the relationship with Christ is, it is in the spirit of I-and-thou or prophetic religion: we have nothing of union or absorption-mysticism. Thus Paul's conception is not in harmony with the extravagant claims of the Greek mystery-religions. In any case, recent scholarship has been hostile to the claim that Paul was deeply influenced by the mystery-religions, though he may have used some of the technical terms of the mysteries (such as salvation, mystery, wisdom, knowledge) in support of his own conception, which was more social, more ethical, more grounded in history, more dependent on faith.[65] The mysteries must thus be ruled out as the source of this Pauline conception, though 'many of the terms he used would have an undertone of meaning which would strengthen the appeal of the gospel to the Hellenistic world'.[66]

[64] e.g. Deissmann, *Religion*, p. 171; cf. Mersch, pp. 103-10.

[65] Just as he used 'circumcision' (Ph 3_3) to oppose circumcision. We must consider motif, not vocabulary, as Nygren would say. For his relation to the mysteries, see Kennedy; Schneider, pp. 107-17; Flew, *Church*, pp. 212-13; Davies, pp. 88-98. Of course, the Pauline conception is not *merely* ethical. Cf. A. S. Peake, 'The Quintessence of Paulinism', in *Bulletin of the John Rylands Library*, IV.2. 22: 'To express a merely moral union he must have chosen other language.'

[66] Davies, p. 98. He also dismisses the theory, represented by E. R. Goodenough, that he was influenced by Jewish Hellenistic mysticism in Philo.

Of the attempts to interpret this along Jewish lines, the most conspicuous is that of Schweitzer. In his view, Christianity was not hellenized until the end of the first and the beginning of the second century, in such writings as Ignatius and the Fourth Gospel. The thought of Paul, like that of Jesus, was altogether Jewish and eschatological. Yet he may be said to be a mystic.[67] But his mysticism, most unusually, is a Christ-mysticism, not a God-mysticism.[68] Schweitzer makes many valuable points in his richly suggestive book, and we may readily agree with him that the mainspring of Paul's thought was Jewish; but the account which he gives of the solidarity of the Elect with Christ is altogether unacceptable. We cannot here examine the many remarkable theories in Schweitzer's treatment of this subject;[69] but the main criticism is that he conceives this solidarity, this sharing in the corporeity (*Leiblichkeit*) of Christ in too physical a way. He employs such phrases as 'the physico-realistic character of the having died with Christ', 'actual physical union between Christ and the Elect', and even 'mystical doctrine of physical union with Christ'; these phrases are not torn from their contexts, but are a fair representation of the argument. It is not surprising that this conception is accompanied by a 'realistic sacramentalism',[70] and that this union is effected by Baptism. Even if he took the obvious step of substituting 'ontological' or 'metaphysical' for 'physical', the doctrine would still be incredible, both in itself and as an account of the thought of Paul. These exaggerations more or less refute themselves; in particular the difficulties about time which we noticed above tell against this theory.

But though the theory is unacceptable in detail, he is surely right in seeking its origin in Jewish antecedents and in Christ's own words. We must not of course assume that the phrase originated with Paul. It occurs three times in 1 Peter: this is not necessarily an imitation of Paul; it may reflect the general usage of the pre-Pauline Church. Theories which see its origin in the words or actions of Christ usually stress the corporate aspect of the experience. Thus Flew says that the roots of the phrase are to be found 'in the action of Jesus, who, as the Messiah,

[67] Schweitzer, *Mysticism*, p. 1, gives his definition.
[68] He dismisses Ac 17_{28} as not genuinely Pauline.
[69] cf. Howard, *The Fourth Gospel in Recent Criticism and Interpretation*, pp. 163-70; Taylor, *FR*, pp. 115-16; Davies, pp. 98-100.
[70] Schweitzer, *Mysticism*, pp. 18, 127, 22.

gathered His followers as the nucleus of the true Israel, and declared their solidarity with Himself'.[71] The sayings in the synoptic Gospels which are cited in this connexion did not indeed at the time of their utterance suggest 'Christ-mysticism' to the disciples, but we can understand how they may have initiated a development of thought and experience which, after the death and resurrection of Christ, led to the phrase 'in Christ' and all the rich Pauline and Johannine conceptions of fellowship.

Flew cites a number of Pauline passages where 'in Christ' is used 'as defining the community',[72] and says that for Paul communion with Christ was 'inseparable from the thought of membership in the Ecclesia. Indeed it was the characteristic and constitutive mark of the Ecclesia'. He does not use the ambiguous ideas that the Church is logically prior to the individual or that communion with Christ is mediated through the Church. We may accept this position of Flew.[73]

A somewhat similar explanation is to connect 'in Christ' with 'Son of Man'. The Son of Man spoken of in Daniel has, it is said, taken flesh in Jesus, but has also taken body in the saints of the Most High, the Church, so that members of the Church may be said to be 'in Christ'.[74] Similarly Manson, in his corporate interpretation of the 'Son of Man' sayings, connects them with the Pauline passages on suffering (Col 1_{24}, 2 Co 1_{5}, Ph 1_{29}, 3_{10}, Gal 6_{17}, 1 Co 12_{26}): thus, though the phrase 'Son of Man' does not occur in Paul, we are said to have the same conception with the difference made by the death and resurrection of Christ. But this view of 'Son of Man' has not found universal acceptance: and though it is right to see 'in Christ' in a Jewish setting, it is doubtful if the connexion with 'Son of Man' is so close.[75]

A somewhat similar idea is to connect the formula with the contrast between the first and second Adams.[76]

Another writer who has stressed the corporate aspect of this formula is Anderson Scott. Deissmann was largely concerned with

[71] Flew, *Church*, p. 214; cf. 80. Schweitzer, *Mysticism*, pp. 105-9, himself had called attention to the chief passages which support this view, which are mostly mentioned also in Taylor, *FR*, p. 135; cf. Davies, p. 101: they are Mt 5_{11-12}, Mk 8_{35-8}, Mt 10_{40}, 18_{5}, 25_{31-46}, Mk 3_{31-5}, Mt 10_{37}, 23_{8-9}.

[72] Flew, *Church*, p. 213.

[73] But see a justifiable note of caution in Taylor, *FR*, p. 115; cf. Davies, p. 87.

[74] cf. Selwyn, pp. 20, 83, 194-5.

[75] Manson, *Teaching*, pp. 232-4, cf. *supra*, p. 109.

[76] cf. Oepke, *KTW*, II.538.

the individual who was 'in Christ', and might not have gone much further than Anderson Scott does, when he says of Christ 'Like the Spirit He is conceived of as a Sphere or Atmosphere within which men may live and move'.[77] But Anderson Scott goes on to enrich this conception, without contradicting it, by showing how this 'local' significance, as it is called, is facilitated by the close connexions which Paul deems Jesus to have not only with the Spirit (as Deissmann would agree) but also with the Church. The phrases 'in Christ',[78] 'in the Spirit', and 'in the Fellowship, Body or Church' represent an identical experience under different aspects.[79]

A view which goes beyond this, and is reminiscent of Schweitzer, is put forward by Robinson.[80] He takes the view that all these varied phrases which indicate a close connexion with Christ rest on the assumption that 'Christians have died in, with and through the crucified body of the Lord . . . because, and only because, they are now in and of His body in the "life that he liveth unto God", viz., the body of the Church'.[81] The Christian through Church and sacraments is so literally part of Christ's body that what happened to that body in the flesh can be repeated in him now. There follows a stimulating exposition of the concept of the Church as the Body of Christ. The concept has been traced to various sources, among which the Christian Eucharist is important; but Paul's thought transcends that of his sources. He has reversed the Old Testament notion that the Remnant or the one can represent the many; now the many are included in the one. He uses a great variety of expressions to make this clear. Here Robinson quotes the 'in', 'into' and 'with' passages, with many others such as we have been considering (e.g. 2 Co 5_{14}, Gal 4_{19}, Eph 4_{13}), and passages on being joined sexually to Christ (1 Co 6_{17}, Ro 7_4; cf. 2 Co 11_2);[82] he then proceeds to the idea of the

[77] Scott, *Christianity according to St Paul*, p. 153.

[78] It is, of course, to the exalted Christ, not to the Jesus of history, that reference is made. cf. Taylor, *FR*, p. 113. Even Ph 2_5, which has been rather avoided in these discussions, can be interpreted in this way, if, as has been suggested, it is translated 'Have this mind among yourselves which you actually have in Christ Jesus'. It is in no way incompatible with this that the subsequent relative clause goes on to refer to the Jesus of history, who is after all the same Person as the exalted Christ.

[79] Scott, op. cit., p. 158. This is immediately followed by his distinctive view of κοινωνία as equivalent to *Chaburah*, but it is independent of that.

[80] Robinson, *The Body*; cf. Schneider. [81] Robinson, *The Body*, p. 47.

[82] He also has Eph 5_{28-32}. The nuptial relationship is intimate, yet it is an I-thou relationship. Moreover κοινωνία could be used for it in secular Greek (Hauck, *KTW*, III.799). cf. Chavasse.

unity of a single flesh, the relation of limbs to a body, and Christians as a single organism. The idea of 'Temple of God' is similar. Paul avoids 'Temple of Christ' as too external, preferring those expressions which imply the relation of part to whole.[83] Then by way of some of the κοινωνία passages, he comes to the idea of Christ as Head of the Body.[84]

Now this is an impressive list of passages, skilfully woven together by the author: and no doubt there are all kinds of subtle links between them: but it is not entirely proved that the idea of the Body is the pivotal idea. It would seem equally possible that the idea of being in Christ should have been the starting-point on which the rest of the structure was built. The occasional occurrence of 'in Christ' in 1 Peter (where there is only one mention of 'body', and that clearly to the physical body of Christ) (1 P 2_{24}) would support this view, especially as the conception 'in Christ', as many think, might fairly easily be derived indirectly from the words and actions of Christ, whereas the idea of the Body, now so familiar, was one which was strange, at least in this precise form, to the ancient world,[85] and might well have taken some time to develop. Moreover, this scheme is open to the objection already considered that there must be limits to the literal and physical understanding of these expressions, in so far as the Christian is not now going through precisely the same experiences as Christ.

There are other theories again which relate the idea of fellowship with Christ to the corporate life of the Church in more moderate ways, and with reference to liturgy and the sacraments. Thus Taylor, after referring to the starting-point of the idea of fellowship in the life of Jesus and the new light thrown by the death and resurrection of Christ,[86] goes on to point out how the corporate life of the early Church, and particularly the sacraments of Baptism and the Eucharist, shaped the New Testament idea of fellowship. Weiss thought that the formula 'in Christ' was derived from the baptismal formula 'into Christ', which was originally the expression for 'belonging to Christ'.[87] Davies, however, has

[83] For Temple of God, cf. 1 Co $3_{16, 17}$ (twice), 6_{19}, 2 Co 6_{16} (twice), Eph 2_{21} (not quite a straightforward example). cf. Phythian-Adams, esp. pp. 194-204. He says that we are not individually temples (p. 199); 'we are (together) the Naos (there can only be one)': but Robertson and Plummer, on 1 Co 3_{16}f., 6_{19}, rightly show that this is also true of every member of the Christian community.

[84] Robinson, *The Body*, pp. 60-6.

[85] Robinson, *The Body*, pp. 49-50.

[86] cf. *supra*, p. 160; Taylor, *FR*, pp. 136-7.

[87] Weiss, p. 469. But see Oepke, *KTW*, I.537; II.430-1.

connected this strand in Pauline thought with liturgy in another way, by calling attention to the liturgy of the Passover. Paul explicitly compared the death of Christ with the Passover Festival (1 Co 5_{6-8}), and the connexion is hinted at in several other passages. It is therefore likely that he will hold the Christian liturgy to stand in the same relation to the death of Christ as did the Passover liturgy to the Exodus. This relationship was well stated by Knox; 'a past event of history (or mythology), embodied in the ritual action, became an "effective symbol" for producing a change in the character of the believer'.[88] Knox was not however referring to the Passover liturgy, but to the proselyte's bath.[89] Knox continues, after the passage quoted, 'This conception had passed from Hellenistic religion into the devotional language of the synagogue;[90] Paul transferred it to the faith of the Church'.[91] Davies warmly accepts the latter point, but disputes the former. 'We need not go outside Judaism',[92] he says, to account for this conception, and cites Amos 3_2, Deuteronomy $26_{5ff.}$, Joshua 24. 'Your fathers' and 'you' are used interchangeably: for example, 'your eyes have seen what I have done in Egypt'. There is no need of any Hellenistic explanation of the precisely similar phenomenon in the Passover liturgy. Davies quotes this at some length;[93] the first words of the first response quite suffice to establish the point: 'We were slaves to the Pharaoh in Egypt'.

We are now in a position to return to Paul. The thought was familiar to him and to his fellow-Jews that those who took part in the Passover liturgy in some sense ('mystically', many would say) share the events of the Exodus. Christianity had already in Paul's day developed a cult, Baptism and the Eucharist, and Christ's death could easily be compared with the Passover. Thus the thought could hardly be avoided that the Christian who took part in this cult shared in some sense in the events, namely the death and resurrection of Christ. This may well be the sole and

[88] Knox, p. 98.

[89] Knox, p. 98. But see the reference to the domestic liturgy of the Passover on p. 28.

[90] Accordingly, Knox, pp. 29-33, thinks that Judaism was assimilated to a mystery-cult to a considerable extent. This might appear to resemble Goodenough. But Knox, pp. ix-x, points out that they differ entirely about Philo. Davies, pp. 97-8, prefers Knox to Goodenough; it is not that Philo or other Jews used Judaism to express mysticism, but that Philo 'used the ideology of the mysteries for the sake of Judaism'. Juadism was assimilated to a mystery-cult for missionary ends. (Is Davies, p. 97 n.7, really consistent with this?)

[91] cf. Knox, p. 181. [92] Davies, pp. 108-9. [93] Davies, pp. 103-4.

sufficient explanation of all the συν- compounds; and from these it is but a slight development to the expression 'in Christ'.[94] This mode of thought is still necessary if we are to understand the Church's worship. 'In its central sacrament', writes Dodd, 'the Church places itself ever anew within the eschatological crisis in which it had its origin. Here Christ is set before us incarnate, crucified, and risen, and we partake of the benefits of His finished work, as contemporaries with it.'[95] He goes on to say that the Church lives always, when it is its most real self, 'within the historical moment of its redemption', and then adds, most pertinently to our theme, 'This contemporaneity must not be confused with the timeless "now" of the mystics'. The Roman Church, in its Collects, sometimes describes the event commemorated as having occurred 'on this day' (*hodierna die*); the Anglican and Methodist liturgies have softened this to 'as at this time' (Whit-Sunday) or omitted it altogether (Ascension Day). The Church's hymns show this characteristic as much as the ancient liturgical material does. An Advent hymn such as 'Come, Thou long expected Jesus',[96] though it may be interpreted as a prayer for Christ to come and rule in our hearts, or possibly, for the hastening of the Second Advent, derives its tone and language from the situation of the Old Israel as it waited for the First Advent of the Messiah.[97] And just as our liturgies go back in imagination (if that is not too weak a word) to the time of the Old Israel, so parts of the liturgy of the Old Israel (the Psalms) can be used by the New Israel. The use of metrical Psalms in which 'David' is made to speak as a Christian is a kind of mixture of these two methods.

Thus the origin of the use of the συν- compounds may be satisfactorily found within Judaism; the phrase 'in Christ' may well be closely connected with them; and moreover, the general principle which runs through these phrases is seen to be one which is of general application in the sphere of liturgy.

[94] The parallel does not apply only to the sacraments. Knox, p. 28, suggests that we have, notably in Ps 78, 136, instances of a Jewish kerygma, and that the canonical account of the Exodus was used in preaching to the Gentiles. Thus there was precedent for the way in which the apostolic preaching used the death and resurrection of Jesus. How far does this support the high Protestant view of the presence of God in His preached Word?

[95] Dodd, *History*, pp. 163-4.

[96] *Methodist Hymnbook*, No. 242.

[97] Hymns for Easter sometimes make use of the imagery of the Exodus, quite in the Pauline manner; e.g. 'The foe behind, the deep before' (*Methodist Hymnbook*, No. 218).

VISION AND KNOWLEDGE

We next consider the terms 'know'[98] and 'see'. Paul from time to time uses γινώσκω with God the Father or Christ as the object, explicit or implicit (Gal 4_9, Ph 3_{10}),[99] and beside this is set the thought that we are known by God, introduced either by way of comparison (1 Co 13_{12})[100] or by way of correction (Gal 4_9). The most significant case is 1 Corinthians 8_3. But we must also consider the uses of γνῶσις and ἐπίγνωσις. γνῶσις is used sometimes with some Person of the Godhead in the genitive:[101] and so is ἐπίγνωσις.[102] These words are also used absolutely in favourable senses (e.g. 2 Co 6_6, Ro 10_2); and also with genitives other than Persons of the Godhead,[103] but γνῶσις is also used (especially 1 Co 8, 13) in an unfavourable sense.

Most of these senses call for no comment. The words are not used of merely theoretical knowledge, but in the sense of ידע which we observed when discussing the synoptic Gospels, namely a personal knowledge, an obedient recognition of God's demanding and gracious will. There is sometimes some theoretical element,[104] but this hardly affects the cases where 'God' or 'Christ' is object of the verb or genitive after the noun. The only senses that cause any difficulty are the use of the verb in the passive of God's knowledge of us, and the unfavourable use of the noun, which occur separately in various places and together in 1 Corinthians 8_{1-3}. The former need occasion no real difficulty. God's knowledge of us is almost equivalent, in the thought of the Old Testament, to His election of us. The most obvious example is

[98] cf. Bultmann, *KTW*, I.688-719; Taylor, *FR*, pp. 122-5; Blackman, *RTW*, pp. 121-2; *supra*, p. 64.

[99] Ro 1_{21} is a reference to the 'natural' knowledge of God possessed by non-Christians, but in 1 Co 1_{21} the world is said *not* to know God, 'know' being understood presumably in a richer sense. In 1 Co 13_{12} 'God' may presumably be understood to be the object. 2 Co 5_{16} refers to a particular mode of knowing Christ, which has now ceased. In Ro 11_{34}, 1 Co 2_{16}, the same quotation from Isaiah in each case, it is implied that we do not know the mind of the Lord, 'know' being presumably used in a more intellectual sense. Parts of οἶδα are also used mostly of those who know not God (Gal 4_8, 1 Th 4_5, 2 Th 1_8); but 1 Co 2_2 speaks of knowing Christ. cf. Seesemann, *KTW*, V.120-1.

[100] The word is ἐπιγινώσκω; for other uses of this, see Ro 1_{32}, Col 1_6.

[101] Ro 11_{33}, 2 Co 10_5, Ph 3_8; but of these genitives, probably the first is subjective, and the last two objective.

[102] Eph 1_{17}, 4_{13}, Col 1_{10}; these genitives are presumably objective.

[103] e.g. 2 Co 4_6, Col 1_9 (of the glory or of the will of God). Genitives are also used in an unfavourable sense, e.g. knowledge of sin, Ro 3_{20}.

[104] Bultmann, *KTW*, I.706-8.

Numbers 16_5 (ידע), quoted in 2 Timothy 2_{19}.[105] The connexion perceived by Weiss with the Hermetic writings is far-fetched. Parallels there may be, but the Old Testament is enough to explain the usage.[106]

As for the latter point, the unfavourable use of γνῶσις, it is clear that Paul was aware of the dangers of Gnostic tendencies, not merely when he wrote Colossians, but at the time of the Corinthian correspondence. He therefore resolves to dissociate himself from the favourable use of the term, and to guard further against misunderstanding both by the use of the verb in the passive, which we have just noticed, and by the stress he lays on love. In 1 Corinthians 8_3 he combines these methods in a single verse, 'If a man loves God, he is known by him',[107] and in 1 Corinthians 13 they are spread through the passage. The 'knowledge' thus condemned is not the knowledge of God spoken of in the Old Testament, but that 'direct' relationship claimed by incipient Gnosticism. This, says Paul, does not in this life exist, but it will exist hereafter: 'then shall I know', but even this in turn is immediately qualified by the passive 'even as also I have been known' (1 Co 13_{12}). Moreover when he uses 'know' or 'knowledge' favourably (e.g. Ph 3_{8-10}), he takes care, by the choice of other expressions in the context, to make it clear that he is not using the words in a Gnostic sense, and this is made abundantly plain by the fact that he is not referring to particular untypical individual experiences, but to the common experience of Christians.[108] We may thus reach the conclusion that it is in harmony with his teaching to speak of our knowing God; but in this life we know 'in part' (1 Co $13_{9,\ 12}$), a fuller knowledge is reserved for the life to come. And the knowledge which we have is the common property of Christians, not an esoteric secret: it is moreover a personal knowledge of God, expressing itself in love and obedience, not a speculative or academic knowledge of propositions.

We must now examine the somewhat similar notion of 'seeing',[109] linked with 'knowing' in the sentence, 'For now we see in a mirror in a riddle, but then face to face; now I know in part,

[105] Bultmann, *KTW*, I.705, also cites Mt 7_{23}, and says that this use, the most alien to the Greek use, was afterwards lost.

[106] Weiss, p. 251. Even the parallels are questioned by Bultmann, *KTW*, I.710 n.78.

[107] cf. Kirk, p. 105; Weiss, pp. 250-1.

[108] cf. Bultmann, *KTW*, I.711.

[109] cf. Michaelis, *KTW*, V.315-81; Kirk, pp. 101-5.

but then I shall know, even as also I have been known' (1 Co 13_{12}). The word for 'see' is βλέπω; this is not generally used in eschatological contexts; it is required in the first clause by the reference to a mirror; it must, of course, be grammatically supplied with 'face to face', but would not normally have been chosen in such a context; moreover, the object has to be supplied, for 'face to face' is to be understood adverbially; and though the 'I have been known' later in the sentence implies a reference to God, it does not follow that God is the object here; the object may be God's plan of salvation or something of that kind. If that is true of the eschatological vision, it follows *a fortiori* of the present vision. Kirk says, 'S. Paul is not here depreciating the vision of God which we already possess',[110] but the words are qualified by two strong expressions, namely, 'in a mirror' and 'in a riddle'; and the whole structure of the sentence suggests a contrast between the imperfect vision which we have now and the perfect vision which we shall have hereafter. Michaelis goes so far as to say that there is no contrast between the present seeing (1 Co 13_{12}) and the present walking by faith in the words 'for we walk by faith, not by sight' (2 Co 5_{7}); the eschatological seeing will not be a continuation and heightening of our present seeing; like all that is eschatological, it will be *totaliter aliter*, wholly other. We proceed to note that the parallelism in I Corinthians 13_{12} might be thought to support the idea that Paul draws no sharp distinction between seeing and knowing; but in fact it is not so much that he is speaking with a Hellenistic freedom of seeing as that he has become chary (through his controversy with Hellenistic opponents) of using even the Hebraic idea of knowing, and is thus led to qualify his references to present knowing, as we have already seen.

The only other passage where Paul can plausibly be said to refer to seeing God is 2 Corinthians 3_{18}. Kirk makes a good deal of this much-discussed passage.[111] But whether κατοπτριζόμενοι means 'seeing in a mirror' or 'reflecting in a mirror', and whatever the links may be with magical mirrors and Hellenistic mysticism, the fact remains that seeing in a mirror is less direct than seeing God face to face; and it seems significant that a mirror is

[110] Kirk, p. 102; but see Michaelis, *KTW*, V.366-7.

[111] cf. Kirk, pp. 103-4, and references there given; Kittel, *KTW*, II.694; Behm, *KTW*, IV.765-6; Michaelis, *KTW*, V.367 n.234; A. D. Nock in (ed.) Rawlinson, *Essays on the Trinity and the Incarnation*, pp. 107-8.

introduced into the only passage where Paul speaks of seeing God. We say 'only' advisedly, despite Kirk's bold statement that Paul 'asserts emphatically that we *have already seen* God'.[112] The only text which he adduces before coming to those which we have already considered is 2 Corinthians 4_6, which actually contains 'knowledge' rather than 'vision', and has no verb of 'seeing', though some of its language tends in that direction. Thus the Pauline literature lends no support to the view that the Christian life is the vision of God,[113] who indeed is described as invisible (Col 1_{15}; cf. 1 Ti 1_{17}, 6_{16}, He 11_{27}).

[112] Kirk, p. 102; his italics.

[113] 1 Co 9_1 is a reference to the special vision of Christ granted to Paul (1 Co 15_8), and is not relevant here; cf. the accounts in Acts, e.g. Ac 9_{1-19}; cf. Michaelis, *KTW*, V.358-62. Occasional visions of the Risen Christ are no basis for the general use of 'vision of God'.

CHAPTER SEVEN

ST PAUL (*continued*)

Κοινωνία

WE TURN to the actual word κοινωνία in Paul, with its cognates. κοινωνός occurs in 1 Co 10_{18}, $_{20}$, 2 Co 1_7, 8_{23}, Philem 17, and συνκοινωνός at Ro 11_{17}, 1 Co 9_{23}, Ph 1_7. Taylor[1] observes that only Ph 1_7 and possibly Philem 17 suggest a common religious experience, but it must be added that some of the other passages have a religious context, whether Christian (e.g. 1 Co 9_{23}) or pagan (e.g. 1 Co 10_{20}). Thus the reference to sharing the richness (or rich root) of the olive tree (Ro 11_{17}) is in a pasasge which we may link with the Johannine use of the Vine and the Branches (Jn 15_{1-6}). The verb κοινωνέω occurs at Ro 12_{13}, 15_{27}, Gal 6_6, Ph 4_{15} (cf. 1 Ti 5_{22}), and συνκοινωνέω at Eph 5_{11}, Ph 4_{14}. Taylor sees no reference here to a distinctively spiritual experience, and it is indeed notable that the words are not followed in any of these instances by references to God or Christ. Nevertheless Ro 15_{27} refers to spiritual blessings, and several instances refer to the financial aid which was one of the fruits of the spiritual κοινωνία.

The noun κοινωνία is more important for us, and occurs in Ro 15_{26}, 1 Co 1_9, 10_{16} (twice), 2 Co 6_{14}, 8_4, 9_{13}, 13_{13}, Gal 2_9, Ph 1_5, 2_1, 3_{10}, Philem 6. It also occurs as a variant reading in Eph 3_9. We have already[2] seen that its uses can be divided into 'having a share', 'giving a share', and 'sharing'. We follow provisionally Seesemann's classification of the passages according to this scheme, and begin with two in which the meaning is 'giving a share'. The translations are given from RV as a basis for discussion.

2 *Co* 9_{13}. ἁπλότητι τῆς κοινωνίας εἰς αὐτοὺς καὶ εἰς πάντας.

The liberality of your contribution unto them and unto all.

Seesemann, after defending the transitive interpretation of κοινωνέω in Galatians 6_6 (not in Ro 12_{13}),[3] observes that the difficulties which

[1] Taylor, *FR*, p. 110. [2] cf. *supra*, p. 133.

[3] Seesemann, pp. 24-8; but see Campbell, pp. 367-70.

have attended the exegesis of this verse disappear when the word κοινωνία is translated *Mitteilsamkeit,* which we may roughly translate 'generosity'. κοινωνία is neither to be translated concretely 'gift', nor to be derived from the meaning 'fellowship' and thus translated here 'expression of fellowship': it is derived rather from the transitive use of κοινωνέω. We may add that the meaning here is not reached by way of the idea of 'sharing in contributing' or 'contribution in which we share'. No doubt the somewhat exalted style and religious vocabulary of the context was an attempt to stir the readers to greater generosity; it would not be right to say that the word is used here in a purely secular sense: nevertheless the meaning of the word here is not derived from the notion of communion with God, however true it may be in fact that generosity is an expression of that communion. The 'religious' use of the word added overtones; but it is important, though disappointing, to say that 'fellowship with God' is not the primary use from which the others are derived.

Ro 15_{26}. κοινωνίαν τινὰ ποιήσασθαι εἰς τοὺς πτωχούς.

To make a certain contribution for the poor.

Seesemann[4] attacks Billerbeck's view that the word κοινωνία is here to be understood by reference to Leviticus 6_2 (LXX) (5_{21} in the Hebrew), where it translates a Hebrew expression which is itself a somewhat obscure hapax legomenon in the Hebrew. He concedes that it here must mean the collection itself, as the verb requires a concrete object. The abstract sense *Mitteilsamkeit,* 'generosity', has been made concrete with the aid of the τινά. The word διακονία, which occurred twice in the context of the similar passage in 2 Corinthians 9_{13}, is represented here by the participle of the verb in the preceding verse. Paul did his best to infuse a religious tone into his appeals for the collection.

We now come to passages where κοινωνία is thought to mean 'to have a share in', *die Teilnahme, das Anteilhaben.* (The verb (συν)κοινωνέω has this meaning in Romans 15_{27}, Ephesians 5_{11} (cf. 1 Ti 5_{22}), with the dative of the thing in which one has a share. More doubtful and complicated constructions occur at Philippians $4_{14,15}$, where the sense may be the same.) We consider nine cases.

[4] Seesemann, pp. 28-31.

1 *Co* 10_{16} (twice). τὸ ποτήριον τῆς εὐλογίας ὃ εὐλογοῦμεν, οὐχὶ κοινωνία τοῦ αἵματος τοῦ Χριστοῦ ἐστι; τὸν ἄρτον ὃν κλῶμεν, οὐχὶ κοινωνία τοῦ σώματος τοῦ Χριστοῦ ἐστιν;

The cup of blessing which we bless, is it not a communion of (*participation in*, mg.) *the blood of Christ? The bread which we break, is it not a communion of* (*participation in*, mg.) *the body of Christ?*

Also κοινωνοί occurs twice in the context. So also μετέχω occurs in the context, and the relation of κοινωνέω to μετέχω and of the corresponding nouns here arises.[5] The view that κοινωνία is the stronger expression was explicitly stated by Chrysostom, who concluded his comment with the interesting words: οὐ γὰρ τῷ μετέχειν μόνον καὶ μεταλαμβάνειν, ἀλλὰ καὶ τῷ ἑνοῦσθαι κοινωνοῦμεν.[6] He thus supports the unbiblical notion of union, like many modern writers. It was once thought that μετοχή meant having a share in something and κοινωνία meant having the whole in company with others. Thus a party of people might have μετοχή of a beautiful view, but κοινωνία of the food which they had brought with them. This would fit this passage quite well, for in it μετοχή is used of actual food and the κοινων- words of things spiritual. But this is not borne out by other passages. The roots are sometimes used interchangeably (e.g. Lk $5_{7,\,10}$); they are not, however, as is sometimes nowadays said, synonyms, for the κοινων- words have meanings which μετέχω and μετοχή lack. The κοινων- words are better fitted to describe something inward; it may be that they also lay some stress on the community with others in the act of participating. In the New Testament the κοινων- words are commoner; in papyri and inscriptions the μετέχω group.

The phrases 'blood of Christ' and 'body of Christ' in this passage have been much discussed. Those theories which link the eucharistic 'body of Christ' closely with the use of the phrase to mean the Church have to explain the reference to the blood as mere parallelism, and then have difficulty in explaining the order of the phrases. But possibly the application of 'body' to the Church may be derived from the Eucharist, and not vice versa.[7]

[5] Seesemann, p. 3 n.1, and the literature there cited; Thornton, pp. 448-50; J. A. Robinson, *HDB*, I.461-2; Hanse, *KTW*, II.830-2 (inadequate on κοινωνία).

[6] *Homilies on Pauline Epistles*, 1 Co, *Hom.* XXIV. Some writers wrongly give the last word as κοινοῦμεν.

[7] cf. A. E. J. Rawlinson and R. G. Parsons in *Foundations*, pp. 184-5; A. E. J. Rawlinson in (ed.) Bell and Deissmann, *Mysterium Christi*, pp. 227-8; Robinson, *The Body*, p. 56.

This discussion would carry us far from our course. Paul was here presumably referring to the exalted Body of Christ, which he conceived as in essence one with His earthly Body, however much it was glorified: but no doubt a cross-reference to the other uses of the phrase 'body of Christ' was in his mind.

Anderson Scott seems to have developed his peculiar interpretation of κοινωνία first of all in an article on this passage, a passage which is apparently unfavourable to it.[8] He takes the second sentence to mean 'Does not the Loaf represent the Fellowship of Christ's Body?', the reference being to His Body, the Church. He admits that in the first sentence a slightly different force must be given to the genitive; it refers to a Fellowship which owes its origin to and is sealed by the Blood of Christ. Scott lays all the stress on the 'horizontal' relationships; thus he translates κοινωνία as 'fellowship', not 'participation', and has to find these other ways of taking the genitive. Jourdan has since put forward a similar view, particularly attacking Lietzmann. Jourdan seems to wish to stress the 'horizontal' aspect of the sharing; yet he uses such expressions as ' "sharing together" in Christ'. He objects however to the 'idea of the consumption by Christians of the Body and Blood of Christ, parallel to the consumption by the heathen of their gods in sacrificial feasts'.[9] Against all this Taylor is surely right in thinking that the idea of the relations between the believers, which occurs in verse 17, is a secondary idea in this passage; the primary argument is against participation in pagan sacrifice, and rests on the parallel between them, Jewish sacrifices, and the Christian Eucharist. Thus inevitably there is a reference to participation in the Body and Blood of Christ, and not merely to the fellowship which arises from them. Thus even Scott is forced to use the phrase 'partners of Demons',[10] which he distinguishes from 'participate in demonic life'. But even the former phrase suggests 'partners with Christ', which would spoil his concentration on 'horizontal' fellowship.

Jourdan, who gives no clear account of the significance of the whole passage, says that Greek religious banquets 'were concerned with an association, or partnership, of the gods with men,

[8] Scott, 'The Communion of the Body' in *The Expositor*, Eighth Series, XVIII. 121-30; cf. his *Christianity according to St Paul*, pp. 182-8; Seesemann, p. 43; Taylor, *JS*, pp. 210-11; Jourdan; Lietzmann, pp. 48-51.

[9] Jourdan, pp. 124, 121.

[10] Scott, in *The Expositor*, loc. cit., p. 123.

not at all of a *communion*, a sharing together in some sacred co-operation'. The instances of cult-meals adduced by Lietzmann he deems to be no parallel to 1 Corinthians 10_{16}. He is very sceptical about the existence in Paul's day of the idea of the devotee consuming his god. Now it is true that these two ideas, that of eating with the god, and that of eating the god, are sometimes confused by modern writers on these subjects, but not by Lietzmann, who gives instances of both, though more of the former. Presumably the latter is involved here, and to that extent the greater number of Lietzmann's cases are not apt. Yet even these go much beyond Jourdan's comment, for in them gods and men had communion and shared together in sacred co-operation. He also attacks the view that θυσιαστήριον in verse 18 is a metonym for 'God', but his own view that it is a metonym for the sacrifices makes poor sense of the verse. It is true, as he says, that Paul never uses the phrase κοινωνία τῶν δαιμονίων, but he does in verse 20 speak of κοινωνοὺς τῶν δαιμονίων. He says that it would never occur to Paul to think that Christians could be κοινωνοί of God. But it is agreed that Paul does not say this. Jourdan spoke earlier[11] with approval of Paul representing our relationship with God as being mediated through Christ; and the reference here to participation in His Body and Blood (not 'in God') is no departure from that principle. Moreover, it is not necessary to Paul's argument that the heathen should themselves share his view, though they probably did; he is arguing *from* the admitted nature of the Christian Eucharist and Jewish sacrifices *to* the nature of the pagan sacrifices. Nor, of course, is he asserting that the Eucharist is a sacrifice. The argument is somewhat *ad hominem*, and is simply concerned with this one point about participation.

κοινωνία then is here best understood in the sense of 'participation', 'having a share in', *das Anteilhaben*. Seesemann, being of the opinion that this is one of the passages where the κοινων-words have a richer significance than μετέχω, wishes to include some element of *Verbundensein*, 'being joined with'. The participation meant is something inward, for which *Teilhabe*, 'having a share' is too weak. But he rejects *Gemeinschaft*, 'fellowship', as liable to misunderstanding. Campbell is even more emphatic that one cannot have fellowship with things, and insists that verse 20

[11] Jourdan, p. 113.

must not be rendered 'to be partners with the demons', but 'to participate in demons', i.e. 'to participate in demon-worship'.[12] We may agree with Seesemann, without endorsing his quotation from Chrysostom, or his use of *Einswerden*, 'being one with'.

This is the first instance we have had of κοινωνία followed by a genitive, with the sense 'participation', and we must notice, here and elsewhere, what are the realities, whether objects or persons, of which the Christian partakes. Here it is the Blood and Body of Christ. The verse is compatible with most later theories of the eucharistic presence; for the categories of 'substance', 'accident' and the like, in which they are phrased, are alien to Paul, and raise questions which he does not answer. But the close connexion between the bread and the Body in verse 17 seems to preclude some of the less realistic theories. 'Bread and wine are for Paul bearers of the presence of Christ'[13] and the connexion thus established carries with it the blessing secured by His death, namely the forgiveness of sins. Paul does not hold, if indeed anyone ever did, that the Eucharist is a mere memorial; whether physically, corporally, really, spiritually, or however it may be, the communicant partakes of Christ. This carries with it the corollary about the 'horizontal' relations between the partakers mentioned in verse 17. The Christians who partake are 'one body', despite the inconvenience (so to speak) of using an expression so recently used in a different sense in the eucharistic phrase 'body of Christ'. The individualistic way in which some people 'make their communion' as an act of private piety is quite out of harmony with the New Testament. In the Free Churches, though the whole membership can rarely be present at once, yet the Eucharist is understood to be the act of the whole local Church, at which all the members ought to be present, and not a mere handful who can attend daily. More frequent communions, though in many ways desirable, are not to be sought at the expense of this principle, which the Free Churches have never lost. It is now to some extent being restored in Anglicanism.

The conception of the Eucharist here found is not to be dismissed as the mere survival of crude and primitive notions; nor can we regard it as simply the intrusion of Hellenistic ideas, for

[12] Seesemann, pp. 43-4 (and for other views pp. 35-43); Campbell, pp. 375-8; Jourdan, pp. 115-16.

[13] Hauck, *KTW*, III.806 (my translation); and cf. 805; Seesemann, pp. 44-6.

this notion of communion with God, though not the word, was one which the Jews shared with the rest of the Semitic world and indeed the whole of the ancient world. Paul takes this common idea, and handles it with a remarkable sobriety.

1 *Co* 1_9. πιστὸς ὁ Θεός, δι' οὗ ἐκλήθητε εἰς κοινωνίαν τοῦ υἱοῦ αὐτοῦ Ἰησοῦ Χριστοῦ τοῦ Κυρίου ἡμῶν.

God is faithful, through whom ye were called into the fellowship of his Son Jesus Christ our Lord.

This is the only New Testament passage where κοινωνία is constructed with the objective genitive of a person, apart from references to the Holy Spirit, who, though theologically a Person, is in Greek grammar neuter. Some deny the possibility of such a construction, and render this 'into a communion belonging to (and named after) God's Son', giving similar translations of the passages relating to the Holy Spirit (Ph 2_1, 2 Co 13_{13}).[14] There are, however, occasional parallels in secular literature to this objective genitive of a person;[15] and thus those who defend the objective genitive here have no need to concede that Paul speaks of Christ as though He were a 'thing'. If this were a genitive of author, κοινωνία would, of course, have to be translated 'fellowship'. We should certainly not follow Scott in seeing here, as he saw in Acts 2_{42}, a designation of the Church, the *Chaburah* of Jesus. Yet those who make this genitive objective and translate 'participation' rightly stress the richness of the expression and hear in it overtones which would justify the translation 'fellowship with'; some indeed go too far, with such expressions as *Einswerden*, 'becoming one with': but Campbell makes no such concession, and thinks that Paul speaks of the risen and glorified Christ in a curiously impersonal way.[16]

As this is one of the passages where the distinction between subjective and objective genitive is important, we may mention here Deissmann's view, which was partly taken from Schmitz,[17] that Paul uses the genitive 'of Jesus Christ' in a peculiar manner,

[14] G. G. Findlay, *EGT*, II. ad loc.; Scott, *Christianity according to St Paul*, p. 160 n.2.
[15] Seesemann, pp. 15-6, 47 n.3; Hauck, *KTW*, III.799.
[16] Seesemann, pp. 51, 56; Thornton, pp. 71-2; Hauck, *KTW*, III.804-5; Campbell, p. 380; Cranfield, *RTW*, p. 82, has no explicit opinion about the construction of the genitive, but says 'It is not certain whether sharing *in* or sharing *with* Christ is meant'.
[17] Deissmann, *Paul*, pp. 162-4; Schmitz; cf. Jourdan, pp. 118-19. This passage is not actually one of those which Deissmann cites.

for which the classification into objective and subjective is insufficient. This he calls the 'mystical genitive' or 'genitive of fellowship'. In these cases the 'of Jesus Christ' is in the main identical with 'in Christ'. This may be somewhat exaggerated, but there is some truth in it; it might be otherwise put in this way, that when a phrase such as 'the love of Christ' is primarily to be regarded as meaning (say) 'Christ's love for us', then the very fact that 'our love for Christ' could in other circumstances be the meaning of precisely that phrase gives the phrase an overtone. It has primarily the one meaning, but that does not exclude the other. Translation is ever imperfect, and the real meaning of these phrases is not to be sought by putting syntactical questions which Paul would hardly have understood. However well the thought of another language is translated, it does not remain quite the same thought. Incidentally, the fact that in German not only the genitival construction but also the compound nouns, like *Christusliebe*, have this ambiguity, increases the appeal of this idea to the German mind.

Is this participation in the Son to be understood as only future or also present? Though the former view has the support of Eusebius and Chrysostom, and might be thought to harmonize with verses 7b-8, yet Seesemann is no doubt right[18] in saying that the verse sums up the whole section from verse 4, and in deducing from the customary associations of the verb 'call' that the participation here spoken of is already enjoyed in the present, thus corresponding to 'in Christ' as well as to 'with Christ'. The clear present reference in the parallel, 1 Corinthians 10_{16}, points to the same conclusion.

But this parallel raises a difficulty. Here (1 Co 1_9) the Christian as such participates in Christ. There (1 Co 10_{16}), by receiving bread and wine, he participates in Christ's Body and Blood. It does not seem that even the Body and Blood of Christ can easily be conceived as greater than Christ Himself, so that the Christian in 1 Corinthians 1_9 is already described as having what sacramental communion might give. It might, of course, be maintained that mediation through bread and wine is necessary for the participation described here (1 Co 1_9), in a passage which does not deal with conditions or mediation. This would, however, be a somewhat artificial exegesis, and it is surely possible to have some

[18] Seesemann, pp. 48-50; Robertson and Plummer, ad loc.

participation in Christ before one first receives the Holy Communion.

There is a similar difficulty about Baptism; indeed it is greater about a sacrament which is unrepeatable and makes a greater change. Holy Communion, being repeatable, must confirm something already existing, which may thus be conceived as existing before first Communion. But the relation between adult Baptism and faith is much more difficult: must not the faith which leads the candidate to seek Baptism itself secure in a measure, at least, the blessing which Baptism purports to convey? These considerations would seem to preclude an altogether 'Catholic' view.[19]

But the difficulty is more logical than real. The Holy Communion is a strengthening of that participation which the Christian already enjoys. These spiritual matters must not be too mechanically conceived; we must neither think that he who once believes possesses Christ so securely that he has no need of means of grace nor that a child (say) who has never received Holy Communion is devoid of Christ. Moreover, he who already participates in Christ must presumably be said to participate in the whole Christ. It is not fitting to separate His Deity from His Humanity. Where Christ is, there He is altogether. But in the Holy Communion we receive Him in another mode or by another channel. But here again, it is easy to mis-state the case. It is sometimes said from the 'Catholic' side that we receive Him both by faith and by the sacraments. But they should not be thus co-ordinated. Faith (and faith alone) is the disposition in the recipient whereby he is able to apprehend the blessing of the sacrament.[20] The sacraments are one of the modes whereby grace is offered rather than a mode of its apprehension parallel with faith.

Hauck rightly says[21] that Paul nowhere dares to speak of an immediate κοινωνία θεοῦ. This is mediated through Christ, and in the Old Testament in various ways, as through the altar (1 Co 10_{18}). Nevertheless, participation in Christ is, to the Christian, participation in the Godhead.

[19] cf. Oulton, pp. 49-68, 125-32; and, on this passage, Seesemann, pp. 50-1.

[20] This requires some modification for infant Baptism. But it covers reception by the faithless, for whatever they receive at the Eucharist, it is not blessing.

[21] Hauck, *KTW*, III.804 n.51.

Ph 2_1. εἴ τις κοινωνία Πνεύματος.

If [sc. *there is*] *any fellowship of the Spirit.*

The interest of the commentators has been somewhat absorbed in the question of the correct reading in this verse, on which hinges the precise translation; but this does not affect κοινωνία Πνεύματος. It is quite in accordance with Pauline thought that the Spirit here occupies a place similar to that which Christ held in the passage last considered. It is generally held that the genitive is similarly objective. There is a certain danger of taking each text in isolation, as also 2 Corinthians 13_{13}, and supporting one's defence of the subjective or objective genitive, as the case may be, by referring to the other two cases as already established, regardless of the fact that the opposing party will challenge all three. Therefore we shall not make any use of the other two texts here. The views of those who hold the genitive to be subjective are summarized by Seesemann, who notes that they mostly tend to render κοινωνία as 'unity', for which Paul would have used ἑνότης.[22] He argues strongly that the genitive is objective,[23] and that the phrase must be rendered 'fellowship with the Spirit' (*Gemeinschaft mit dem Geist*) or, more precisely, 'participation in the Spirit' (*Teilnahme, Anteilhaben am Geist*). He argues from 1 Corinthians 1_9, an argument which we have agreed not to use, and also cites a number of passages from the writers of the early Church in which κοινωνία Πνεύματος or some kindred phrase is used, in all of which the meaning must be 'participation in the Holy Spirit'. He also argues from the context that the four expressions in this verse must be taken in two pairs; the last two, namely κοινωνία Πνεύματος and σπλάγχνα καὶ οἰκτιρμοί refer to something present in man; to take Πνεύματος as genitive of author would mean that the third phrase out of the four would refer to an objective power, which would not fit the context. We may add that the matter is not complicated, as it is in 2 Corinthians 13_{13}, by two genitives in the immediate context. There is indeed one, παραμύθιον ἀγάπης, itself not easy to classify, but it is not sufficiently prominent in the sentence to affect the construction here. On the whole we hold Πνεύματος to be objective genitive.

[22] Seesemann, pp. 58-60; cf. 56-7. He does not remark that this does not apply to Scott, *Christianity according to St Paul*, p. 160; cf. Jourdan, pp. 118-19.

[23] Seesemann, pp. 60-2, supported by Hauck, *KTW*, III.807; Thornton, pp. 70-1.

2 *Co* 13_{13}.[24] Ἡ χάρις τοῦ Κυρίου Ἰησοῦ Χριστοῦ καὶ ἡ ἀγάπη τοῦ Θεοῦ καὶ ἡ κοινωνία τοῦ Ἁγίου Πνεύματος μετὰ πάντων ὑμῶν.

The grace of the Lord Jesus Christ, and the love of God, and the communion of the Holy Ghost, be with you all.

In this, at once the most famous and the most difficult of all the passages in which κοινωνία occurs, we have again the problem whether the genitive is objective or subjective, but the difficulty of taking it as objective is much increased by the apparent parallelism with the other phrases in which 'Jesus' and 'God' are presumably subjective genitives. Moreover the parallelism seems to the modern mind, at least, not merely grammatical, but, as it were, theological, the three Persons of the Trinity being naturally co-ordinate, though it is doubtful how far Paul thought along those lines. But to take the genitive as subjective would not make the three phrases exactly parallel; for the subjective and the possessive genitive, though both opposed to the objective genitive, are not identical. Now the second phrase is precisely subjective, corresponding to 'God loves us';[25] and the first phrase corresponds, though not quite so precisely, to 'Christ is gracious to us'. But the third phrase, even if the genitive were said to be other than objective, would not quite correspond; it might be translated 'the fellowship which belongs to the Holy Spirit', in which case the genitive would be possessive rather than subjective, like 'John's house' rather than 'John's love'; and even if it were translated 'the fellowship which the Holy Spirit creates', there would still be no verb corresponding to 'loves' and 'is gracious to'.

In favour of the objective genitive, Seesemann[26] adduces the evidence of the Fathers and the liturgies; but that of the Fathers has been shown by Jourdan to be at best ambiguous; and that of the early liturgies is also somewhat confusing. Some liturgies supplement κοινωνία by adding after it 'and the gift' or 'and the visitation'.[27] Seesemann argues that there are instances of

[24] Some editors call this 2 Co 13_{14}.

[25] It would theoretically be possible to take it as objective, but this is not likely; but see Oulton, pp. 63-4.

[26] Seesemann, pp. 72-3.

[27] e.g. the liturgy of St James, cited by Seesemann from Brightman, I.49. The quotation from that of the Syrian Jacobites, which Seesemann takes from A. Rücker, can be found in Brightman, I.85.

Πνεύματος being constructed differently with two nouns, with κοινωνία as objective and the other ('gift' or 'visitation') as subjective,[28] and this is supposed to mitigate the difficulty that κοινωνία has here an objective genitive whereas 'grace' and 'love' have not. But the point is not the same, for the difficulty here lies in the relationship to the preceding 'grace' and 'love' with their own dependent genitives, not, as in the liturgies, in any noun supplementing κοινωνία. Seesemann has a much more apt parallel when he quotes 2 Thessalonians 2_{13}. Later, with considerable ingenuity, he argues that 'gift' could not possibly be combined with κοινωνία if the latter meant *Gemeinschaft, societas.* This is probably true, and we admire the skill with which he draws an argument for Πνεύματος being objective genitive from the insertion of a phrase with which he takes it as subjective. But in a construction so mixed, it might be genitive of apposition, 'gift consisting of the Spirit'. But these expansions are not so much proof that κοινωνία takes an objective genitive as that the writers were puzzled by the expression and sought to clarify it. We have some sympathy with the Armenian liturgy, which sweeps, as it were, the question aside with the words 'The grace, the love, and the divine sanctifying power of the Father and the Son and the Holy Ghost'.[29]

A further point is that, if κοινωνία means anything like *societas* or 'Church', the parallelism is destroyed. The phrase 'sense of membership' avoids this difficulty, but is a subjective and excessively psychological phrase which puts the case for the subjective genitive at its worst.[30] The difficulty might perhaps be met by 'fellowship created by the Holy Spirit', understood neither concretely as the Church, nor psychologically, but as a relationship with others.

On the whole, however, we may follow the general view that the genitive is objective,[31] and translate it 'participation in the

[28] Seesemann, p. 70. He also quotes πᾶσαν τοῦ ἁγίου Πνεύματος τὴν ἐνέργειαν καὶ κοινωνίαν from Methodius, *de Resurrectione*, III.16, 9.

[29] Brightman, I.435.

[30] It was used by Plummer, p. 384, and J. A. Robinson, *HDB*, I.460; and was rightly disapproved by Thornton, p. 84n. The subjective genitive was also approved by H. W. Robinson, p. 18, and by Hopwood, p. 224, who misunderstands the construction and meaning of κοινωνία throughout.

[31] So Seesemann, pp. 62-73; Hauck, *KTW*, III.807 (who, however, is rightly criticized by Thornton, p. 450, for calling it objective genitive of the *thing* shared: 1 Co 1_9 shows that a *person* can be used in this construction); Thornton, pp. 69-84; Lietzmann, ad loc.; Campbell, pp. 379-80; Oulton, pp. 62-4; and many others.

Holy Spirit'. Even if the genitive is objective, the translation might be 'fellowship with', but that would be better expressed by μετά.

We might indeed take the view that Paul himself could not have decided this issue, and so come again to Deissmann's 'mystical genitive'; but Seesemann observes that we never have a genitive which is with the same noun at once objective and subjective. It is further argued that the words have become fused into one concept, *Geistesgemeinschaft*, 'spirit-fellowship'.[32] A somewhat similar view is taken by Jourdan,[33] who, fearful lest the support of an objective genitive should afford the opportunity 'for some to insist that the spiritual benefit indicated is a quality inherent in man', concludes, in connexion with this and other passages, that the concept is too large to be confined within such arguments. It has

'a quality of signification which is capable of being applied simultaneously in an internal and in an external direction, that is to say, of being used at the same time with an objective and subjective force. It can mean, at one and the same time, the "having a share", the "receiving of a share", and the "granting of a share".'

This is attractive, but it is perhaps simpler to keep to the theory of an objective genitive.

2 *Co* 8_4. μετὰ πολλῆς παρακλήσεως δεόμενοι ἡμῶν, τὴν χάριν καὶ τὴν κοινωνίαν τῆς διακονίας τῆς εἰς τοὺς ἁγίους.

Beseeching us with much intreaty in regard of this grace and the fellowship in the ministering to the saints.

This seems to mean 'begging of us the favour of being allowed to share in the ministry to the saints'. The context is the collection for the saints at Jerusalem, in which connexion we have had instances of κοινωνία meaning 'generosity' or even concretely the 'collection' itself; here, in a similar context, it seems to mean 'participation in'. The context, however, gives a religious tone to it. χάριν καὶ κοινωνίαν may be a hendiadys; or the καὶ may be regarded as epexegetic.[34]

[32] This view is discussed in Seesemann, pp. 66-9.

[33] Jourdan, pp. 116-19.

[34] cf. Seesemann, pp. 67-8; Hauck, *KTW*, III.809.

Ph 1_5. ἐπὶ τῇ κοινωνίᾳ ὑμῶν εἰς τὸ εὐαγγέλιον.

For your fellowship in the furtherance of the gospel.

There have been two main lines of interpretation. According to the first, it means 'your co-operation towards (in aid of) the gospel',[35] with which we may compare Romans 15_{26}, 2 Corinthians 9_{13}. This interpretation is usually taken almost exclusively in a financial sense so that κοινωνία might almost be translated 'alms' or 'generosity', which are certainly possible translations. The εἰς here is reminiscent of the εἰς in the two passages which we have just mentioned, though there is a slight difference; it may here be rendered 'in furtherance of', but we should hardly translate Romans 15_{26} 'in furtherance of the poor'. There are, however, various objections to this view, the chief of which is that Paul is not accustomed to give thanks in the opening paragraphs of his letters for such achievements, though the force of the argument is diminished if the financial side is not stressed.

The other line of interpretation[36] is to take the εἰς clause as equivalent to another genitive, so that the words mean 'your participation in the Gospel', which is almost equivalent to 'your faith'. The argument is that Paul was compelled to turn the sentence in some such way, as two genitives together would be misunderstood, or would be impossible.[37] This is probably correct;[38] yet it is curious that Paul should use εἰς after κοινωνία in such very different senses; and it might be thought that so distinctive a preposition must mean 'in furtherance of'. Certainly we feel that this is not a reference to almsgiving, but we may wonder whether we have not here the rare case of κοινωνία used absolutely in the sense 'fellowship' (cf. Ac 2_{42}, Gal 2_9), so that the translation would be 'your fellowship in furtherance of the gospel'.[39] Thus we cannot be certain that the gospel is here the thing of which they partake.

[35] So Lightfoot, *Philippians*, ad loc.

[36] So Seesemann, pp. 73-9, who has convinced Dibelius, *Philippians*, ad loc., though not by his use of Chrysostom.

[37] A possible answer to this lies in Ph 1_7; but as this is variously translated 'partakers with me in grace' and 'partakers of my grace', the point is not clear, though the former is to be preferred.

[38] So Hauck, *KTW*, III.805, as far as the translation goes, but I cannot accept his reference to Dibelius or the account of the grammar which he implies in his reference to his own p. 798.

[39] cf. Thornton, p. 32; Taylor, *FR*, p. 111.

Philem 6. ὅπως ἡ κοινωνία τῆς πίστεώς σου ἐνεργὴς γένηται.

That the fellowship of thy faith may become effectual.

A wide variety of interpretations is possible here.[40] The genitive πίστεως might be that of author; it might then mean 'the fellowship (with others? with me?) that springs from your faith' or 'the generosity (or kindness) which springs from your faith'. To translate it 'the faith which unites you with Christ' is theologically sound, but hard to reconcile with the grammar. If the genitive πίστεως is objective, then does κοινωνία mean 'communication',[41] or, in the usual way, 'participation'?[42] Others, again, take σου more closely with κοινωνία than with πίστεως: 'your participation in the faith.' Campbell takes it as the participation of the saints who have just been mentioned.[43]

This instance is so difficult to classify that it is of little help to the argument.

Ph 3_{10}. τοῦ γνῶναι αὐτόν, καὶ τὴν δύναμιν τῆς ἀναστάσεως αὐτοῦ, καὶ κοινωνίαν παθημάτων αὐτοῦ.

That I may know him, and the power of his resurrection, and the fellowship of his sufferings.[44]

The passage does not throw much new light on the grammatical aspects of κοινωνία, for here there can be little doubt that the following genitive is objective. Even so, Anderson Scott wishes to translate it 'partnership in', not 'participation in'.[45] These sufferings are, of course, shared *with Christ*, but that point is not verbally expressed. The meaning is not that Christ's sufferings create a fellowship, though that is true, but that we may share with Christ in His sufferings. The Hebrew use of ידע, which we have already considered, provides a sufficient basis for the use of 'know' here; there is no need for Seesemann to bring in Reitzenstein. But what the passage lacks in grammatical interest, it

[40] cf. Taylor, *FR*, p. 111 n.2.

[41] So Thornton, p. 38.

[42] So virtually Seesemann, pp. 79-83, who departs for once from the patristic interpretation, and takes ἡ κοινωνία τῆς πίστεως closely together, σου going with the whole phrase, as a stronger expression for 'faith' in the subjective sense of the word; cf. Hauck, *KTW*, III.805.

[43] Campbell, p. 370; cf. Moffatt, ad loc.

[44] Some minor variants in the text do not affect the translation.

[45] Seesemann, pp. 83-6; Scott, in *The Expositor*, Eighth Series, XVIII.121.

makes up in devotional value. It is curious, and contrary to the Pauline custom, that the resurrection is mentioned before the sufferings of Christ; and this might be taken to mean that the reference to the sufferings was something of an afterthought. But it is the new life which is lived in the power of His resurrection which makes it possible to share His sufferings.[46] We are in the realms of thought which are associated with the συν- compounds, one of which occurs in the next phrase; 'being conformed (συμμορφιζόμενος) unto his death'. Up to this point Paul is referring to experiences of the Christian in this life, and these are to be distinguished from the experience mentioned in the next verse: 'if by any means I may attain unto the resurrection from the dead.' By the phrase 'participation in His sufferings', Paul does not mean merely that the Christian experiences the sufferings of Christ after Him in thought, imagination, or sympathy, nor merely that his own actual sufferings are endured with Christ or for the sake of Christ (though all these ideas are present), but that his own actual sufferings are a real participation in Christ's sufferings, suffered by virtue of his communion with Christ.[47]

This is the last of many passages in which κοινωνία denotes a close inner participation. Seesemann says that it has almost the character of 'becoming one' (*Einswerden*); but we would stress that it never has that completely.

There remains one Pauline passage where κοινωνία bears a different sense.

Gal 2_9. δεξιὰς ἔδωκαν . . . . κοινωνίας.

Gave the right hands of fellowship.

This passage affords no difficulty. It is similar to Ac 2_{42}, though there the meaning of the word is disputed. It is used absolutely, without any dependent genitive or similar phrase, and means neither 'having a share' nor 'giving a share', but 'fellowship', in the sense of partnership or joint participation in a common enterprise, in this case, spreading the gospel. Paul and

[46] Dibelius, *Philippians*, ad loc.

[47] This is borne out by Col 1_{24}, Ro 8_{17}, and 2 Co $1_{5, 7}$ (where the expression is very similar to that used here); cf. 1 P 4_{13}; cf. Seesemann, pp. 83-6; Hauck *KTW*, III.806-7 (but I should not use the word 'mystical'). The topic has been fully investigated by Schneider, pp. 48-61, who also mentions Gal 6_{17}, 2 Co 4_{10-11}, Eph 3_{16}, Ph 2_{17}, 2 Ti 2_{11}.

Barnabas are accepted as partners. There is no reference, explicit or implicit, to a religious experience, save in so far as the common enterprise was a religious one. It therefore goes rather too far to say that Paul is recognized as a κοινωνός of Christ: he was in fact that, but what is meant here is that he was recognized as a partner of the original apostles.[48]

We have left out of account 2 Corinthians 6_{14}, where κοινωνία is used in a non-religious context, as a synonym for μετοχή.[49]

Seesemann says that Paul never uses the word in a secular sense; it is for him a religious term. Taylor says of the κοινων- words in general that in forty-three passages only nine, or at most twelve, use the words 'of a distinctively religious or mystical experience'.[50] From what he says in the immediately preceding passage, we gather that his figures for the use of κοινωνία in Paul are that out of twelve passages four or possibly six refer to a religious experience. But there is no real contrast.[51] The six rejected cases refer, on Taylor's own showing, either to 'co-operation or partnership in respect of the Gospel' or to 'contributions or almsgiving'; and these, though the reference may not be to a religious experience of Christ or the Spirit, are religious contexts in which κοινωνία is often linked, as Seesemann points out, with such words as χάρις and ἀγάπη. But the interpretations we have adopted would cause Philippians 1_5 and Philemon 6 to be taken somewhat differently, the former of sharing in the Gospel and not merely co-operation in respect of it, and the latter not of alms-giving, but of participation in faith.[52] Thus, to put it at its lowest, κοινωνία has a certain religious flavour in Paul, though it does not always refer to participation in Persons of the Godhead.

Seesemann is of the opinion that the various Greek uses of the word, including those of the Stoics and Philo, do not provide any parallel to the Pauline use,[53] though the usage of the rest of the

[48] But cf. Seesemann, pp. 86-7; Hauck, *KTW*, III.809.

[49] Seesemann, p. 67 n.1, regards the un-Pauline use of the word as an additional reason for regarding the passage as not genuine. But see Hanse, *KTW*, II.831. Thornton, pp. 11-15, attaches great significance to the passage.

[50] Seesemann, p. 99; Taylor, *FR*, p. 111, who tacitly agrees with the omission of 2 Co 6_{14}.

[51] The two doubtful cases are 2 Co 13_{13}, Ph 2_1; and by taking these genitives as objective, we are entitled to add them to the four cases of religious experience.

[52] 2 Co 8_4 might also be taken rather differently.

[53] Seesemann, pp. 100-3; cf. Hauck, *KTW*, III.799-800, 803-4.

New Testament does not diverge from the usual Greek use. The use of the κοινων- words as technical terms in connexion with the heathen sacrificial meals is an exception; for Paul is obviously influenced by this (1 Co 10); and this may have been the origin of his usage; in particular, the unusual use of κοινωνία with the genitive of the person (e.g. 1 Co 1_9), may easily have been derived from the use of the phrase κοινωνία τοῦ αἵματος or τοῦ σώματος τοῦ Χριστοῦ (e.g. 1 Co 10_{16}). κοινωνία gradually became a technical term for the Eucharist, as 'communion' still is,[54] but the Pauline use remained peculiar to him, and it remained possible to use the word in secular contexts.

With the latter part of these views of Seesemann we may agree, but the earlier sentences call for some comment. First, he somewhat exaggerates the contrast between the Pauline usage and that of the rest of the New Testament. For not all the Pauline uses are distinctive; Galatians 2_9, for instance, is very similar to Acts 2_{42}. Moreover all the extra-Pauline New Testament uses are religious; indeed if we may make such comparisons, the instances in 1 John 1 are more 'religious' than (say) Romans 15_{26}, which merely derives a certain religious flavour from its context. It is true that the meaning 'participation' is uniquely Pauline within the New Testament, but that is not the distinctively Pauline feature which Seesemann wishes to stress in relation to Greek usage in general. And indeed the use of the term in the rest of the New Testament is so slight that it is difficult to make any inference with regard to the ways in which those authors regarded the word, save only that it was not with them a prominent conception. The contrast between the Pauline use of κοινωνία and the ordinary Greek use is also too sharply drawn by Seesemann. He admits, with examples, that κοινωνία is used in ordinary Greek to indicate that which man has or ought to have in common with God. It is true that these instances do not speak of sharing in God (*das 'Anteilhaben' an Gott*), and that they may not have influenced the Pauline usage; they are nevertheless 'religious' uses, more 'religious' than some of the Pauline instances. The real differentia of the Pauline use is not that it is religious whereas the other New Testament and the general Greek uses are not; but that *some* of the Pauline uses, those which bear the meaning 'participation' (*Anteilhaben*), do not, except for 1 Corinthians 10_{16}, find precise

[54] Seesemann does not make this point, which is inapplicable in German.

parallels elsewhere. The other Pauline uses are indeed in a general sense religious, but so are some at least of the non-Pauline uses both in the New Testament and elsewhere. Seesemann speaks as though Paul used the word as a religious technical term in a uniform way, which made the secular use of the word for him impossible. One might as well say the same of the whole of the New Testament usage, for the other instances, though not conforming to the meaning 'participation', are all 'religious'. But in fact it is impossible to say, from the comparatively few uses of the word in the New Testament, whether or not the New Testament writers would have felt free to use the word in a secular sense.

We cannot say, as some have done, that κοινωνία is a key-word for Paul. It does not play the part in his thought which is played, for instance, by 'in Christ'. Yet it was a word of varied meaning. By the use of this word the Christian is said to participate in Christ (1 Co 1_9), the Body and the Blood of Christ (1 Co 10_{16}), as well as His sufferings (Ph 3_{10}); he is also twice said to participate in the Holy Spirit (2 Co 13_{13}, Ph 2_1). It is true that some of these passages are prayers, aspirations and the like; but presumably these are quite normal or possible experiences for the Christian. The word is not used in Paul of participation in God the Father. Though it is not a central phrase in Paul, it is used in important passages, and is entirely in harmony with his thought. It preserves an I-thou relationship. Moreover, though the meaning in so many passages is 'participation' rather than 'fellowship', it does not lack a certain corporate flavour, for its absolute use (e.g. Gal 2_9) gives it certain overtones which it can never entirely lose. The alternation between 'Christ' and 'the Spirit' as the subsequent genitive is in harmony with Paul's treatment of the Trinity. Its use in eleemosynary contexts keeps alive the ethical note. We may, perhaps, add that the alternation between religious and semi-secular uses (which indeed derive a religious flavour from the context) prevents it from becoming entirely a religious term into which some further significance such as mystical absorption could easily be poured.

THE CORPORATE ASPECT OF COMMUNION WITH GOD

When we dealt with the synoptic Gospels, we saw that our theme could not be separated from the themes of the Church, the

Ministry, and the Sacraments. This is even more true in dealing with Paul. Though a full treatment of these themes would take us far beyond the compass of the present work, yet hardly anything more needs to be said to show that the experience which we have been discussing is a corporate experience, for that has emerged in the discussion at every point. The experience of being 'in Christ' is not to be separated from that of being a limb in the Body of Christ, and the former conception may even be derived from the latter. The same word, κοινωνία, is used to describe the participation in Christ and in the Holy Spirit which is the hallmark of the individual Christian and that fellowship with each other which the members of the Church enjoyed. We have rejected the view that κοινωνία is almost a synonym for the Church; but the translation 'participation' does not mean that individuals can participate in Christ in isolation from each other. Almost all the varied theories which we have in various connexions considered have in greater or less degree stressed the corporate aspects of Paul's thought; and though an exclusive stress on the forensic aspects of his doctrines has sometimes obscured this, it is now impossible for the serious student of Paul to do otherwise than to view him as a great Churchman.

The doctrine of the ministry, though much light is shed on it by various casual references in the Pauline letters, is not so relevant to this scheme as are the sacraments. Of the ministry, it need only be said that no claim that communion with God is mediated exclusively by Christian ministers could find any basis in his writings. Indeed a passage such as 1 Corinthians 12_{28-31} seems to suggest that almost anyone in the Church would have some kind of ministry, in a diversity ranging from apostleship to the gifts of tongues, all being classed together by implication as lesser gifts. But the sacraments are far more closely linked with fellowship with God, so closely indeed that we have already dealt with them by implication.

As regards Baptism, it is a mistake simply to quote 1 Corinthians 1_{17}, and to assume that this theme was of no importance for Paul. The central passage for his view of Baptism is Romans 6_{1-4}, with which Colossians 2_{9-13} is closely parallel. Now it is just these passages which contain the most notable uses of the συν- compounds which we have already considered. Only anti-sacramentalist prejudice could deny the important part played by Baptism in this process of dying and rising with Christ. Being buried with Him is explicitly stated to be *through* (διά) Baptism; Baptism is no mere illustration used for the purpose of the argument; it is the means whereby the process is effected. Moreover the statement that we are baptized *into* Christ cannot be disconnected from the phrase 'in Christ'; Baptism is surely *the* means, or at the least *a* means, whereby we come to be in Christ. (The phrases 'body of Christ', 'put on Christ', 'they that are of Christ', all belong to the same circle of ideas.) These points come from the Romans passage; Colossians 2_{12} uses ἐν where Romans 6_4 has διά, and Colossians keeps διά for 'through faith'; but the connexion of Baptism with the whole process is equally close. The fact that Paul could thus use 'baptism' and 'faith' interchangeably after the word διά shows that there was no sharp opposition between them in his mind. Yet they should not be co-ordinated; διά is not used with both in the *same* passage; for they do not fill the same role in the process. We have already seen this in connexion with the Eucharist. What Paul would have said if he had been asked whether it was possible to have this communion with God by faith without Baptism, we can only conjecture; but it is quite clear that he lays an equal stress on faith, and would have denied efficacy to Baptism unconnected with faith, for mention of faith is explicit in the Colossians passage, and the verb πιστεύω appears also in the Romans passage (Ro 6_8).[55] Prominent as Baptism is in these passages, there is nothing in this prominence to show that Paul borrowed his sacramental teaching from the mystery-religions; our former conclusions on that subject still stand.[56]

The relation of communion with God to the Eucharist in Paul has already been considered in connexion with 1 Corinthians 10_{16}. The Holy Communion, as we now significantly call it, is a participation of the Body and Blood of Christ; yet the Christian is said to participate in Christ or the Holy Spirit in other contexts where there is no reference to the Eucharist; nor are the references to the Eucharist parallel to those to Baptism; there is no place where the decisive entry on the Christian life is said to be effected *through* the Eucharist. This is only to be expected, for the Eucharist

[55] For his view of a purely external rite, see Gal 6_{15}. In the case of infants the appropriating faith is usually said to be subsequent to the Baptism, though some hold it to be in some sense implanted in the infant, while others refer to the vicarious faith of the parents or of the Church.

[56] cf. Flemington, pp. 76-9; and, on the whole question of Baptism in Paul, pp. 52-84.

is a sacrament of continuance rather than of entry. Ought not a greater place to be given to Baptism than to the Eucharist in the life of the Church to-day? This eucharistic passage may possibly be the whole origin of the distinctively Pauline use of the word κοινωνία (as also of the use of 'body'); but there is no reason to suppose that participation in the Godhead is only possible through the Eucharist, or that participation in Christ is a less real or vivid experience than participation in His Body. This is not to deny that the Eucharist is, by virtue of its divine institution, unique among the means of grace that relate to continuance in the Christian life, or that it was possibly more prominent in the thought and experience of Paul than the comparatively few references to it would suggest.

THE NATURE OF COMMUNION WITH GOD

We may now ask of Paul the same questions which we put about the synoptic Gospels and the early Church. First, what type of piety is to be found here? Was Paul a mystic? The opinion of Schweitzer is well known that 'Paul is the only Christian thinker who knows only Christ-mysticism, unaccompanied by God-mysticism'.[57] This raises incidentally the question, which Schweitzer discusses in the following pages, whether we do not find God-mysticism in Paul's speech at Athens (Ac 17_{28}; cf. 1 Th 1_1). Leaving aside the question whether this is a genuinely Pauline utterance, we may note that its significance as a turning-point has been very variously conceived. It is true enough that the phrase here used is not characteristic of Paul and may well be of Stoic origin. It purports, of course, to describe the position of all men, not merely of Christians; and, whether genuine or not, throws no light on Paul's conception of the Christian experience, and would probably not have attracted so much attention, had it not been for its almost accidental resemblance in form to the phrase 'in Christ'.

The use of 'in Christ', is, of course, far more important. We have rejected Schweitzer's eschatological explanation, as also its derivation from the Hellenistic mystery religions. The Pauline conception is something rarely found at least so explicitly in Christian writers, yet developed from Jewish antecedents, and

[57] Schweitzer, *Mysticism*, p. 5.

fully harmonious with the Christian Gospel. So many other themes have since occupied the minds of Christians that the Pauline teaching on dying and rising with Christ and being in Christ has been in danger of being overlooked. Apart from the idea of the New Birth, brought in by the Fourth Gospel, the Pauline writings themselves have been the source of other modes of expression. In particular, the stress on justification, and still more the legalistic distortion of this teaching, have distracted attention from these elements in Paul. Many think, using both words in a very loose way, that the 'forensic' aspects of his theology were of more importance than the 'mystical'. But Paul's so-called 'mysticism' is fundamental to his thought: nevertheless, it would not be even plausible to suggest that he was out of touch with the main stream of Christian tradition or went to any dangerous lengths of 'mysticism'; this element in his teaching has only to be emphasized afresh for us to see how essentially Christian it is.

If we are to classify it according to the scheme with which we began, we readily perceive that it cannot be put under type one (unio-mysticism) or type three (a faith-relationship falling short of communion). It belongs to type two (an I-thou communion with God), and within this type it approaches more nearly the frontier with the first type than that with the third. It exactly fits the description which we originally gave: 'When piety of this second type approaches the frontier with type one, then its language becomes warm and intimate. Though there is no talk of union, yet it speaks of mutual indwelling and the like.' When this classification is used, the question about 'mysticism' becomes unimportant; but it is more convenient to confine that word to unio-mysticism. The consensus of writers who use the term 'Christ-mysticism' of Paul is indeed so great that it is tempting to employ that usage after all, especially as many of these writers are fully aware of the distinction between this and absorption-mysticism. But various tendencies, particularly their proneness to use the phrase 'mystical union', induce us to leave the word entirely alone in connexion with Paul.

This may raise the question how it is that Paul's way of speaking of communion with God is more warm and intimate than that of Christ Himself, which we were compelled to classify under that part of type two which adjoins the frontier with type three, or, in other words, the strongly prophetic conception of communion with God. It is only natural that the Christian after the death and resurrection of Christ should have both an actual communion with God and also an intellectual conception of it richer and more intimate than had been possible to the disciples before those decisive events had occurred. What is remarkable is that our conclusions might seem to suggest that Paul's conception of communion with God was richer than the conception of Christ Himself, and even that Paul actually enjoyed a richer communion. Unless some reason can be found for this, Paul will, after all, have to be accused of introducing dangerous notions of intimacy into Christian piety. We must, however, remember that there were some traces of a richer conception in the teaching of Jesus, and Paul may be said simply to have been developing these in the light of the cross and resurrection. As for Christ's own communion with God, we have to remember that it included the Cry of Dereliction, the expression of an experience which may not have been confined to that moment. Christ bore vicariously, and that not only on the cross, the sin of the world, from which all Christians, including Paul, have thus been freed, even though they may still share in their present experience in the sufferings of Christ. There was a certain paradox or polarity about Christ's experience of the Father, as there is about the whole Incarnation. This is in a way mirrored in the experience of every Christian with its twin notes of suffering and triumph. Paul did not, of course, really enjoy a richer intercourse with God than Christ did with the Father, but the expressions which he used to describe that experience on its richer and more joyous side naturally create an impression of greater intimacy than those which Christ used in emphasizing the other aspect. Yet perhaps the net result of these tensions (if the phrase does not improperly resolve the paradox) was that Paul had a greater preponderance of joy over sorrow than Christ. 'He that believeth on me, the works that I do shall he do also; and greater works than these shall he do' (Jn 14_{12}). It may be that the believer thus enjoys, in some respects, a more joyful experience. However that may be, enough has been said to clear Paul of the charge of being a dangerous innovator. It must, however, be said that he was the first to have this insight. The investigation which we have already conducted into the Acts of the Apostles has not led us to think that the early kerygma struck this note; it was rather of the 'prophetic' type; nor do the Pauline letters themselves suggest that it was a feature of the Gentile Churches before Paul. The phrase ἐν Χριστῷ may have been earlier: but its use in 1 Peter shows none of the richness associated with it in Paul: nor do the faint traces of other similar ideas in 1 Peter contain anything like the conception of dying and rising with Christ found in Paul: so that even if 1 Peter gives indirectly some indication of pre-Pauline thought, Paul's substantial originality is not impaired. Paul was not 'the second founder of Christianity', but he struck a note which had not been struck before.

We turn to the question whether 'communion' or some other word would best describe this intercourse with God. The word 'vision' is as inappropriate as we found it to be in the synoptic Gospels; and the word 'knowledge' has its own difficulties and ambiguities for Paul. The word 'union', though often used by writers on Paul, particularly in the phrase 'mystical union', has no basis in his vocabulary. Anderson Scott says 'Another name for the Koinonia is the Unity (ἑνότης)',[58] and refers to Ephesians $4_{3, 13}$, (and ἕνωσις in Ignatius, *Ph*, 4.) These are indeed the only New Testament occurrences of ἑνότης, unless we read it also in Colossians 3_{14}. Scott is here influenced by his own theory about κοινωνία; in any case the references are not sufficient to justify the phrase 'mystical union', from which indeed Scott is here free.

The word 'incorporation', which we have not previously had occasion to consider, has here something to be said for it. In so far as the phrase 'body of Christ' is Pauline and seems to be linked in Paul's thought with the phrase 'in Christ', the word 'incorporation' is appropriate. But though we may speak of 'incorporation into Christ' we cannot speak of 'incorporation into God', so that a phrase equivalent to 'communion with God' is still lacking. Moreover our aim is not simply to find a phrase to fit the Pauline conception, but to check by the Pauline conception such phrases as generally commend themselves. 'Incorporation' might do for the Pauline species, but it will not serve as the generic word.

The word κοινωνία, though not very frequently in Paul, is sufficiently common, and linked sufficiently closely with the

[58] Scott in (ed.) Streeter, *The Spirit*, pp. 140-1; cf. Scott, *Christianity according to St Paul*, p. 161. We may add that ἑνόω is not used in the N.T.; εἷς is often used in religious contexts, but never so as to imply that we are one with God. 'United' occurs in the R.V. of Ro 6_5, but the Greek is σύμφυτοι, and no part of ἑνόω.

phrase 'in Christ' and with the συν- compounds to be obviously important. The fact that it occurs in Paul and not in the synoptic Gospels may indeed correspond to the transition from one type of piety to another within our type two. Thus if we appropriate this word as characteristic of the Pauline species of piety, we automatically imperil its use as the generic word. The Pauline type of piety is indeed characteristically Christian, and to some extent normative; coming after the death and resurrection of Christ as the words of Christ do not, it has some claim even to be considered as more typical of Christianity than that of the synoptic Gospels. Nevertheless, we cannot rule the 'prophetic' end of type two to be unchristian, and therefore some generic word must be left which will cover both extremes of type two. It is best in English to keep 'communion' for this purpose. It is in any case not the best word for Paul, for though κοινωνία might summarize his piety, that has been shown to mean in most cases 'participation'; but to call Paul's piety 'participation' would be verbally awkward, and to call it 'communion' might suggest a mistranslation. But what will not do as a specific word may serve well enough as a generic expression: 'communion' and 'fellowship' carry with them in English the varied associations not only of Paul's use of κοινωνία, but also of Acts 2_{42}, and of the Johannine uses, while they seem appropriate also to cover the piety of those books like the synoptic Gospels which never use κοινωνία. They are broad terms, as generic words should be, and yet warm and colourful; moreover 'communion' serves very well to distinguish type two from type one ('union'), and is also too strong for type three. If then we are right in maintaining that all the Christian piety which we have so far examined falls into one or other part of type two, then 'communion' is the best word both to describe part two as a whole and for a generic description of all genuine forms of Christian piety.

We must now ask what term can be used specifically to describe the Pauline piety, and, more widely, all those instances of piety within type two which border on type one. Possibly some adjective before 'communion' might serve as differentia. As the other extreme within this type can conveniently be called 'prophetic', so there is a natural tendency to use here the word 'mystical', whether before 'union', 'communion', or 'incorporation'. If 'mystical union' were kept for type one, then 'mystical communion' might do for this; but 'mystical' is unscriptural (the occurrences of μυστήριον being irrelevant) and apt to mislead. 'Ontological' is equally unscriptural. We may be sorry that there is no adjective corresponding to 'in Christ', as this is so central and characteristic a phrase. We might indeed describe Paul's conception as one of 'indwelling communion'; for the rest we must rely on longer paraphrases.

THE MEDIATION OF COMMUNION WITH GOD

Finally, is communion with God, according to Paul, mediated or unmediated? It is, of course, clear that Christ and the Holy Spirit play a determinative part in communion with God, but we are not considering these questions here. Nothing (despite Ro 1_{20}) suggests that Paul had any conception of communion with God in nature. Personal relationships were to him important, but rather as the fruit or outworking, or indeed the illustration, of our dealings with God or His with us. Actual communion with God may indeed suffuse a man's whole life, but it is mediated by 'religious' activities. Above all, in Paul the sacraments play a larger part than they have done in the other strands of the New Testament which we have considered. Baptism is a means, indeed *the* means, whereby we die and rise again with Christ; and the Lord's Supper is also an important, if not a unique, means of communion with Him.

CONCLUSION

Paul has thus a full and rich conception of communion with God in Christ. Nevertheless, something is reserved for the life of bliss. Though the Christian may die and rise with Christ, he is not yet with Christ. Piety of our second type stops short in this life, reserving something for the next. But that does not mean that it speaks of an experience of type one in the next life, that there at last the frontier is crossed and mystical absorption attained. Even there this type still speaks of an I-thou relationship. Paul does not conceive even the next life in as 'absorptionist' a way as some writers have conceived this. Thus neither as regards this life nor as regards the next is Paul quite at the frontier with type one. But he is as near as he ought to be; we must now see whether anything nearer is to be found in the rest of the New Testament.

CHAPTER EIGHT

THE JOHANNINE WRITINGS

INTRODUCTION

WE TURN to the Johannine writings to see how far the new insights into communion with God which characterized Paul find an echo there, and what fresh insights were vouchsafed to the writer of the Fourth Gospel. It is not necessary for our purpose to consider how far the Johannine Epistles were from the same hand. We must take them into account, as they issued from the same circle. So, perhaps, did the Apocalypse; but it stands somewhat apart, and cannot be thought to be by the same author; so it will be considered later.

Many writers have considered whether these writings reflect Jewish or Greek ideas. This question indeed arises about the three main strands of New Testament thought outside the synoptic Gospels and Acts. We have already considered it in relation to Paul, and it arises again in connexion with the Epistle to the Hebrews. It does not fall within our sphere to investigate the general question, though, as with Paul, the results reached about communion with God will supply some additional evidence. We may note, however, that there now is a general, though by no means universal, tendency (again as with Paul), to lay greater stress on the Jewish element. Apart from the Prologue, which does not seem deeply to have influenced the rest of the Gospel, there seems no reason to see much trace of Greek philosophy or of Philo; and their influence even on the Prologue is very doubtful. Similarly, Howard, after considering Hellenistic mystery religions, Mandaean Gnosticism, and the Hermetic writings, concluded

> 'The most that can be said is that, in commending Christianity to the surrounding pagan world, terms belonging to the religious vocabulary current in these regions were sometimes borrowed. . . . But the more closely the Johannine writings are studied the more clearly does the Jewish character of both language and thought stand out.'[1]

There has been a somewhat similar discussion whether the dominant theme in the Fourth Gospel is eschatology or mysticism.

[1] Howard, p. 30.

(Here again we may compare the similar problem about Paul.) It has been too easily assumed that the two are incompatible with each other, and that as the Fourth Gospel is 'mystical' (not, of course, in the extreme sense of that word), therefore it cannot be eschatological. In fact, the Fourth Gospel has some futurist eschatology in the form of references to the last day, to the future coming of Christ, and so on. More often, the eschatology is 'realized', and the expressions which some have used about the 'transmutation' of eschatology may mean no more than this. But 'realized eschatology' is still eschatology, and expressions such as 'judgement' or 'eternal life' (that is, the life of the age to come) still carry with them their eschatological associations. Nevertheless, it is true that a wholly 'realized' eschatology would promote a different type of piety from that proper to a futurist eschatology. A more intimate account could be given of communion with God, if there were nothing left to look forward to. The vestiges of futurist eschatology remaining in the Fourth Gospel mean that that is not altogether the case here. Yet it is true that this is a subordinate element; and if it is true that 'mysticism' is, however paradoxically, often found in combination with futurist eschatology,[2] it follows, *a fortiori*, that it can be combined with realized eschatology. Yet an outlook which arises from the view that the expected end has come will not altogether lose the flavour which belonged to that tradition at an earlier stage when the end was still awaited; the Hebraic outlook cannot be simply transformed into the Platonic by the fulfilment of its prophecies. We shall therefore expect that the Johannine piety will be neither wholly futurist-eschatological nor wholly mystical, but rather realized-eschatological; that is to say, warm and intimate, but not absorptionist, and holding something back for the world to come. The eschatological note is even stronger in the first Epistle.

THE PRAYERS OF JESUS

As in the synoptic Gospels we have here recorded prayers of Jesus. Two are brief and may be briefly treated.

Father, I thank thee that thou heardest me. And I knew that thou hearest me always: but because of the multitude which standeth around I said it, that they may believe that thou didst send me (Jn $11_{41\text{-}2}$).

[2] cf. Howard, pp. 201-4, and (on the whole question) pp. 106-28.

This prayer occurs in the story of the raising of Lazarus, of which the historicity has been much doubted. The first part of the prayer, is, however, very characteristic of Christ. The simple vocative 'Father' has synoptic parallels, and the note of thanksgiving is strongly reminiscent of Matthew 11_{25}. The words appear to refer to a prayer previously offered, presumably silently, at some point (not stated) earlier in the narrative, or indeed constantly offered since He heard of the death of Lazarus. This earlier unspoken prayer must have been a petition for the recovery of Lazarus, a definite request fully in the 'prophetic' tradition. To offer thanks for the fulfilment of the prayer before that fulfilment is made apparent goes indeed beyond what is customary, but an expression of confidence is quite in accord with the 'prophetic' tradition: indeed it is fully harmonious with the teaching of the synoptic Gospels on intercessory prayer (esp. Mk 11_{24}).

The difficulty of the passage is caused by the second part of the prayer.[3] Does 'I said it' mean 'I uttered the earlier petition', or 'I uttered the earlier petition aloud' or 'I uttered this thanksgiving' or 'I uttered this thanksgiving aloud'? What step would have been omitted were it not for the crowd? It has sometimes been asserted that the Johannine Christ was incapable of genuine prayer; on that view, no prayer at all would have been offered, not even an unspoken prayer, had it not been for the crowd. It is, of course, true that the Fourth Gospel has a high Christology which sometimes imperils the stress he intends to lay on the Humanity of Christ. Nevertheless, to assert that He is so conceived in this Gospel as to be incapable of prayer goes altogether beyond the evidence; and this very passage itself precludes it. Whatever the motive which is supposed to have led Jesus to utter this thanksgiving aloud, He refers in it to the Father hearing Him always, which implies not simply the intimate relationship of Persons within the Godhead, but constant prayer. The fact that prayer is always answered does not make it any the less prayer.[4] If then we affirm that Jesus did in fact pray, there seems no reason to deny that He may have offered this thanksgiving, or (prefer-

[3] Bernard, ad loc., adopts a variant reading, of which the main point is that 'I said it' is replaced by 'I do it'; but it is weakly attested, and does not entirely avoid the difficulties.

[4] This point is well brought out by Hoskyns, ad loc., but he does not seem to feel how jarring the passage nevertheless is.

ably) may have offered this thanksgiving *aloud* simply for the sake of the crowd; what is intolerable is that He should have used this very prayer to convey that fact. Anyone may offer aloud a prayer which in the absence of others would have been offered in silence, not indeed with the purpose of letting others know that he needs to pray or does pray, but in order that they may join in the prayer; but it is no mark of devotion to use the prayer to 'preach' at the bystanders. We are thus driven to regard these words as 'a comment or interpretative gloss of the evangelist',[5] which has somehow[6] got into the text of the prayer. If that is so, we can ignore it for our purpose.

The second prayer is:

Now is my soul troubled; and what shall I say? Father, save me from this hour. But for this cause came I unto this hour. Father, glorify thy name (Jn 12_{27}).

This is not placed in Gethsemane, but occurs in a short discourse in which Jesus describes His state of mind to Andrew and Philip, who had come on quite other business; but in spirit it is remarkably parallel to the synoptic account of the Agony in the Garden, which it is meant to improve and replace. It may be based on what the author read in Mark, or be a piece of independent tradition. The reference to His soul being troubled is anti-docetic. It is not really of very great importance whether a question mark is placed after 'Father, save me from this hour'. As the words correspond in spirit to the synoptic 'Remove this cup from me', it would be better to omit it,[7] at least as an account of what probably occurred. It would, however, be quite in harmony with the nervousness of this Evangelist about the Humanity of Christ that he should insert a question mark. But, if the prayer is uttered as a prayer, it is 'crushed, almost before it is uttered, into an act of complete surrender',[8] just as

[5] So Bernard in his comment on the received text before he comes to the reading which he prefers.

[6] Unfortunately, merely to alter 'I said' to 'he said' would not put things right. It looks as though the transformation of the comment into part of the prayer took place in the mind of the Evangelist.

[7] If the question-mark is correct, this confirms the point that the Markan version was not likely to be invented. Westcott, ad loc., tries to justify the words completely as the true answer to the preceding question, by pointing out that the prayer is for deliverance out of (ἐκ), not from (ἀπό) this hour. The synoptic parallel does not support this general view.

[8] Hoskyns, ad loc.; cf. Heiler, p. 267.

in the synoptic parallel. The two prayers, if they are to be counted as two, are in both the synoptic and the 'prophetic' traditions. Their terseness, their use of 'Father', but above all the complete frankness of the first and the complete surrender of the second, are all familiar features; and the contrast between the two prayers need not be further discussed, as the synoptic parallel has already raised the same question.

We do not find here, as in John 11_{42}, any statement that Jesus prayed only for the benefit of the bystanders; but it is interesting to notice that almost immediately afterwards Christ is depicted as making a similar comment on a Voice from heaven, namely, 'This voice hath not come for my sake, but for your sakes' (Jn 12_{30}). These words are not so jarring as those in John 11_{42}, for they neither occur in a prayer nor refer to a prayer. Here again it seems likely that some theologically-motivated comment has found its way into the text. We are told in the preceding verse that the multitude said that it thundered, though others ascribed it to an angel, from which we may deduce that they heard a sound, but did not grasp the meaning of the words or recognize it as words. This consideration makes the remark that it was for their sake quite pointless; it is the invention of a docetic mind. This author indeed attacked Docetism, but was himself influenced by what he attacked. Some commentators, as at John 11_{41-2}, go so far as to infer that the Johannine Christ was incapable of genuine prayer. Bauer, for instance, says, 'The spoken words of Jesus are no genuine prayer, as the immediate discarding of the thought and the *Not for my sake*, which follows in verse 30, prove'.[9] 'The immediate discarding of the thought' belongs, in this context, as we have already seen, to the essence of prophetic prayer; verse 30 is a far more serious difficulty. But if we are right in thinking that verse 30, in its disharmony with verse 29, is some kind of insertion into the tradition, then 'the Johannine Christ', as represented by the prayer itself, is fully capable of prayer; and the synoptic tradition about Gethsemane is strikingly confirmed, though indeed it is difficult to feel sure whether the incident actually happened as recorded here in addition to that recorded in the synoptics.

'We now come to what is, perhaps, the most sacred passage even

[9] Quoted in Hoskyns, ad loc. Here again Hoskyns is right in his disapproval of commentators of this kind, but he does not seem to see how unsuitable verse 30 is.

in the four Gospels',[10] the prayer recorded in John 17. This is important as being the only lengthy prayer of Jesus which is recorded. The question naturally arises how far the report is accurate, and this must depend largely on the general view which we take of the Fourth Gospel. We cannot claim to have here a verbatim report, or rather translation from the Aramaic; but to regard it as the free composition of the evangelist 'would be to ascribe the deepest thoughts in the Fourth Gospel to the disciple rather than to the Master'.[11] Words spoken on so memorable an occasion would be easily remembered, and it seems reasonable to suppose that we have here at least the substance of what Jesus said, preserved and perhaps to some slight degree transformed in the memory of the Apostle John, and finally conveyed to the author of the Gospel, if (as we take it) the actual author was other than the Apostle. It has been called 'The High-Priestly Prayer' and 'The Prayer of Consecration'. It is hardly an actual consecration prayer for the Eucharist, composed subsequently and then put back on to the lips of Jesus; nor was it the 'Consecration Prayer', in that technical sense, of the Last Supper itself, seeing that it followed the taking of the elements. Nevertheless, it has a certain significance, not only as, in substance, the actual prayer used on this occasion, but as a general expression of Christ's relation to the Father, and as a model prayer for the Church, though in this connexion it cannot rank with the Lord's Prayer.[12]

At first sight, the prayer seems very different from the prophetic prayers recorded in the synoptic Gospels, and it might be thought that with its somewhat repetitive phrasing it is an example of mystical contemplation. Certainly it lacks the terseness of the synoptic prayers, but a closer examination of its contents shows remarkable parallels to the synoptic Gospels, in His use of 'Father', in His praying for Himself and for His disciples, and in echoes of Matthew $11_{25ff.}$ and of the Lord's Prayer.[13] Moreover, the whole theme of the prayer is not adoration and contemplation, but petition and intercession. He begins, quite in the prophetic tradition, with petition for his own immediate needs. These were spiritual, and we do not find the petitions for material benefits which often characterize the prophetic tradition. Moreover,

[10] Temple, p. 307.
[11] Bernard, ad loc.
[12] cf. Hoskyns, ad loc.
[13] Details in Bernard, ad loc.

some of the sentences seem to be devotional comment, and it seems likely that verse 3 is an insertion of the Evangelist. Secondly (verses 9-19), He prays for the disciples. The words in verse 9, 'I pray not for the world', are at first sight surprising, but must mean that He was not praying for it on that occasion. He did pray even for His enemies (Lk 23_{34}) in accordance with His own teaching (Mt 5_{44}). Moreover the whole purpose of that sanctification of Himself with which this section of the prayer concludes (verse 19) was the ultimate sanctification of the world. However, verse 9 seems to have influenced Christian liturgy in as much as the intercessions contained in the main eucharistic rites are for the most part in the form of prayers for the Church rather than for the world; when, as in the Anglican and Methodist rites, those in authority, the sick, and so on are mentioned, it is in their capacity as members of the Church, as the Bidding shows; and there is no prayer for men's conversion.[14] The third section of the prayer is for the Church in general, those who come to believe through the testimony of the first disciples. This section contains some indication of the mode of communion with God which the Christians are to enjoy, and must be considered later: but we may say that, right to its close, the prayer, though meditative, is in the prophetic rather than the mystical tradition.

THE TEACHING OF JESUS ON PRAYER AND THE SPIRIT

The example of Jesus counts for more than His teaching, but this Gospel does not lack distinctive teaching. The words προσεύχομαι and δέομαι never occur in the Johannine literature: αἰτέω and ἐρωτάω are the favourite words in this connexion. The great new point made in the Fourth Gospel is contained in the Upper Room discourse, and is well summed up in the verse 'And whatsoever ye ask in my name, that I will do, that the Father may be glorified in the Son' (Jn 14_{13}). Similar teaching is contained in several other parts of the same discourse (Jn 14_{14}, 15_{16}, 16_{23-7}).[15] The thought is twofold; first, that prayer is always to be offered 'in the name of Christ'; and, second, that such prayer will always be answered. The first thought is new; 'Until now you have not asked anything in my name' (Jn 16_{24}). The phrase 'in my name'

[14] cf. our previous discussion of Lk 23_{34}. The point arises again in 1 Ti 2_2.
[15] In Jn 15_7 it is related to mutual indwelling, to be considered later.

is indeed found in the synoptic Gospels (e.g. Mk 9_{39}), but it had not been associated explicitly with prayer. It is, however, reminiscent of 'Hallowed be thy name'. To pray in Christ's name means to pray as His representatives, but we are truly His representatives only when we pray in the spirit in which He prayed and for His purposes. We are to pray for the doing of His will and the coming of His kingdom. The Lord's Prayer is thus the supreme example of prayer in His name; and what is there implied is here stated in another way. The injunction has been taken literally, so that many Christian prayers end 'in the name of Jesus Christ'; and it is fitting that they should, though not essential, as the Lord's Prayer itself shows. The expression has more warrant than 'for Jesus Christ's sake': but, of course, what matters is not the verbal addition of the formula, but the spirit behind the words.

The second point follows from the first. The synoptic Gospels had already contained injunctions to pray in faith, believing that they will be answered, and promises that such prayers will be answered (e.g. Mk 11_{24}): and these promises must naturally be qualified in our thought by the condition that the prayer must be such as Christ can approve. Here that is made explicit. If the prayer is really in Christ's name, it is natural that the Father will answer it.

On prayer in general we may note these particular points. Requests are normally made to the Father. But in John 14_{14} we read, 'If ye ask me anything in my name'. This is in apparent verbal contradiction to John 16_{23}, 'And in that day ye shall ask me nothing'. It is true that the Greek verbs are not the same, but nothing should be made of this, as this writer often uses synonyms interchangeably, despite many commentators.[16] But in John 14_{14} the 'me' is omitted by some MSS., while others omit the whole verse. On the whole the weight of evidence supports it. John 16_{23-4} contains a variation in the thought: 'If you ask anything of the Father, he will give it you in my name'. God's answer, as well as our prayer, is in Christ's name. Shortly afterwards we read 'And I say not to you that I will ask the Father concerning you, for the Father himself loves you'. Here, despite the fact that Jesus speaks of what He will *not* do, we have a trace of that triadic arrangement

[16] cf. Howard, *The Fourth Gospel in Recent Criticism and Interpretation*, pp. 120-1, 254. For the vocabulary for prayer in general, see Greeven, *KTW*, II.805-6.

of the Father, Christ, and the Christians, which we shall find again in this Gospel.[17]

The same teaching that we are certain to obtain what we ask in accordance with God's will is contained in the Johannine Epistles (1 Jn 3_{21-2}, 5_{14-15}): 'in accordance with his [God's] will' is a useful commentary on 'in his [Christ's] name': they come to the same thing.

The Gospel also contains teaching on worship (Jn 4_{21-4}), which culminates in the injunction to worship 'in spirit and truth'.

About the Holy Spirit, this Gospel does not imitate the comparative silence of the synoptic writers. This Gospel and the first Johannine Epistle, like the Pauline Epistles, are full of references to the Spirit, as we should expect of any writing in the early Church which does not attempt, as the synoptic writers do, to put itself back into the atmosphere before Pentecost. Some of the teaching on the Spirit is highly distinctive, notably the five Paraclete sayings, and also the difficult account of the insufflation (Jn 20_{21-3}). Yet the Spirit is not closely connected with the language of indwelling communion. ἐν πνεύματι occurs (Jn 1_{33}, 4_{23-4}), but, apart from the fact that it does not always refer to the Holy Spirit, the phrase is not comparable with the Pauline 'in Christ'. 'The Spirit' is once followed by the distinctive Johannine word 'abide' (μένω), followed by ἐπί, not ἐν (Jn 1_{33}); but there are several 'indwelling' passages of a triadic nature, where the absence of any reference to the Spirit is conspicuous. Nor is there any such reference to 'participating' in the Spirit as we find in Paul. Thus the teaching on the Spirit, though important in itself, does not bear on our theme as closely as we might have expected.

INDWELLING COMMUNION

We now turn to those words and phrases which are used to describe communion with God. The Pauline 'in Christ' does not explicitly occur, but its place is taken by the phrases 'abide in' (μένειν ἐν) (Jn 6_{56}, 14_{10}, $15_{4, 5, 6, 7}$, 1 Jn $2_{6, 24, 27, 28}$, $3_{6, 24}$, $4_{12, 13, 15, 16}$) and 'be in' (εἶναι ἐν) (Jn 14_{10}, $17_{21, 23, 26}$, 1 Jn 2_5, 5_{20}).[18] In the Gospel μένειν is used chiefly of abiding in

[17] cf. Temple, pp. 297-8.

[18] Conveniently set out in Taylor, *FR*, pp. 120-2, who points out the greater frequency of the use of μένειν in 1 Jn; in the Gospel it is used in this way only in the Allegory of the Vine and in the Eucharistic Discourse, to which we must add Jn 14_{10b}. To these lists in general we may add passages where εἶναι is to be supplied: Jn 10_{38}, $14_{11, 20}$.

Christ; as He is often the speaker, the words 'in Christ' do not appear in this connexion: it is often 'in me'. But there are three passages in the Gospel (Jn 6_{56}, 15_{4-5}) where such a reference is immediately followed by a reference to Christ ('I') abiding in the Christian ('him' or 'you'). In the Epistle, which is not of course from the lips of Christ, 'me' naturally becomes mostly 'him', which refers back sometimes to Christ and sometimes to God; in 1 John 2_{24} it is explicitly said 'ye shall abide in the Son and in the Father', and there are other explicit references to abiding in God. Here also the indwelling is mutual; there are references to God abiding in us; and in 1 John 3_{24} the 'he' who is said to abide in us may be 'Christ', though this is not certain. Other things are said to abide in us, and we to abide in them; thus, for instance, God's word should abide in us, and we in Christ's word (Jn 5_{38}, 8_{31}).[19] We may particularly notice the references to abiding in love, and love in us (Jn 15_{10}, 1 Jn 3_{17}). It must also be noticed that some of these references are to the mutual indwelling of the Father and Christ (Jn 10_{38}, $14_{10, 11}$).[20] We may leave the Christological implications of this, but clearly this use in Christological contexts exalts the other uses of the phrases to a very high level; it cannot be said that the use of the same phrases is accidental, for the Gospel also uses 'triadic' formulae, in which the disciples take the third place. There are two clear instances of this;[21] John 14_{20}, 'In that day ye shall know that I am in my Father and ye in me and I in you'; and John 17_{21}, 'that they all may be one, even as thou, Father, art in me, and I in thee, that they also may be in us'. The disciples take the third place, which in other contexts might be given to the Spirit. Moreover, the second of these passages introduces the idea of unity. Jesus does not indeed say that the disciples are 'one' with Him or with the Father, or that He or the Father is 'one' with them; and thus He avoids expressing communion in terms of union, just as Paul uses κοινωνία, but never ἕνωσις. He does, however, compare the unity which He desires for the disciples with the unity which He has with the Father (Jn 17_{22}; cf. Jn 10_{30}). His use of the word ἕν in a context of indwelling is significant. Those who are 'in' each other are in at least some

[19] Other instances in Taylor, *FR*, p. 121: cf. Oepke, *KTW*, II.539.

[20] These are all with εἶναι to be supplied, but Jn 14_{10b} has a reference to the Father indwelling the Son which uses μένειν.

[21] Oepke, *KTW*, II.539, mentions also Jn 17_{26}, 1 Jn 2_{24}; but these are not quite of the same type.

instances 'one'; unity and indwelling are not mutually exclusive terms; nevertheless this makes His reluctance to say that He is 'one' with the disciples[22] the more significant. The significance of these ἐν sentences is further qualified by Oepke, when he says that they are on the whole as much non-ecstatic as non-eschatological. He would call them 'mystical' in a broader sense; this is not, however, the sense in which we think it best to use that word. It is, however, he goes on, concerned with personal ethical fellowship of will (*persönlich sittliche Willensgemeinschaft*); here Oepke refers to the κοινωνία passages in 1 John, and to the similar formations with ἀγάπη and λόγος. This is true as far as it goes, but perhaps a stronger phrase would be justified. But there is a certain artificiality in trying to decide how to describe the relationship expressed by the simplest of words, ἐν; the phrase remains very much clearer than the explanations. The 'strong ethical note which so decisively distinguishes this teaching from the characteristic utterances of Hellenistic piety,'[23] is, however, unmistakable.

In general, there are marked resemblances to, and marked differences from the Pauline teaching. The use of ἐν is common to both, but in John it is preceded by μένειν or εἶναι, whereas in Paul it is used to qualify a great variety of verbs. In both John and Paul the relationship described is reciprocal or mutual, but in John the Father is often mentioned in these formulae, whereas in Paul the commonest phrase of this kind is 'in Christ'; variants occur such as 'in the Lord' or 'in the Spirit', but only seldom 'in God the Father'; there are thus no such triadic formulae as occur in John. The ethical note is common to both. The connexion which exists in Paul between these formulae and the συν- compounds,[24] that is, with the whole idea of dying and rising with Christ, is lacking in John, who does not use these modes of thought at all. The Pauline teaching is perhaps the richer, but we would not gladly do without the Johannine, which finely complements it.

[22] That is, the reluctance of the author to put such an expression on His lips. A similar adjustment must be made elsewhere.

[23] Taylor, *FR*, p. 122. Oepke points out there are few parallels in Hellenistic mysticism and in Gnosis.

[24] But on three significant uses of μετά (Jn 13_8, 15_{27}, 17_{24}) see Lohmeyer, pp. 234-5.

KNOWLEDGE AND VISION

We must now consider the Johannine use of the terms 'know' and 'see'.[25] Of the terms for 'know', ἐπίγνωσις and ἐπιγινώσκω are not found, either in the Gospel or in the Johannine Epistles. γινώσκω is unusually frequent; γνῶσις does not occur. οἶδα occurs frequently, and is apparently almost interchangeable with γινώσκω. We have already seen Paul battling against incipient Gnosticism, and therefore using the word γνῶσις sometimes in a favourable and sometimes in an unfavourable sense. The complete absence of the word in the Johannine writings is no doubt a sign that the battle was more intense; and indeed the frequency of the verb is, in a different way, evidence of preoccupation with the same topic. Nor is this a mere conjecture; for the Johannine Epistles do in fact contain a sustained polemic against antinomian and Gnostic tendencies, against the man who says 'I know him' and does not keep his commandments;[26] the test is always ethical, the keeping of God's commandments, or love.

In fact the word γινώσκω is most intimately related both to πιστεύω and to ἀγαπάω. There is no opposition between 'faith' and 'knowledge', though they perhaps may be related as seed to fruit,[27] and love is the test of both. The main uses all occur together at John 10_{14-15}, where we read of the mutual knowledge of the Father and the Son, and of the Son (the Good Shepherd) and His sheep. To this we may easily add instances of men knowing God the Father (e.g. Jn 17_3);[28] there is also an instance of men knowing the Spirit of truth (Jn 14_{17}).

From these contexts it is clear that γινώσκω does not mean mere academic knowledge, nor a mystical vision divorced from ethics.[29] It is in fact very much akin to the Hebrew ידע, and on man's side refers to the grateful and obedient acceptance of God's act of love in Christ. Bultmann[30] has, however, a careful fourfold argument to show that γινώσκειν does not correspond

[25] For 'know', the references are given under Paul; for John, add Howard, pp. 164-8; Bernard on Jn 1_{26}; Dodd, *The Johannine Epistles*, pp. 29-32.

[26] 1 Jn 2_4; cf. 1_6 (false claim to κοινωνία), 2_6 (test of the claim to abide in him), 2_9 (false claim to be in the light), 3_{18} (wrong kind of love), 4_1 (wrong kind of faith), 4_3 (wrong kind of confession), 2_{20} (wrong claim to knowledge).

[27] Blackman, *RTW*, p. 122.

[28] These cases are more frequent in 1 Jn.

[29] cf. Bultmann, *KTW*, I.711.

[30] Bultmann, *KTW*, I.712-13, cf. *supra*, p. 66.

precisely to ידע, but has acquired some of the meaning which it has in Hellenistic-gnostic usage. First, it is often combined with verbs of seeing, e.g. John 14_7; secondly, it is often followed by a ὅτι clause, e.g. John 7_{26}; thirdly, it cannot *mean* obedience, for love (obedience) is its criterion; fourthly, it stands in a particular relation to πιστεύειν, which is not used of the mutual relationship of the Father and the Son. πιστεύειν is the first turning to God, corresponding to ידע, to which, if it endures, γινώσκειν is promised. This does not, of course, mean that the Johannine writings have gone over to the Gnostic viewpoint; the polemic against it is indeed more explicit in 1 John than in the Gospel; but there is no reason to suppose that the author of the Gospel (whether he be the same or another) was more favourable to it. Indeed the third of the reasons given above for supposing that the Johannine use is influenced by the Gnostic use is itself taken largely from 1 John; but this use of love as the criterion is also the strongest reason for saying that the writer did not take the Gnostic point of view. This is simply the common case of an author coming as near as he can to the terminology of his opponents in order to refute them. As Bultmann says, he accepts their putting of the question. His own position is amply safeguarded, by the positive content of what he says, by his avoidance of the noun γνῶσις, and also by his cautious use of verbs of 'seeing', to which we now turn.

When we turn to 'seeing', we may well start from Kirk's enthusiastic assertion, 'If there is some slight hesitation in S. Paul as to the possibility of receiving the vision of God in this life, it has disappeared altogether in the fourth evangelist'.[31] We begin with the passages which seem to contradict this, the chief of which is, 'No one has seen God at any time' (Jn 1_{18}; cf. Jn 6_{46}, 1 Jn $4_{12, 20}$). The point of this passage, according to Kirk, is that God is not visible to the physical eye: 'in the sense in which he here uses the words the vision of God is at all times impossible.' This is true, but it does not follow, as he seems to imply, that God is visible to the eye of intelligence or of faith; the contrast is better pointed by the author of the Fourth Gospel himself when he concludes the verses by referring to the Son[32] declaring Him.

[31] Kirk, pp. 105-6: cf. 105-10; Michaelis, *KTW*, V.362-8; Blackman, *RTW*, p. 223; Taylor, *FR*, p. 126.

[32] Christ is meant, but the reading is doubtful.

The invisible God has been made visible by Christ.[33] The other relevant passage is 'We know that if he is manifested we shall be like him, because we shall see him just as he is' (1 Jn 3_2).[34] This seems to imply that such a vision is lacking at present. The verse is, perhaps consciously, reminiscent of the Beatitude about the pure in heart (Mt 5_8; cf. He 12_{14}), and likeness to God corresponds roughly to purity of heart; the passages differ, however, in that, in the following verse in Matthew, being sons of God seems to be given a like eschatological significance, whereas here it is a present (νῦν) possession. Kirk deals with the passage thus:[35] 'here what is implied is only a difference of degree and not of kind—the *uninterrupted* vision of the future will give a clearer knowledge of the nature of God than any which to-day is within our grasp.' This seems rather to minimize the passage. He further thinks that 'the vision of God makes the Christian like the Father (as in S. Paul's mirror analogy)'; this depends on the idea of the Hellenistic mystery-religions that knowledge or vision confers deification. This requires us to take the 'because' clause as qualifying 'we shall be like him'. But it is possible to take it as qualifying 'we know': on this view likeness to God is taken as a prerequisite to the vision of God, as Michaelis supposes: this would also rest on a Hellenistic presupposition, 'Like is known by like'. But, whatever the presupposition, the writer has written a sentence which is 'the model for all our thinking about the life to come'.[36]

Kirk is, however, right in observing that beyond these passages there is no need to make exceptions. God is made visible in Christ. This is made clear in a host of well-known passages, and the clearest possible statement is put on the lips of Christ Himself, 'He that

[33] The implication of Jn 5_{37-8} is somewhat similar. There is a reference to seeing God's glory in Jn 11_{40}.

[34] Michaelis, *KTW*, V.367, supports the translation 'if *it* is manifested', viz. 'what we shall be', supplied from the earlier part of the verse. He also thinks that the reference is to God the Father, not to Christ at the Parousia. But Dodd, *The Johannine Epistles*, ad loc., refers it to Christ and takes it to be based on Jn 17_{24}. F. C. Synge, in *Journal of Theological Studies* (N.S.), III.79, has suggested that by changes in the punctuation the verse should read 'Now are we sons of God, and he has not yet been made manifest. What we shall be we know, because if he is made manifest we shall be like him, because we shall see him as he is'. This does not vitally affect the present issue.

[35] Kirk, p. 107.

[36] Dodd, *The Johannine Epistles*, ad loc.; cf. A. D. Nock in (ed.) Rawlinson, *Essays on the Trinity and the Incarnation*, pp. 106-8; cf. 2 Co 3_{18}. A mystery-religion would speak of an immediate deification; here the change is reserved for the Parousia.

hath seen me hath seen the Father' (Jn 14_9; cf. Jn 1_{14}, 12_{45}, 14_7, 1 Jn 1_{1-3}).[37] We thus, rather unexpectedly, find more emphasis on seeing God in the Johannine writings than in the rest of the New Testament. Indeed the whole notion of seeing is common in them, quite apart from seeing God the Father. There are frequent references to seeing or not seeing Jesus (e.g. Jn 6_{40}, 12_{21}, 14_{19}, 16_{16-19}, 20_{29}), which are not confined to any one Greek verb. The words vary between physical sight and spiritual insight,[38] and can be followed by a 'that' clause (e.g. 1 Jn 4_{14}). We have already noticed that γινώσκειν is often combined with, or interchanged with, verbs of 'seeing'; and this surely is the clue to the frequency of the verbs of 'seeing'. Just as the author went as far as he could in the use of the Gnostic word 'to know', in order that he might differ from the Gnostics the more decisively at the crucial point, so he went as far as he could with the terminology of seeing; those who claimed to see God were right—yet with two most important qualifications: God is visible only in so far as He reveals Himself in Christ; and the vision of God thus granted can be tested by its ethical fruit.

It does not follow that 'knowledge' and 'vision' are very suitable words by which to describe the Johannine conception of communion with God. 'Knowledge' is the safer, because its other uses, and in particular the Old Testament use, give it, both for the author and perhaps still more for us, certain helpful overtones. 'Vision' is a more doubtful word; its comparative absence in the rest of the New Testament makes it rather dangerous here. We can imagine that the author would protest vigorously at any statement to the effect that he, unlike the other New Testament writers, believed in the vision of God; it would be fairer to him to use only the phrase 'vision of God in Christ'.

OTHER SIMILAR EXPRESSIONS

'Seeing' and 'knowing' are not, of course, the only words which describe the relationship of the Christian to God. Three times we find the striking phrase 'has' (ἔχει); 'he who confesses the Son has also the Father' (1 Jn 2_{23}); 'he who abides in the teaching

[37] That 'see' is sometimes not to be understood in any very exalted sense is clear from Jn 15_{24}. Contrast 1 Jn 3_6, 3 Jn 11.

[38] So Michaelis, *KTW*, V.362-5; he chose verbs of 'seeing' to bring out the existential character of meeting Jesus.

[of Christ] has both the Father and the Son' (2 Jn 9); 'he who has the Son has the life' (1 Jn 5_{12}). And (in the same three passages) 'everyone who denies the Son has not the Father'; 'everyone who goes ahead and does not abide in the teaching of Christ has not God'; 'he who has not the Son of God has not the life'. There are some remote parallels,[39] but the expression is perhaps derived from the use of μετέχω, and is felt to be related to the uses of κοινωνία and μένειν ἐν; very likely it was taken from his Gnostic opponents, who made the same claim without justification.[40] But in the New Testament it stands on its own, though 'have' is frequently found in John with such objects as 'love', 'joy', 'peace', 'light', and 'life'.

We have already mentioned 'believing' or 'trusting' in God (e.g. Jn 14_1); the Christian also comes to the Father through Christ (Jn 14_6), will ask in Christ's name (Jn 16_{26}), bears witness, and proclaims (1 Jn 1_2), ought to walk in the same way in which Christ also walked (1 Jn 2_6), does the will of God (1 Jn 2_{17}), keeps God's commandments (1 Jn 5_3), loves God (1 Jn 5_2), hears from the Father (Jn 8_{38}), and so on. This list is not complete; yet if we leave out the ethical expressions about doing God's will and so on, which are fairly numerous in the Epistles, it could not be prolonged very much. The Christian is much more being acted on in the accusative, than he is the subject of action or experience in the nominative, as is significantly symbolized in the verse, 'You have not chosen me, but I have chosen you' (Jn 15_{16}).

Κοινωνία

We turn now, however, to the one remaining word which is germane to our theme: κοινωνία. The word and its cognates do not occur in the Gospel; in the Epistles it occurs four times, and κοινωνέω occurs in 2 John 11. These occurrences of κοινωνία are all within the space of a few verses,[41] as follows:

1 *Jn* 1_3. ὃ ἑωράκαμεν καὶ ἀκηκόαμεν, ἀπαγγέλλομεν (καὶ) ὑμῖν, ἵνα καὶ ὑμεῖς κοινωνίαν ἔχητε μεθ' ἡμῶν· καὶ ἡ κοινωνία (δὲ) ἡ ἡμετέρα μετὰ τοῦ πατρὸς καὶ μετὰ τοῦ υἱοῦ αὐτοῦ Ἰησοῦ Χριστοῦ.

[39] Hanse, *KTW*, II.823, mentions Mt 26_{11}, Mk 2_{19}, 14_7, Jn 12_8, He 4_{14-15}, 8_1, 10_{21}, 1 Jn 2_1.

[40] Hanse, *KTW*, II.824.

[41] The main references are in the Bibliography, section D. The relevant pages for these occurrences are Seesemann, pp. 92-9; Hauck, *KTW*, III.808.

That which we have seen and heard, proclaim we also to you, that you also may have fellowship with us. And our fellowship is with the Father and with his Son Jesus Christ.

1 *Jn* 1_{6-7}. ἐὰν εἴπωμεν ὅτι κοινωνίαν ἔχομεν μετ᾽ αὐτοῦ, καὶ ἐν τῷ σκότει περιπατῶμεν, ψευδόμεθα καὶ οὐ ποιοῦμεν τὴν ἀλήθειαν· ἐὰν δὲ ἐν τῷ φωτὶ περιπατῶμεν ὡς αὐτός ἐστιν ἐν τῷ φωτί, κοινωνίαν ἔχομεν μετ᾽ ἀλλήλων καὶ τὸ αἷμα Ἰησοῦ (Χριστοῦ) τοῦ υἱοῦ αὐτοῦ καθαρίζει ἡμᾶς ἀπὸ πάσης ἁμαρτίας.

If we say that we have fellowship with him and walk in darkness, we lie and do not the truth; but if we walk in the light as he is in the light, we have fellowship with one another, and the blood of Jesus (Christ) his Son cleanses us from all sin.

In verse 3 the 'we' (understood) and the 'us' (ἡμῶν) are the 'we' of authorship: but the 'our' (ἡμετέρα), of course, includes the readers.[42]

There is an important textual variant in verse 7. For μετ᾽ ἀλλήλων (with one another), the original hand of A probably read μετ᾽ αὐτοῦ (with him), which is supported by Clement of Alexandria and Tertullian. The more common reading certainly introduces a new thought rather abruptly into the sentence, which is not then sustained by the following phrase about the blood of Jesus. But this very fact would account for the alteration to an easier reading. Moreover, it may be argued that, though the author is fond of parallelism, he is not simply repetitive, and thus it is quite in his manner to introduce a new idea into the sentence. On the other hand it is argued for the reading 'with him' that the change to 'with one another' is more easily explicable than at first appears, for the mention of 'fellowship with him' might appear repetitive after the reference to 'walking in the light' if it were not recognized that this last refers (as on this view it must) simply to an ethical standard, and not to anything synonymous with fellowship with God. But this seems to us the less likely change; the attestation heavily supports 'with one another', and so, despite Seesemann, we prefer that reading. That being so, we take the meaning to be that we Christians have fellowship with one another, which harmonizes with the uses of ἀλλήλους in 1 John 3_{23}, 4_7, $_{12}$, 2 John 5, not, as it has sometimes been taken to mean

[42] On the Johannine use of 'we', see Dodd, *The Johannine Epistles*, pp. 9-16.

in the interests of parallelism, that God and we have fellowship one with another. To make the relationship with God mutual in that way would be quite contrary to the Johannine idiom; had he wished to say that, he would have written 'We have fellowship with him and he with us'. It might also be taken to mean 'We have fellowship (sc. with him) in company with one another'. But the 'with' (μετά) which follows κοινωνία in every one of these four Johannine instances must surely be understood every time in the same sense. Fortunately, the use of κοινωνία in the Johannine writings of relations between men, does not depend on the reading in, or translation of, this verse, for it is already plain in verse 3.

Seesemann classifies this use of κοινωνία with Acts 2_{42}, Galatians 2_{9}; he says that it is undisputed that here it means *Gemeinschaft*. Hauck comes virtually to the same conclusion, though he classifies it with instances of having a share in something with someone. At first sight the construction whereby κοινωνία is followed by a preposition might be thought to resemble that of Philippians 1_{5}. But to translate by 'participation' here would not lead to that result. It would mean that the first occurrence in verse 3 would need to be rendered 'that you may participate with us [sc. in the Father and in Christ]', but what should we then make of the second use in that verse? One possibility is that the μετά, like the εἰς in Philippians 1_{5}, is a mere substitute for a genitive, made necessary by the need for emphasis or by the suggestion of ἡμῶν contained in ἡμετέρα: but this would have the disadvantage, already referred to in another connexion, of taking the two instances of μετά in different senses; moreover μετά would be an impossible preposition to follow 'participation': μετά cries out for the translation 'fellowship'. The other possibility is that it has here the same meaning which (on this hypothesis) it has in the first part of the verse, that is to say, that the reference is to participation with the Father and with Christ; but this inevitably raises the question 'In what?', to which no satisfactory answer can be given. Thus the meaning of the second part of the verse must be 'our fellowship is with the Father', and then it becomes extremely probable that the first part of the verse refers to 'fellowship with us'. The same reasoning applies even more strongly to κοινωνίαν . . . μετ' ἀλλήλων in verse 7, where only extreme ingenuity could find a reference to participation in something else. Even so, it is in fact true that the basis of the best human fellowship is an interest in some third person or thing, in this case the Father and Christ, and even fellowship with God may be said to arise from a common concern for the will of God. Nevertheless, 'fellowship' is the right translation, and there is no need to speak of omitted genitives.

The thought contained in the two references to fellowship with God (and once also to Christ) is paralleled in the Fourth Gospel, and elsewhere in the Epistles, as Seesemann points out, by that Johannine teaching on mutual indwelling which we have already considered. What we have here is simply a substantive form of that which is elsewhere expressed by verbs, except indeed once (Jn 13_8), where it is expressed by the noun μέρος. The author indeed usually avoided abstract nouns.[43] Thus the comparative infrequency of κοινωνία in the Johannine literature[44] is easily explicable: the thought is present, and the word, though not common, is quite apt as an expression of his conception of intercourse with God.

We have here, as in the other Johannine phrases and as in Paul, an I-thou relationship, not absorption. It is, however, so rich a conception that the next life is conceived as a continuation of it; he does not reserve another expression for that, as Paul keeps 'with Christ' for it.[45] As compared with the Pauline uses of κοινωνία, we note that the Johannine writer speaks of fellowship with God, whereas Paul never says 'participation in God', just as Paul says 'in Christ', and not 'in God'. But too much must not be made of this: 'it may be just as wrong', as Taylor[46] says, 'to describe the Johannine teaching as "God-mysticism" as it is to distinguish the Pauline doctrine as "Christ-mysticism".' There is some verbal justification for this distinction (to leave out of account the word 'mysticism'); but Paul was well aware that the Christian was in touch with God (to use a most general expression); and the Johannine writer, though he speaks here of fellowship with God, speaks of fellowship with Christ in the same passage; and in the passages which we have considered about seeing and knowing God

[43] Seesemann refers to πίστις and γνῶσις; the former occurs once in the Epistles; otherwise they do not occur at all; there may be something in this, but we have seen a better reason for the avoidance of γνῶσις.

[44] Hauck, *KTW*, III. 808, somewhat exaggerates when he refers to it as a favourite expression.

[45] So Seesemann, p. 95 n.3. Jn 14 has no parallels to 1 Co $13_{9f.}$, Ph 1_{23}.

[46] Taylor, *FR*, p. 126.

and in the 'indwelling' passages, particularly in the triadic formulae, there is no doubt about the part which Christ plays.

Another example of the links between the various strands of the New Testament is that here, as in two other places (1 Co 10_{16}, He 2_{14}), a κοινων- word is used in a context which refers to blood. We are thus reminded that κοινωνία rests on the sacrificial death of Christ.

The Johannine author here associates fellowship among men (between himself and his readers and among Christians generally) very closely with our fellowship with God; and makes both dependent on 'that which we have seen and heard', the apostolic witness to the messianic event of the incarnate life, just as 'fellowship' is connected with 'the apostles' teaching' (Ac 2_{42}).[47] Paul does indeed use κοινωνία absolutely (Gal 2_{9}), and in meanings which relate to doing good amongst men; but he never associates these meanings with fellowship with or participation in Christ in the same context. But this is simply a matter of his verbal use of κοινωνία; for the thought is by no means alien to him. Nevertheless it comes out with unusual force in these Johannine verses; and the rapidity of the transition from the one kind of fellowship to the other, within verse 3 and again in verses 6 and 7, marks the very close association of the two ideas: those who have fellowship with God are thereby brought into fellowship with each other. This strikingly echoes the combination of the two ideas in their verb-forms in the High-Priestly Prayer 'that they all may be one, just as thou, Father, art in me, and I in thee, that they also may be in us' (Jn 17_{21}).

THE CORPORATE ASPECT OF COMMUNION WITH GOD

What was said about the Church in connexion with Paul may be applied, *mutatis mutandis*, to the Johannine teaching on the Church,[48] namely that the experience which we have been discussing is a corporate experience. There is no need for us to ask what part the Church plays in communion with God. The very form of the question is misconceived, and the passages from 1 John which we have last been considering put the matter in its true setting; those who have fellowship with God in Christ have thereby fellowship with each other. The fellowship of the Church is

[47] cf. Thornton, pp. 156-7. [48] cf. Howard, pp. 132-7; Taylor, *FR*, pp. 127-30.

the result of, rather than the means to, fellowship with God in Christ; yet the two aspects are inseparable; a man does not first come to Christ, and afterwards 'decide to join the Church'. The 'vertical' and 'horizontal' fellowships go always together. Yet even the most extreme High-Churchman must surely admit that the vertical relationship has at least a certain logical priority. The chief Johannine passages referring to the Church are the allegory of the Shepherd and the Sheep, the allegory of the Vine and the Branches, and the High-Priestly Prayer (Jn 10, 15, 17; cf. also Jn 3_{29}); and these are all full of those expressions such as 'abide in' which we have already considered. The writer is deeply interested in the unity of the Church, as various passages show, but especially the High-Priestly Prayer. This does not, of course, mean that he contemplates the government of all Christians by a centralized ecclesiastical bureaucracy;[49] but equally we cannot suppose that the author of this exalted prayer would have been content with the grudging toleration or even apathetic indifference which sometimes pass for Christian courtesy and charity in relations between the denominations.[50]

Though this author is not silent on the doctrine of the ministry, nothing that he writes on it is especially relevant to our theme. He attaches considerable importance to Baptism, notably, according to the almost universal interpretation of the verse, in John 3_5, which is probably not an exact reproduction of a saying of Christ.[51] We have already seen that his teaching on communion with God makes no use of the idea of dying and rising with Christ which is so prominent in Paul, and with which Paul associates Baptism. The Fourth Gospel, instead of this, associates Baptism with the idea of birth, not strictly speaking *re*-birth, but simply birth from above, birth of water and the Spirit. Resurrection and birth are indeed the two great possible metaphors to describe renewal, and we may regard it as providential that of the supreme theologians of the apostolic age the one used one and the other the other, so that neither was neglected. There is no need to see in either phrase any mere borrowing from Hellenistic religion.

[49] cf. Howard, p. 137.

[50] The New Testament never discusses relations between denominations, because there were then no denominations. The divisions so strongly reprobated in 1 Co were not those between denominations. The permanent existence of denominations, however friendly to each other, is thus difficult to justify from the New Testament.

[51] See also 1 Jn 5_{6-8}; cf. Howard, pp. 143-50; Flemington, pp. 85-96.

This baptismal context does not however yield any new phrase for communion with God; only the initial entry is covered by the metaphor of birth.

The teaching on the Eucharist in John 6 (cf. also Jn 15) is curiously similar. On each sacrament his teaching is allusive, or even elusive. It is introduced in each case in a context remote from the actual institution or celebration of the rite in question; there are ambiguities in the teaching, which is given in the form of a controversial dialogue with a Jew or Jews. In each case Jesus begins with an uncompromising assertion, which evokes, partly through its ambiguity, a question beginning with the words 'How can——?' The reply is as uncompromising and exclusive as ever, 'Verily, verily, I say unto you, unless——'. If these assertions were taken strictly (and why make them so emphatically unless to establish this?), then the sacraments of Baptism and the Eucharist respectively would be the indispensable media of salvation. Only he who is born of water and the Spirit enters the kingdom of God: only he who eats the flesh of the Son of Man and drinks His blood, has life in himself (Jn 3_5, 6_{53}).[52] Communion with God, on this view, essentially requires the sacraments. Yet in each case the passage contains references to the Spirit which culminate in a contrast between flesh and spirit, so worded as to point in an opposite direction (Jn 3_{6-8}, 6_{63}). No doubt the historical situation which confronted the author explains this hesitation; he is fighting on two fronts at once, against a neglect of the sacraments and against an unethical sacramentalism. In such a case it is always easy for the modern heirs to these disputes to claim that the author's main emphasis lay this way or that; but the proportion of the passages would suggest that he was in general sympathy with sacramental religion, though aware of its dangers.[53] Leaving now the comparison between Baptism and the Eucharist in this writer, we notice that the passage on the latter contains one of the phrases used to denote communion with God: 'He that eats my flesh and drinks my blood abides in me and I in him' (Jn 6_{56}). This links Holy Communion (as we have come to call it) with communion with God in a manner strongly reminiscent (though not verbally

[52] cf. Howard, pp. 204-5.

[53] Cullmann, especially in *Urchristentum und Gottesdienst*, has recently discovered a very large number of liturgical and sacramental allusions in this Gospel, but their veiled and ambiguous character remains.

so) of 1 Corinthians 10_{16}. Participation in the Eucharist is clearly *a* means of communion with God. This verse in itself, however, (leaving out the 'unless' sentence in the context, which we have already considered) would not suggest that it was the sole means of communion with God: the fact that the phrase 'abide in' is the very phrase so common in other contexts suggests rather that the same kind of communion could be attained, not indeed by neglect of the Eucharist, but at the other means of grace as well as at the Eucharist.[54]

THE NATURE AND MEDIATION OF COMMUNION WITH GOD

When we put to this writer the same questions which we have already put to the other strands, we shall be interested to see how the Johannine differs from the synoptic Christ, and how the Johannine writer differs from Paul. The first question is, What type of piety is to be found here? Was this writer a mystic? We have already seen that some use the word 'mystic' so widely that even the synoptic Christ is a 'mystic': and many more use the word about Paul. All these naturally see mysticism in the Fourth Gospel. But even those who do not see mysticism elsewhere in the New Testament often find it here. The Fourth Gospel is widely acclaimed as the mystical book *par excellence* in the New Testament. Again, it is very widely held that we have Christ-mysticism in Paul and God-mysticism here. Neither of these statements is right. The first rests partly on the view that a book must be either eschatological or mystical, and that as the Johannine writer is not eschatological, he must be mystical; or even, that as he is not Hebraic, he must be Hellenistic. We have already considered these erroneous views, and our conclusion was that on the basis of his general outlook we should expect the Johannine piety to be neither wholly futurist-eschatological nor wholly mystical, but rather realized-eschatological; that is to say, warm and intimate, but not absorptionist, and holding something back for the world to come.[55] This forecast has been exactly fulfilled by the passages which we have studied; the only qualification is that the modes of expression which we have studied do not make it explicit that something is reserved for the life to come.

[54] cf. Temple, p. 95: 'The sacrament is normally necessary; but it is the communion alone that is vital.'

[55] cf. *supra*, p. 197.

The author does not reserve a special word or phrase for this, as Paul reserved 'with Christ', and to some extent the word 'see'. The Johannine author uses up, so to speak, the phrase which he might have kept. That something was reserved for the future has thus to be inferred from the futurist-eschatological hints in his general outlook.

We may thus say that the Johannine piety is of our type two (an I-thou communion with God), approaching the frontier with type one, a position which we defined by the words 'Though there is no talk of union, yet it speaks of mutual indwelling and the like'.[56] We were able to apply these words to Paul also: and indeed it is now time to affirm that there is no great difference between the Pauline and Johannine conceptions of piety. There are differences indeed of expression, and we note particularly that in the Johannine writings dying and rising with Christ is absent, but that more is said of being in God. But we have seen that there is no ground for any great dichotomy between Christ-mysticism and God-mysticism: Christ is frequently mentioned in the relevant Johannine passages. The Pauline 'in Christ' and the Johannine mutual indwelling are not very dissimilar modes of describing precisely the same relationship; moreover the Johannine *Epistles* share with the Pauline the use of κοινωνία. This resemblance of the Johannine conception to the Pauline carries with it the conclusion that the Johannine way of speaking of communion with God is (as we said of the Pauline)[57] 'more warm and intimate than that of Christ Himself'. For the explanation of this unexpected conclusion we may also refer to what we said about it in connexion with Paul. But whereas we were there comparing Paul's experience of God with that of Christ, we are not now so much comparing the experience of this author with that of Christ as comparing Christ as depicted in the Fourth Gospel with Christ as depicted in the synoptic Gospels. Our conclusion thus amounts to this, that Christ is depicted in the Fourth Gospel as having a richer and more intimate communion with God than He is depicted in the synoptic Gospels as having. We must not here enter on the problems of Christology or of the historical accuracy of the Fourth Gospel, which verge on our theme; but we may say that the Fourth Gospel may not be wholly inaccurate at the purely historical level in supplementing the synoptic picture of Christ.

[56] cf. *supra*, p. 12. [57] cf. *supra*, p. 191.

The synoptic Gospels were concerned to emphasize some aspects of the incarnate Life; and the Fourth Gospel others. The former are indeed our chief source, and there may be a slightly docetic flavour in the latter, for all its fundamental belief in the Incarnation; nevertheless it may be that Christ's own communion with God may have contained some notes which the synoptic Gospels do not depict, and to that extent the difficulty which we noticed in connexion with Paul is diminished. It remains true that in comparison with the outlook of the synoptists and of the primitive kerygma, Paul and the Johannine writer stand together for a richer conception. Nothing need here be added to what has been already said about the actual use of the word 'mysticism'.

What word, we now ask, would best describe this intercourse with God? We have already rejected 'knowledge' and 'vision' though the corresponding verbs are found. There is no case for 'union', nor can we use 'incorporation', which might have done for Paul. κοινωνία is not as common as in Paul, but we have seen that it is the substantive equivalent of the very common expressions about mutual indwelling; thus, as for Paul, we may approve the phrase 'communion' or 'indwelling communion'.

Finally, what activities (if any) are the media of this communion? What was said in connexion with Paul[58] may here be repeated without qualification, except that Baptism is no longer associated with dying and rising with Christ.

The Johannine writer has thus a conception as warm and rich as that of Paul. He has moreover the advantage in the Gospel that he is able to expound this theme in more intimate connexion with the life of Christ; to give us, for example, the High-Priestly Prayer. The writings are thus the climax of the New Testament teaching on this theme.

[58] cf. *supra*, p. 195.

CHAPTER NINE

OTHER STRANDS IN THE NEW TESTAMENT

THE OTHER New Testament writings may be treated more briefly.

THE EPISTLE TO THE HEBREWS

Many writers have described how this Epistle combines a copious use of Old Testament imagery with a Platonic strain. The Jewish cult is swept away 'once for all' by a unique act in time; but we are not told that the New Age has come; we read rather of 'the greater and more perfect tabernacle not made with hands' (He 9_{11}), of 'the pattern shown in the mount' (He 8_5); and we are reminded of the Platonic ideas laid up in heaven, in which the particulars in this world but dimly participate. We read indeed in Plato (*Republic*, 476a), when he is speaking about just and unjust, good and evil, that 'each in itself is one, but by reason of their κοινωνία (participation?) in actions and bodies and each other, they appear everywhere and each seems many'.[1] This is so to speak the Biblical idea in reverse; the heavenly is said to participate in the earthly. No trace of this linguistic usage is to be found in the Epistle, but the Platonic thought is there.

As the Epistle contains a good deal about the cult, we might suppose it would contain much material bearing on our theme; and it might be thought that there would be a good deal about the vision of God when the veil is removed, corresponding to the Platonic conception; whereas the realized eschatology implied in the 'once for all' passages might be thought to lead to conceptions of piety of an intimate, but more Hebraic, kind. In fact, however, there is less material of either kind than might have been expected.

Much is said about 'entering' and 'approaching', for instance, into God's rest (He 3-4). We draw near (ἐγγίζω) to God (He 7_{19}); the word 'approach' (προσέρχομαι) is common (He 4_{16}, 7_{25}, 10_1, $_{22}$, 11_6, 12_{18}, $_{22}$), as is the word 'boldness' (παρρησία)

[1] In the same context at 476d μετέχω occurs. Thus in its interchange of the two words it resembles 1 Co 10. But here the idea has κοινωνία in the particulars, whereas the particulars μετέχουσι in the ideas.

(He 3_6, 4_{16}, $10_{19, 35}$). Faith forms the theme of a whole chapter (He 11), not in the Pauline sense; it describes a hope in and grasp of the unseen largely found in Old Testament saints; boldness is more characteristic of the New Covenant, though Christians must still have faith (e.g. He 10_{22}). Despite all this, there is very little description of the kind of communion with God which those who boldly approach then enjoy. Indeed, the Epistle is taken up with the theological argument, and its descriptions of the Christian life are short and simple. Worship and prayer (He 13_{18}) are recommended, but there is no phrase generally descriptive of its piety like the Pauline 'in Christ'. The Christian who boldly approaches by the 'new and living way' (He 10_{20}) has come 'unto mount Zion and unto the city of the living God, the heavenly Jerusalem' (He 12_{22}). No one who reads these and the tremendous numinous phrases which follow can doubt that intercourse with God was conceived as a profound and stirring experience, intimate and close, yet awe-inspiring: yet we lack a fuller account of it. We are, however, able to say that there is no trace in these words of mystical absorption such as the Greek vein in his thought might have led us to expect: it is an I-thou experience, lacking indeed something of the warmth of the Pauline and Johannine descriptions.

We may pass then immediately to our linguistic investigations. The author uses λατρεύω (serve) more frequently than any other New Testament writer, sometimes indeed of the old dispensation (e.g. He 8_5), but sometimes also of the new (e.g. He 9_{14}, 12_{28}); it is a word naturally suggested by the topic of the cult; but it will not do for a general description of New Testament piety; and its English equivalent has ethical and non-liturgical connotations which are lacking in the Greek.

Of the whole range of 'know' words, ἐπίγνωσις occurs once (He 10_{26}), followed by 'of the truth'. The only other occurrences that are closely relevant are both in Hebrews 8_{11}, where both γινώσκω and οἶδα occur, both in a quotation from Jeremiah 31_{34}. Thus this Epistle says virtually nothing of the knowledge of God.

The words of 'seeing' fare a little better. βλέπω, which occurs several times in irrelevant contexts, appears once followed by Jesus and a participle; 'we see Jesus crowned' (He 2_9). This may be that construction whereby verbs of seeing take an accusative and participle in place of the accusative and infinitive which follow verbs of saying: thus it may mean 'we see that Jesus is crowned'. In any case, it corresponds to the 'we see not yet' (οὔπω ὁρῶμεν) of the previous verse, where the object is not a person. θεάομαι does not occur, and θεωρέω not significantly. εἶδον is not here important, but there are several important uses of ὁράω. We may omit Hebrews 9_{28}, which is a reference to the Second Coming. Moses is said to have endured, 'as seeing him that is invisible' (τὸν . . . ἀόρατον ὡς ὁρῶν) (He 11_{27}). This is qualified both by the ὡς and by the description of God as invisible. The verse begins with 'By faith', and elsewhere faith is described as the ἔλεγχος (proving? conviction?) of things not seen (He 11_1). Faith has 'a power of realization, by which the invisible becomes visible and the future becomes present. While hope is the confident anticipation of a future regarded as future, faith appropriates that future as an experience of the present.'[2] Thus what is said of Moses is quite in accordance with the author's basic conception of faith, though only here is the invisible extended to include God. At the climax of the passage on faith we are exhorted to look away (ἀφορῶντες—a rare word) unto (εἰς) Jesus (He 12_2). The idea seems to be that we should turn even from the Old Testament saints and concentrate our attention on Him: the sense and the preposition 'unto' thus prevent this from being a statement that we see Jesus. The reference to 'the sanctification, without which no one shall see the Lord' (He 12_{14}) is ambiguous: it may refer to such a vision in this life or in the next; ordinary grammatical usage shows that the future tense is not decisively in favour of the latter; thus one might write 'if you do not have faith, you will not be justified'; the tense would be future, but the reference would be to the present. This sentence must thus be left as ambiguous.

κοινωνία appears once; this is the only appearance of it in the New Testament which we have still to consider.

He 13_{16}. τῆς δὲ εὐποιΐας καὶ κοινωνίας μὴ ἐπιλανθάνεσθε· τοιαύταις γὰρ θυσίαις εὐαρεστεῖται ὁ Θεός.

But to do good and to communicate forget not: for with such sacrifices God is well pleased.[3]

[2] Peake, *Hebrews*, p. 210.

[3] The Methodist *Book of Offices* has this in the Offertory sentences, following its usual policy of substituting R.V. for the Prayer Book Version, which here has 'distribute': but in this connexion R.V. risks being misunderstood as meaning 'receive Holy Communion'.

This is one of the least controversial of the uses of the word. It is here used absolutely, but bears a meaning somewhat like that in Romans 15_{26}, 2 Corinthians 9_{13}. It might be held that it here means 'generosity' considered as a sign of fellowship, but it is generally held to derive directly from the possible meaning 'giving a share'. We may compare the use of the verb in Galatians 6_6. It refers to the action of contributing rather than to the concrete 'collection' or 'contribution',[4] (as in Ro 15_{26}, 2 Co 9_{13}). It is best rendered 'generosity' or turned with a verb, as in R.S.V., 'to share what you have'.

The verb κοινωνέω (He 2_{14}) and the noun κοινωνός (He 10_{33}) occur once each; they are part of the linguistic evidence the conclusions of which we have already assumed,[5] but they throw no light on communion with God.

The former of these two passages contains also the verb μετέχω, which here (cf. 1 Co 10) is used with little or no distinction of meaning; it occurs also at Hebrews 5_{13}, 7_{13}. More theologically significant is the use of μέτοχος, which this author alone among the New Testament writers uses, apart from an unimportant instance in Luke 5_7. There are three important instances out of five.[6] Christians are partakers of 'a heavenly calling' (He 3_1), of 'Christ' (He 3_{14}), and of 'Holy Spirit' (He 6_4). These are strikingly like the Pauline references to participation (κοινωνία) in Christ (1 Co 1_9) and in the Holy Spirit (2 Co 13_{13}, Ph 2_1). They serve to support the idea that the two roots are used practically synonymously; the Hebrews passages support also the way in which the genitives are taken in the Pauline passages; but, more important, they supply in Hebrews a kind of theological equivalent to the Pauline expressions. Hitherto, we have found nothing in this Epistle so warm and intimate as in Paul. These two passages alone cannot raise the temperature to Pauline heights, but they are the warmest, most intimate, and most Pauline expressions in this Epistle. He is also the only New Testament writer to use μεταλαμβάνω in theological senses, of receiving blessing from God (but the subject is 'the land') (He 6_7) and God's holiness (He 12_{10}). Somewhat similar is the use of 'taste'

[4] cf. Campbell, pp. 373-4; Seesemann, p. 24; Hauck, *KTW*, III.809.

[5] cf. Campbell, pp. 362-4.

[6] The other two are He 12_8, 1_9. The latter is from Ps 45_7, where the Hebrew uses the root חבר, which is also the Hebrew equivalent for κοινωνία; cf. Hanse, *KTW*, II.831-2.

(γεύομαι), both with the genitive and with the accusative. Elsewhere in the New Testament, apart from secular uses, the word is most commonly used, as indeed once in Hebrews also (He 2_9), in the phrase 'taste death', but here it is used of 'the heavenly gift' and 'the good word of God' (He 6_{4-5}).[7]

That the experience of the Christian is corporate is clear in this Epistle. It twice uses the phrase 'the people of God' (ὁ λαὸς τοῦ Θεοῦ) (He 4_9, 11_{25});[8] the recipients are urged not to neglect the gathering of themselves together (He 10_{25}); an exalted account is given of the heavenly Jerusalem in corporate and ecclesiastical terms (He 12_{22-4}). Those who have the rule over them, that is, the ministers, whom they are urged to remember, are described as having spoken to them the word of God—a very unsacerdotal conception of the ministry (He 13_7). There are also notoriously controversial references to Baptism and the laying on of hands (He 6_{1-2}, 10_{19-22})[9] and possibly to the Eucharist (He 13_{10});[10] yet on the whole the sacraments play little part in his thought despite the prominence of the idea of sacrifice and priesthood. Certainly 'the Epistle of Priesthood', as it has been called, gives no support to the ideas of priesthood found in 'Catholic' circles to-day.

To what type of piety does this author belong? The word 'mystical' has indeed been used of him, but could only be justified in the broadest sense of the word. His piety is of our type two; it lacks the characteristics of Pauline and Johannine piety; and were it not for his use of the word μέτοχος, we should be inclined to put it in that half of type two which borders most nearly on type three; but in view of the use of this word, we may perhaps place it in a central position in type two.

When we consider in the light of this evidence what word might best be used to describe our intercourse with God, we receive no great help from this Epistle. 'Participation' is the most likely word, and this is at least compatible with 'communion', which we have provisionally decided to use.

As for the question how it is mediated, there is no trace here of mediation through nature or anything of that kind. The writer's

[7] μέτοχος is used in the same passage.

[8] Otherwise found, mostly in N.T. only at 1 P 2_{10} (without the article), though 'my people' is found in O.T. quotations where God is the speaker, also 'his people' with reference to God.

[9] cf. Flemington, pp. 97-9; Lampe, pp. 77-8.

[10] cf. Taylor, *ANTT*, pp. 153-62.

interests are liturgical; yet it cannot be said that he conceives of communion with God as being mediated through the cult of which he speaks: for that cult is the sacrificial cult which was superseded by the 'new and living way' (He 10_{20}) which Christ consecrated. Yet he stresses corporate Christian worship: and it was presumably chiefly in this that he sought that 'participation' in Christ in terms of which he conceived communion with God.

THE FIRST EPISTLE OF PETER

Much has been written in recent times by way of introduction to this Epistle:[11] and the view is widely held that the Epistle does not contain, as was once supposed, diluted Paulinism, but rather reflects the general mind of the primitive pre-Pauline community. Its resemblances to the Pauline Epistles may well be due to the use of common sources, mostly liturgical and catechetical: it is not, however, lacking in the impress of an individual mind, which may well be that of Peter himself assisted by Silvanus.

The strength of the Epistle lies in its close connexion between theology and ethics, but it shows very little interest in those themes which concern us here. Selwyn has well written

'In its close association of ethics with theology, this Epistle is one of the seed-plots of the *theologia perennis* of Christian ethical thought, immune alike from the mysticism which tends towards the absorption of the human soul in the divine and from the moralism which finds its classical expression in the works of Kant'.[12]

We shall, therefore, without further discussion of its characteristics look immediately at those few phrases and ideas which have any bearing on our theme. We notice first that considerable importance is attached to prayers (1 P 3_7, 4_7), which are mentioned in the plural, 'as though he thought of prayer as consisting in definite acts and occasions':[13] it is associated with watching, as in Mark 14_{38}.

The phrase ἐν Χριστῷ occurs three times (1 P 3_{16}, 5_{10}, $_{14}$).[14] Christ is the atmosphere, climate, and environment of the Christian life.[15] We have already referred to the use of the phrase

[11] cf. Taylor, *ANTT*, pp. 35-48; Selwyn; Cranfield.

[12] Selwyn, p. 64.

[13] Selwyn, p. 110.

[14] ἐν ᾧ in 1 P 1_6 probably does not refer to Christ.

[15] Selwyn on these passages.

in this Epistle, and suggested that the phrase may be pre-Pauline, part of the general view of the primitive Church.[16] We may accept this without following Selwyn in his view that it is connected with the corporate interpretation of the phrase 'Son of Man'.[17] In any case it is agreed that the phrase is not developed as in Paul and John: there is no doctrine of what is popularly called 'mystical union'. There are somewhat similar phrases about the Spirit (1 P 1_2, $_{12}$)[18].

The ideas of seeing and knowing God are altogether lacking: indeed we read these explicit words about Christ; 'whom not having seen ye love; on whom, though now ye see him not, yet believing, ye rejoice greatly . . .' (1 P 1_8). κοινωνία is altogether lacking; but there are significant uses of the cognates. We read 'insomuch as ye are partakers (κοινωνεῖτε) of Christ's sufferings, rejoice' (1 P 4_{13}). A somewhat similar thought lies behind the sentence, 'The elders, therefore, who are among you I exhort, who am a fellow-elder, and a witness of the sufferings of Christ, who am also a partaker (κοινωνός) of the glory that shall be revealed' (1 P 5_1). These passages raise no new questions about the grammatical properties of the κοινων- words: the meaning is the ordinary one of 'participation'. But the former passage seems parallel to various Pauline passages, particularly the reference to participation in Christ's sufferings in Philippians 3_{10} (a κοινωνία passage),[19] and the notion of dying and rising with Christ (Ro 6). Both these Petrine passages have been compared with Ro 8_{17}.[20] But Taylor is emphatic that the idea in the former passage is not 'mystical' but concrete and practical, and that there is no analogy to the Pauline idea of dying with Christ.[21] This is borne out by the fact that the author is concerned in other passages also (e.g. 1 P $2_{20ff.}$), with the simple imitation of Christ. Yet the two themes are not to be too sharply separated, and it may be that here, as with the phrase 'in Christ', we have a pre-Pauline[22] theme which Paul was able to take and mould to new

[16] cf. *supra*, p. 159.
[17] Selwyn on 1 P 3_{16}; also pp. 20, 83.
[18] cf. Selwyn's note on ἐν at 1 P 1_2.
[19] cf. Seesemann, p. 85 n.4; Schneider, pp. 121-3.
[20] So Hauck, *KTW*, III.807.
[21] Taylor, *ANTT*, p. 44; *FR*, pp. 110-12. But he allows that 1 P 5_1 suggests a common religious experience. cf. Selwyn on 1 P 4_{13}, also p. 20.
[22] This does not, of course, mean that this Epistle was written before the Pauline Epistles, but that it contains modes of thought relatively uninfluenced by Paul and of an earlier date, the common stock of the early Church.

ends. But the latter passage (1 P 5_1) raises further problems. Hauck,[23] still with Romans 8_{17} in mind, thinks that the Apostle bears witness to the sufferings of Christ by his whole life and activity, including his own sufferings, and thus has a present certainty of partaking in the glory that is to be revealed. But were it not for the influence of the supposed parallel in Romans, it would be natural to take the first part of the verse to mean only that he was an eye-witness of the sufferings of Christ.[24] But the more vital question is the meaning of the second part of the verse. Selwyn observes that commentators usually write as though ἐσόμενος were to be understood. He takes the view that we have here a reference to the Transfiguration.[25] The Transfiguration may have been indeed a foretaste of the glory of the Parousia; but it seems doubtful whether we should see such a reference here. But whether we take this view or not, it must be conceded that the theme of sharing the experiences of Christ, the so-called mystical union (one is almost forced to use the language so common among the commentators) plays no such part in this author as it does in Paul. At the most, we have only these passing references to it.

This non-mystical imitation of Christ, which is the heart of the author's ethic, is to be lived within the Christian community; the Church (though that word does not occur) is described in a rich and eloquent passage in the second chapter as 'a spiritual house', 'a chosen race, a royal priesthood, a holy nation, a people for God's possession', 'God's people', whose task is 'to offer spiritual sacrifices' and to declare God's wonderful deeds (1 P $2_{5, 9, 10}$). They have a ministry of elders (1 P 5_{1-5}), who are conceived in a non-sacerdotal way. They practise Baptism (1 P 3_{21}),[26] but there is no mention of the Eucharist, though no doubt they observed this too. But the sacraments are not prominent as media of communion with God.

We turn to ask our usual questions. To what type of piety does the author belong? His piety is of our type two. His lack of 'mysticism' in even the broadest sense of that word might seem to

23 Hauck, *KTW*, III.807.

24 This view assumes the Petrine authorship, but a pseudonymous writer might intentionally give the impression of having been with Christ. Hauck's view does not require Petrine authorship, though Hauck apparently accepts it.

25 Selwyn, ad loc. His statement that 'κοινωνός, with its correlatives, is a word that normally connotes in the New Testament some kind of *concrete experience*' is not entirely borne out by the facts, or by the citation which he gives from Taylor.

26 cf. Flemington, pp. 99-101.

put him into that half of type two which is nearer to type three: the phrase 'in Christ' and the use of κοινων- words may, however, weigh against this consideration, and a final verdict must depend on the detailed exegesis of the passages we have considered; but on any view the full Pauline thought is absent. He may call our attention to the presence in the Church of pre-Pauline strands which Paul was able to adopt: but he himself must be classed with the part of type two which is nearer to three, being just a little to that side of the central point of class two.

There is nothing in this Epistle to overthrow our existing conclusions about the choice of a word to describe our intercourse with God; its occasional use of κοινων- words is quite compatible with our provisional decisions.

There is nothing in this Epistle to suggest the mediation of this communion through nature or anything of that kind. Nor, on the other hand, are the writer's chief interests liturgical, like those of the writer to the Hebrews; his interest in ethics is so strong that he might well have thought that we have communion with God in imitating Christ; but this nowhere finds explicit expression. The fact is that communion with God is not a central theme in his mind at all.

THE EPISTLE OF JAMES

This Epistle contains nothing that is really relevant to our purpose. It is strongly ethical in tone, and its definition of 'pure religion and undefiled' (Ja 1_{27})[27] is in purely ethical terms. Its interest in worship is largely concerned with the avoidance of class-distinctions in the meeting for worship (Ja $2_{1ff.}$). There is, however, a strong stress on prayer (Ja 1_{5-8}, 4_{2-3}, 5_{13-18}), which extends to the recommendation of two practices which have been much further developed in 'Catholic' Christendom, namely, the anointing of the sick, and the confession of sins to each other; not, of course, to a priest. But there is no developed 'Catholicism' here, and very little Churchmanship at all; only one passing reference to presbyters of the Church (Ja 5_{14}), and nothing about Baptism or the Eucharist. There are no κοινων- words; nor do any of the rival expressions appear. We come no nearer to intercourse with God than such expressions as 'bless the Lord' (Ja 3_9) and

[27] θρησκεία ('religion') might be translated 'worship'; cf. Schmidt, *KTW*, III. 155-9.

'draw near to God'. Abraham is described as 'God's friend' (Ja 2_{23}, an allusion to Is 41_8). As will be found in the investigation of almost any doctrine, this book is not typical of the New Testament, and does not cause us to modify our conclusions.

THE EPISTLE OF JUDE

This late Epistle, apart from an interesting use of κοινός in verse 3 ('our common salvation'), and a reference in verse 20 to praying in the Holy Spirit, contributes to our subject only a verse complicated by textual problems. He writes 'to those that are called, beloved in God the Father and kept for Jesus Christ' (Jude 1). Neither part of the phrase has an exact parallel, whereas an 'in' with Jesus Christ would be common usage. It is not, therefore, surprising that many Greek MSS. read 'sanctified (ἡγιασμένοις) in God the Father', which is a more normal expression than 'beloved' (ἠγαπημένοις), and some of the versions imply 'in' before 'Jesus Christ'. But the best MSS. support the reading implied above. It is, however, possible that at some stage 'in' was accidentally omitted before 'Jesus Christ' and then wrongly inserted before 'God', which had been meant to be dative of agent. In any case, we have an echo, more or less faint, of the Pauline usage.[28]

THE SECOND EPISTLE OF PETER

This late and pseudonymous book, in many ways similar to Jude, is comparatively full of relevant material. It seeks to controvert heresies rather than to make any major contribution to our doctrine; but it seems almost to stumble into using significant phrases.

The chief instance is the verse which John Wesley read on the morning of May 24th 1738: 'whereby he has granted[29] to us his precious and very great promises, that through these you may become partakers of the divine nature (θείας κοινωνοὶ φύσεως), having escaped from the corruption that is in the world through lust' (2 P 1_4). Of all the things or persons in which the Christian is said, by the use of κοινων- words, to participate, this is the most startling. None of the parallels quoted by the commentators (He 3_{14}, 6_4, 12_{10}, 1 Jn 1_3, 1 P 5_1, 2 Co 3_{18}) is precise; but there are

[28] cf. Mayor, ad loc. [29] Taking δεδώρηται as middle.

many Platonic parallels for 'divine nature',[30] and these, as also the parallels in Philo and others, often have the *idea* of participating in it. Sometimes some other phrase is used, such as θεῖα μοῖρα; we have not found a passage in which θεία φύσις actually occurs with a κοινων- word. The idea became increasingly common in the Fathers, particularly Athanasius, until the idea of deification arose. The isolated occurrence of this phrase here need not be taken too seriously; the author was clearly influenced by his Hellenistic environment. His style is always ambitious and artificial; he never used a simple word when a complicated one would do. His phrase may have been partly responsible for the growth of later ideas about deification; but they would probably have arisen in any case, and we need not credit him with any intention of starting a theological revolution.

He also shows a strong tendency to use words relating to 'knowledge'. Apart from unimportant uses of γινώσκω and οἶδα, we have ἐπιγινώσκω twice in one verse, governing 'the way of righteousness' (2 P 2_{21}), γνῶσις three times (2 P 1_{5-6}, 3_{18}), and ἐπίγνωσις four times (2 P 1_{2}, $_{3}$, $_{8}$, 2_{20}). Two of the uses of γνῶσις are absolute, and occur in a list of virtues (cf. 2 Co 6_{6}). The other instance of γνῶσις and all those of ἐπίγνωσις are followed by a genitive of some Person of the Godhead. Thus the author does his best to safeguard the use of the words against Gnostic error; nevertheless, the frequency with which he uses them is perhaps indicative of strong Gnostic elements in his environment.

The author is not interested in the idea of seeing except to assert that he saw the Transfiguration. This was part of his technique as a pseudonymous writer; naturally he describes it in terms largely derived from the synoptic Gospels. It has no value as a source.

He contributes nothing to our ideas on prayer.

In general, he contributes nothing new, but is prone to use impressive phrases related to our subject without giving much thought to their implications.

THE PASTORAL EPISTLES

We take the view, as in Harrison, that these are not by Paul, though they may incorporate fragments of his work. They

[30] Kleinknecht, *KTW*, III.122-3; cf. Mayor, ad loc.

contain many echoes of his thought, but breathe a different spirit, and reflect a later stage in the development of Church life.

This can be illustrated, as by much else, so by those phrases which pertain to our theme. Thus the characteristically Pauline 'in Christ' is frequently found, but always in the form 'in Christ Jesus' (1 Ti 1_{14}, 3_{13}, 2 Ti $1_{1, 9, 13}$, $2_{1, 10}$, $3_{12, 15}$). Paul uses this addition sometimes, but was not bound to it. The Pastorals use ἐνώπιον with a Person of the Godhead more frequently, relatively to their length, than Paul.[31]

The chief phrase connected with knowledge is 'knowledge of the truth' (ἐπίγνωσις ἀληθείας), which occurs four times (1 Ti 2_4, 2 Ti 2_{25}, 3_7, Tit 1_1; cf. He 10_{26}).[32] Paul is fond of this word for 'knowledge', but he never has 'of the truth' to follow it; the Pastorals have nothing else, and thus never have 'knowledge of God (or Christ)'. 'Knowledge of the truth' may mean simply the intellectual acceptance of the Christian faith. The question which troubled Paul whether to use the word γνῶσις in a good or bad sense is here plainly settled by the phrase 'knowledge falsely so-called' (τῆς ψευδωνύμου γνώσεως) (1 Ti 6_{20}). Similarly we read of those 'who profess to know (εἰδέναι) God' (Tit 1_{16}). We also have 'I know (οἶδα) him whom I have trusted' (2 Ti 1_{12}), and a reference to God's knowledge (γινώσκω) of us (2 Ti 2_{19}; cf. Nu 16_5).

The thought of the vision of God is far from the writer's mind. God is plainly said to be 'invisible' (1 Ti 1_{17}), One 'whom no man has seen or can see' (1 Ti 6_{16}).

κοινωνία does not occur, despite its use in Paul. κοινωνέω is used characteristically, but not with reference to God (1 Ti 5_{22}).[33] κοινωνικός, meaning 'generous', makes its only appearance in the Greek Bible (1 Ti 6_{18}).

The most striking reminiscence of Paul's teaching on these subjects is, 'Faithful is the saying: If we died with him, we shall also live with him; if we endure, we shall also reign with him, (2 Ti 2_{11-12}). This seems to be a rhythmical saying, perhaps a kind of hymn. We have here three συν- compounds, quite in

[31] 1 Ti 2_3, $5_{4, 21}$, 6_{13}, 2 Ti 2_{14}, 4_1, against seven instances in the genuine Pauline letters. Luke, Acts, and Revelation are also fond of it; it was possibly a Semitism.

[32] Also the verb ἐπιγινώσκω occurs with 'the truth' in 1 Ti 4_3; the verb does not otherwise occur in the Pastorals.

[33] cf. Seesemann, p. 32.

the Pauline manner, all of them actually used by Paul. The grouping in pairs is also quite Pauline; and the reference to dying with Christ is presumably to Baptism rather than to martyrdom, if the Pauline parallels are to be considered.[34] Yet here the use of two future tenses, though not unparalleled in Paul, is noteworthy, for Paul put these verbs in the future only sparingly. The greater use of the future here may indicate a certain weakening in the sense of present possession, which may also be indicated by the rather scanty references to the Holy Spirit.

The Pastorals have several instructions about prayer; and some of these have had a considerable influence on Christian liturgy, notably the instruction to pray for kings (1 Ti 2_2); as these were not at that time Christians, this is a prayer for the world, going beyond John 17_9. Since the conversion of Constantine rulers have often been included in the prayer for the Church; but it is right to pray for them even when they are not, as persecuted modern Churches have indeed done.[35] Prayer is sometimes seen as the special duty of a particular class (1 Ti 5_5).

There are some references to the Church and to Baptism (Tit 3_5), and many to the ministry. We read of 'the gift of God which is in thee through (διά) the laying on of my hands' (2 Ti 1_6) and of 'the gift which was given to thee through (διά) prophecy[36] with (μετά) the laying on of the hands of the presbytery' (1 Ti 4_{14}; cf. 5_{22}). We must not go into subsequent controversies about ordination; but even when all allowance has been made for various uncertainties (some, for instance, take 2 Timothy to refer to confirmation) and for the qualifications which the contexts may suggest, it does seem that we have, particularly in 2 Timothy, the notion of a spiritual gift being mediated by the laying on of hands, which is a different idea of mediation from that which is common in the New Testament. We are reminded indeed of the διά referring to Baptism in Romans 6_4, but that at least refers to a sacrament instituted by Christ.

Thus the Pastorals contain some scattered fragments of the Pauline theology, but themselves reflect a later, less vivid, and more institutionalized form of the Christian experience.

[34] cf. Lock, ad loc.; on the tenses, cf. *supra*, p. 151.

[35] cf. *supra*, p. 202.

[36] Presumably the prophetic utterance of those taking part.

THE REVELATION OF ST JOHN THE DIVINE

This, certainly in relation to its length, contains as little for our purpose as any New Testament book. As it describes a vision, 'I saw' and 'I heard' are extremely common, but throw no light on the vision of God in this life.[37] The author does not speak of knowing God or being in Christ; he once says 'in Jesus' (Rev 1_9), and speaks occasionally of being 'in the Spirit' (Rev 1_{10}, 4_2, 17_3, 21_{10}), though his doctrine of the Spirit is slight. He is prone to the use of ἐνώπιον followed by a Person of the Godhead. συνκοινωνός is used (Rev 1_9) in a reference to his 'horizontal' relationship with his fellow-Christians in regard to suffering, and συνκοινωνέω is used of participating in something evil (Rev 18_4; cf. Eph 5_{11}). He has much about prayer, and the heavenly worship, but no important teaching on these points. The prayer of the departed for vengeance (Rev 6_{10}) goes beyond the teaching of Luke 18_{1-8}; in Revelation 5_8, 8_3, we have the prayers of the living mediated by elders and angels respectively.[38]

If the book has a distinctive feature in connexion with this theme, it lies in the use of μετά with the genitive, sometimes in connexion with such verbs that it must be deemed a Hebraism.[39] 'I will sup with him, and he with me' (Rev 3_{20}) is faintly reminiscent of the Johannine mutual indwelling, and there is a faint flavour of the Johannine triadic formulae in the following verse (Rev 3_{21}).[40] σύν never occurs.

The book, then, is not interested in our theme, but the triple prayer for the coming of Jesus (Rev $22_{17, 20}$) makes a fitting close to the New Testament.

κοινωνία and its cognates were not in use again for some while after the Biblical writers.[41]

[37] cf. Michaelis, *KTW*, V.352. On the next life, see Rev 22_4; Michaelis, *KTW*, V.367-8.

[38] These passages can be understood only in the light of their Jewish antecedents, for which see Charles, ad loc.

[39] cf. Charles, I.cxxxiii.

[40] Lohmeyer, pp. 233-4, refers also to Rev 3_4, 14_1, 17_{14}.

[41] Lacey, p. 251.

CHAPTER TEN

CONCLUSION

IT REMAINS to sum up what we have found and to consider its bearing on more general questions of theology.

SUMMARY

Jesus came into a world in which there existed various conceptions of communion with God. The Old Testament writers, in whose tradition He stood, and particularly the prophets, had richly experienced it. Such conceptions as the Fatherhood of God, and the Covenant between God and Israel, and God as the Husband seeking an erring wife, implied it. Moreover, individuals had certain particular experiences. These were at first described in crude and anthropomorphic terms, as when God was conceived as walking in the garden or when Moses was said to have seen His back; but the later writers spoke mainly of hearing the Word of the Lord. The prophets, who thus wrote, also occasionally had visions, not so much, usually, of God Himself, as of particular objects, such as an almond-tree, which conveyed a message to them. The messages which they thus received, whether by hearing or seeing, were always for publication, without any of that secrecy or incommunicability which marked other traditions of piety. But close as their connexion with God thus was, there were limits to its intimacy. God was more often conceived as Father and indeed as King than as Husband; and the Covenant was certainly not a contract between equal partners. There were thus limits to the language which they used about their intercourse with God. They spoke freely of 'knowing' Him, but there were certain words which they did not use; in particular, they never used in this context the Hebrew word which would have been translated by κοινωνία (which we often render as 'communion' or 'fellowship'), so that that Greek word never appears in any important sense in the Septuagint. Side by side with this prophetic piety there went the sacrificial system, partly, at least, to remove taints or defilements which would have prevented intercourse with God, but partly as a medium for it. But various views were taken of this system, even within the Old Testament itself; and prayer played at least an equal part as a means of communion.

The rest of the ancient world had very different conceptions. Some things they had in common with the Jews, for instance sacrifice, though no doubt with a somewhat different conception; but they had nothing at all closely resembling the Hebrew prophets. They had lively conceptions of communion with the deities in which they believed, but the difference between, say, the crude but entertaining polytheism of Homer and the virtual monotheism of Plato makes it impossible to generalize. On the whole, their conception of communion with their gods was much less restrained than that of the Jews. Their gods were morally hardly superior to their heroes, and it was natural to think of intercourse with them more along the lines of one's everyday intercourse with one's friends than as the approach to a great King who made heaven and earth. Thus it was possible to 'see', 'hear', and 'know' them. But this did not give the average citizen of the Greek-speaking world of the time of Christ any very lively sense of being in touch with the gods; the 'established religion' of sacrifice had degenerated into the kind of superstition which Paul met at Athens. They did not meet the gods as the Homeric heroes had done. Those who sought the thrill of a more intense personal experience had recourse to the mystery-religions, perhaps to several, for they were not exclusive. There, without any such ethical demands as the Hebrew prophets made, they were initiated into strange, exotic, half-oriental cults, from which they emerged forbidden to tell what they had seen and heard. Among such people, as indeed in most of the world's religions apart from Judaism, some spoke in the most intimate terms of their intercourse with the deity, even to the point of claiming to be united or identified with or absorbed in him.

Into this world came Jesus, and to Christians, who believe Him to be the only Son of God, His practice and teaching alike are of supreme importance. His message was that the expected kingdom of God had come; He announced the New Age for which the prophets had longed. Naturally we should expect that He would inaugurate some new and more intimate kind of communion with God; and that is what we in fact find. He spent much of His life in unostentatious private prayer; and a few prayers, spoken in crises of His life, have been preserved for us. They breathe the spirit of Jewish rather than of Greek or Oriental piety; but their use of a familiar, homely way of addressing God reveals a more intimate trust than anything contained in the Old Testament. God had been known mostly as King, and only in moments of rare inspiration as Father; His only Son addressed Him as Father with simple confidence. Yet this trust is combined in one of these prayers with a frank statement of His own desires and in another with a cry of dereliction, in such a way as to raise all the profoundest problems of prayer. The answers are linked with the deep mystery of the Incarnation itself, but the lesson for subsequent piety is clear: the Christian need not hesitate to pour out his needs in the frankest way before God, so long as with his petitions there goes also a loyal and active acceptance of God's will.

In the teaching, as distinct from the practice, of Jesus, the chief item is the model prayer which He gave to the disciples. Here again the first phrase 'Our Father' breathes a spirit of simple trust. The intimacy which was natural for the Only Son was fitting also for those who were God's children by adoption and grace. Jesus gave men a sense of kinship with God, and within this family relationship communion was more rich and intimate than the children of Israel had ever conceived to be possible. The clause of the Lord's Prayer 'Lead us not into temptation' again raises profound questions about the nature of petition, and encourages us to be simple, naïve, and childlike in our requests. The prayer is in the prophetic tradition in that, despite the new intimacy, it has no trace of absorption into God. The rest of the teaching of Jesus on prayer is in the same tradition; short, simple, unostentatious prayer is recommended. Mark adds that it should be accompanied by 'watching', for, though Jesus announced the New Age, there is a further consummation yet to come. The source Q continues the Old Testament idea of 'knowing' God. Matthew's special source lays stress on the certainty that our prayers will be heard, while Luke's special source recommends importunity in prayer.

An important point of a somewhat different kind is that Matthew's special source, in some sayings of which the authenticity has sometimes been doubted, speaks of a future presence of

Jesus in the midst of His disciples, and thus paves the way for very different conceptions after the ascension.

Towards the sacrificial system (as distinct from its underlying ideas) the attitude of Jesus was, at best, somewhat cool, for He knew that this would be altogether changed by His death. The Jews would indeed continue to practise it till Jerusalem fell; but His death secured effectively that forgiveness of sins which the sacrifices had sought in vain.

The communion with God which He practised and preached (not, despite a well-known Beatitude, to be described as the Vision of God) was henceforth to be enjoyed corporately, that is, by the body of disciples whom He constituted into the new Israel, the Christian Church; within this He instituted the ministry and the two sacraments, though certainly not as exclusive media of communion with God. The Christian, as a member of this body, would find in private prayer, in public worship, and also in the service of those in need, that communion with God which Jesus came to deepen and to make available not only for the Chosen People, but for all mankind.

After the death, resurrection, and ascension of Christ, the early Christians received on the day of Pentecost the gift of the Holy Spirit, at first with some ecstatic accompaniments; and henceforth their conception of communion with God was connected with the Holy Spirit. The apostolic preaching suggested rather than explicitly mentioned the idea of communion with God. The life of the body which Christ had founded, was characterized, as we are told in a famous description of it, by 'fellowship' (κοινωνία).

The meaning of this word has been much disputed, but it seems to mean primarily that men share with each other a common possession. Thus it sometimes means 'giving a share', i.e. alms-giving; sometimes it means simply 'sharing' or 'fellowship'; and sometimes it means 'having a share', or 'participation'. Its emphasis may lie primarily on its 'horizontal' aspect, the people with whom they share, or on its 'vertical' aspect, the thing or indeed person which or whom they share or have in common. In this famous description of the early Church it means 'fellowship', with a primarily horizontal reference, though the two aspects can never be separated; we are not here told, however, what or whom they had in common; we shall find this explicitly stated in Paul. These early Christians enjoyed a rich communion with God, indeed a richer communion than they had had in the lifetime of Jesus before the decisive series of events from Calvary to Pentecost; but their intellectual conception of this communion had not been greatly developed.

That development was the work of Paul. He stood in such close contact with that other, Greek, world of which we have spoken that it has sometimes been supposed that his conception of piety was deeply influenced by it, and certain new modes of thought which he introduced to Christendom lend some colour to this view. It seems, however, more likely that this thought was fundamentally in the Jewish and prophetic tradition, a careful examination of which shows unexpected antecedents to Paul's conceptions; and the use he made of other vocabularies may simply be the use which in controversy we all make of the vocabulary of our opponents. However that may be, he certainly introduced striking changes into the conception of communion with God. He was deeply influenced by his conversion-experience, which may indeed have been largely the basis of his subsequent conceptions. He knew what it was to agonize in prayer, and introduced the idea of the Spirit interceding for us when we do not know how to pray, which is a fresh contribution to the problems of petition and intercession.

His main contribution to this subject, perhaps indeed to theology in general, was his frequent use of the phrase 'in Christ', with which is linked the idea that we die and rise with Christ, even though it cannot be said that in this present world we *are* with Christ. Round these phrases there cluster many others (such as the description of the Church as the 'body of Christ'), the precise relationship of which to each other has been in some dispute. Paul speaks little of 'seeing' God, and only cautiously of 'knowing' God; but he uses the word κοινωνία more frequently than any other New Testament writer, usually in the sense 'having a share', 'participation'. He definitely implies that the Christians participate in Christ, in the Holy Spirit, in the Body and Blood of Christ, and in the sufferings of Christ; these are the most notable of the relevant expressions. This intimate sharing in Christ is another way of describing the relationship expressed by 'in Christ'.

Paul was thus the first to find richer expressions to describe the more intimate communion with God which, as a result of the events from the death of Christ to the descent of the Holy Spirit, Christians had since Pentecost enjoyed. It was not, of course, richer than that of Christ Himself; but it was richer than that of the disciples in the lifetime of Christ and richer far than that of the Old Testament. Yet there was still a certain restraint. Something was reserved for the future bliss of heaven. Moreover, the Christian remained himself; it was an I-thou relationship which avoided, in this life and the next, that absorption in, or identification with, the deity to which pagan piety was prone. Like all Christian piety, Paul's piety was essentially corporate; and the phrases like 'body of Christ' with which he enriched the doctrine of the Church are closely linked with those which we have been considering. Moreoever, the two great sacraments are deeply intertwined with the same vocabulary and the same passages. Our sharing the experiences of Christ, our dying and rising with Him, are inaugurated through Baptism, and sustained by participating in the Lord's Supper.

Paul's great contribution has deeply influenced subsequent piety; yet it is not entirely normative. Many writers, even within the New Testament, have not risen to these heights; and many later writers who have read Paul have thought that his chief emphasis lay elsewhere. But it is right to see in these conceptions the centre of his thought and one of the high-water marks of all Christian theology.

The Gospel according to St John and the Epistles commonly ascribed to the same author raise many similar questions; and here again we do well to see a Jewish rather than a Greek background. This Gospel resembles the synoptic Gospels in containing some recorded prayers of Jesus, among them a variant, placed elsewhere, of the prayer in Gethsemane. These shorter Johannine prayers raise various difficulties and add little to our knowledge of Jesus; but we have also here the longest prayer ascribed to Him, a whole chapter of this Gospel. We can neither suppose it to be a verbatim transcript of what He said in the Upper Room, nor yet a free composition of the Evangelist; and if its style is at first sight very unlike that of the synoptic Gospels, a closer examination reveals many points of contact between it and the Lord's Prayer.

Similarly we find marked resemblances to the Pauline teaching.

The spatial metaphor 'in' is still in use, but in somewhat different constructions and contexts. Particularly, the phrase 'abide in' is common; but 'in Christ' is not used in conjunction with a multiplicity of verbs, as in Paul. There are more references than in Paul to Christ being in us, and the Father is brought into these formulae in an un-Pauline manner. The writer speaks frequently of 'knowing' God, though he avoids the word 'knowledge'; he speaks of 'seeing' God, but only in so far as He is revealed in Christ. The word κοινωνία is used in the Epistles: here it cannot be translated 'participation', but must be translated 'fellowship', fellowship with God the Father and with Jesus Christ and with one another. The Pauline language about dying and rising with Christ is, however, not found. This fellowship is a corporate experience, as the mention of 'one another' implies; it is enjoyed within the Church with its sacraments; and a famous Johannine metaphor about the Church, that of the Vine and the Branches, is itself another way of describing that indwelling in Christ which the author, like Paul, so greatly stresses. It is a mistake to suppose that this author was chiefly concerned with the Father, and Paul with Christ; both were concerned with our communion with God revealed in Christ.

The other New Testament writings add but little. The Epistle to the Hebrews, with its strong liturgical interests, speaks occasionally of participation in Christ, though it uses a different vocabulary. The first Epistle of Peter, with its predominantly ethical interest, has occasional traces of the Pauline vocabulary, notably 'in Christ', but shows very little interest in communion with God, though the use of the Pauline phrases raises the question whether they are not after all pre-Pauline material. The Epistle of James contributes only a strong interest in prayer. Whereas the Epistle of Jude contributes nothing important, the second Epistle of Peter, which is largely akin to it, contributes a number of striking phrases, including 'partakers of the divine nature', which points forward to later theories about deification. It does not seem, however, that the author intended to make any great theological advance, but was rather led by his literary style to use impressive phrases from other traditions. The Pastoral Epistles contain many echoes of the Pauline teaching in a rather different setting. The Apocalypse is too much concerned with visions of the future to throw much light on normal communion with God in this life. After the New Testament period κοινωνία and its cognates went out of use for a while.

Thus the New Testament never again reached the heights attained by Paul and the Johannine writer; and the same may be said of the Fathers.

The New Testament as a whole presents a picture of a rich intimate communion with God which is not the peculiar privilege of a few, but the normal life of the Christian. It was far richer than had been enjoyed in Old Testament times, but it stood in the same tradition, lacking the extravagances of absorption into the Deity. The increased intimacy was inaugurated by Jesus, with His sure grasp of the Fatherhood of God; it was made available for all men by His death and resurrection and the gift of the Holy Spirit; and was intellectually described first by Paul, who had to strain the resources of language to give expression to it. Man in his sin does not deserve to enter into this communion, but he can receive it as an undeserved gift by putting his whole trust in what Christ has done for him. He enjoys this communion in fellowship with his fellow-Christians, and particularly through prayer and the sacraments. His prayer should be a childlike outpouring of his wants to the Father in simple trust and acceptance of His will. He knows God revealed in Christ; he is in Christ, and Christ in him; he partakes of Christ and of the Holy Spirit; hereafter he will be with Christ and will see Christ in glory. The fruit of this communion is his love for others, which serves also as the test of its reality.

THE CHOICE OF METAPHORS

This intimate relationship, though sometimes described in language reminiscent of the piety of a small band of mystics, is the typical, normal Christian experience. There are other terms which refer to this relationship; those which describe God's attitude or act, as that He chooses, loves, blesses, justifies, sanctifies us; and those which describe our own attitude or act, as that we love, fear, trust, hope in God. There are analogies, as that God is Shepherd, King, Judge, Husband; and the greatest of these is Father. All these are consistent with the relationship described by κοινωνία, 'in Christ', 'dying and rising with Christ', and are likewise expressions of an I-thou relationship. Nowhere do we move into the language of absorption, identity, deification, or even union. Yet κοινωνία and such expressions go beyond what is usually implied by even the closest of the other analogies. Thus, for instance, we do not usually speak of participating in a father, of being in him, or dying and rising with him. The devotional language of the New Testament is the language of personal relationships raised to its highest possible level. These expressions are of course metaphors or analogies; apart from the so-called way of negation, there is no way of speaking of these high matters which is not analogical. What do we think of the choice of metaphors?

The use of 'in', as in the phrase 'in Christ' or in its Johannine uses, is the simplest and neatest possible device for this purpose. It is largely a spatial metaphor, but it had in Greek other meanings also, for instance, of the instrument or accompanying circumstance. Similarly in English, there are expressions, like 'in a hurry', where no spatial significance is apparent; and there are prepositions like 'by', which alternate between the local and the instrumental. In Greek and English 'in' is as good a choice as any; and the Johannine use of 'abide' in this connexion suggests a peaceful permanence.

Paul, having already used 'in', and also 'dying and rising with Christ', was hard pressed when he had to find an even more intimate phrase to describe the life of heaven. His 'to be with Christ' does not sound more intimate; we must sympathize with him in his linguistic difficulty, and infer the intimacy from the context. Yet the use of a phrase which *sounds* less intimate than 'in Christ' is providential, for it emphasizes most clearly the continuance of the I-thou relationship even in the life beyond. He who is with Christ has certainly not had his personality absorbed.

The distinction between 'hearing' and 'knowing' in this life and 'seeing' hereafter is somewhat similar. The New Testament writers had to do the best they could to keep one metaphor in reserve for the life to come; and the reticence of the Old Testament about 'seeing' in this life had prepared the way for the New Testament choice. For *this* life the 'knowledge' of God is a convenient phrase, but it lacks the intimacy of such phrases as 'in Christ'.

As the Old Testament had been reticent about 'seeing', so it had been reticent also about the use of the root corresponding to κοινωνία (חבר); but here the New Testament pursues a different course; it does not reserve this for the life of heaven, but uses it for the Christian experience in this life, as equivalent to 'in Christ'.

In general, the choice of κοινωνία is very suitable. It is derived from κοινός, 'common'. It is thus in one sense a vague and indeterminate word, deriving its significance from the genitive or whatever construction it is that follows it. If we merely say that κοινωνία Χριστοῦ means that we 'have Christ in common', then the 'have' is an intrusion. κοινωνία is a colourless word which derives warmth and intimacy from its contexts. Yet the word 'common', in Greek as in English, is not without its significance in the matter. From the meaning 'shared by many people', it acquires also the meaning 'unholy, profane'. And thus we may see in κοινωνία the idea that the Christian's relationship to God is not something exclusive or esoteric, but something intended for the common man; the old Jewish ideas of exclusive holiness are broken down in Christ. To the Christian there is nothing common or unclean; all things become holy for him in Christ.

The fact that κοινός is itself derived from σύν, 'with', suggests a further train of thought. Most of the uses of κοινωνία in the New Testament do not indeed suggest that we are partners with God, as the mention of חבר might suggest. What Paul means is that we are partners *with* each other, sharing together *in* Christ, or the Holy Spirit. Even where the word is used absolutely, the partnership is a 'horizontal' one, with our fellow-Christians, but an important vertical reference is implied to Christ, or the Holy Spirit, as the common possession. But the Johannine Epistles go beyond this and refer to fellowship with the Father and with Christ as well as with one another; we are all partners together, including God.

How is it to be translated? The words 'share' and 'participate', with their suggestion of 'shearing' a thing into parts, are inadequate, for there is no suggestion that we have only a part of Christ. 'Fellowship', originally 'laying down a fee' in partnership, is also not quite suitable, especially as it stresses those with whom we share rather than that in which we share. The fact that it is widely used in current religious writing is really a further disadvantage, as it has lost its original 'edge', and has a very indeterminate meaning.

'Communion' is perhaps a better word, though English usually prefers Saxon words for its fundamental notions. *Communio* in Latin contains *cum*, 'with', which is equivalent to the σύν which lies behind κοινωνία, whereas the other part of the word probably goes back to a root meaning 'bind' and hence 'unite', which is somewhat similar to the idea of חבר. *Communio*, like κοινωνία in Paul, is often used in such a way that joint participation *in* some possession is stressed rather than fellowship *with* each other. On the whole, then, 'communion' is the best translation, as κοινωνία is the best word. But no English word can be used in precisely the same constructions.

COMMUNION AND THE DOCTRINE OF THE TRINITY

Is 'communion' also a proper and adequate description of the relations between the Persons of the Trinity? The discussion of the piety of Christ Himself brought us near to this question. He who stood in a unique relation to the Father is also a particular instance of human piety, whom we presume to judge as showing this or that degree of nearness or aloofness in his relationship to God. Indeed we judge Him to have been of the 'prophetic' rather than the 'mystical' type; yet He who thus stood aloof from all notions of mystic absorption was, we believe, Himself in closer touch with God than any mystic. That His *conceptions*, as recorded in the synoptic Gospels, were less warm and intimate than those of Paul, we have already noted; the Cross and resurrection to some extent account for this. But a deeper problem remains, which would present itself even if He had expressed conceptions richer than those of Paul.

This problem arises from the fact that He prayed and thus is a 'type of piety' at all; but that was inseparable from His becoming Man. As Man, He shared our experiences to the full, except that He did not sin. But the life of even perfect man involves a certain separateness, even aloofness, from God. God is Creator, man is creature; they are not identical. We must probably say that Jesus as Man shared this separation and illustrated it in His prayer-life, while at the same time as God the Son He enjoyed the closest relationship with God the Father. This is, of course, a paradox, but that is not surprising when we are dealing with the Incarnation; and it does not restrict us to any particular account of the relationship of the two natures in Christ.

The Cry of Dereliction suggested a further thought to us. If Christ not only took our human nature but also bore the consequences of our fallen state, then He may have had also that further sense of alienation and estrangement from God which is the worst penalty of sin. It matters little whether we say that He bore this for us vicariously or that His becoming Man in a fallen world inevitably involved it. He may well have had it all the time as Man, even while both as God the Son and as Man He had communion with His Father. In the Cry of Dereliction one of these elements came to expression; at other moments the other. The prayer in Gethsemane had already illustrated the juxtaposition of two such elements. We could, of course, take a strongly kenotic view and deny that He was always in perfect communion with His Father; we might think that this communion was a gradual and partial achievement of Christ as Man. Or we might take a more Chalcedonian line. But the point is that communion and alienation are both there.

But all this must not suggest that as God He had communion with the Father, but as Man was separate and therefore prayed; for communion and prayer are not opposed. But we do not conceive of the pre-existent Christ as praying, though at the ascension Christ took our Manhood to heaven and thus still intercedes. Thus we may say that as God the Son He had a communion with the Father of a kind which did not need prayer; as Man, He was separate from the Father (even apart from His connexion with fallen man), and yet had communion with the Father by prayer.

This raises the major question: if God the Son can be said to be in communion with the Father, how far is the κοινωνία language generally applicable to the relations of the Persons of the Trinity? How far may we speak, moreover, of Christ as 'sharing' our human nature? The Bible does not use κοινωνία in any such senses; and to say that Christ shared our human nature, attractive as the phrase in many ways is, raises many questions which are avoided by simply saying that He became Man.

The 'in' language is different. It is disputed whether in 2 Corinthians 5_{19} Paul speaks of God being 'in Christ', for it is probably right to take 'in Christ' with the whole clause and regard 'was . . . reconciling' as a periphrastic imperfect. But certainly in Paul the phrases that we are in Christ and Christ in us are interchangeable; and in the Johannine literature the language of mutual indwelling is used both of the Father and the Son, and of the Son and the believers; sometimes it is used of both these relationships in the same sentence, in triadic formulae such that the unwary reader might almost suppose that the believers were the third element in the Trinity. But all this applies only to believers. Neither the Father nor Christ dwells 'in' unbelievers; the Incarnation evokes rather the phrase 'God *with* us', and Christ died '*for*' (ὑπέρ) mankind in general. As therefore we had better not describe the incarnation as Christ 'sharing' our human nature, so also we must avoid the idea of His being 'in' men in general. This harmonizes with a sound doctrine of His Work. He is our Representative rather than Inclusive Man or the Idea of Man in a Platonic sense; and, though His Incarnation may have had some effect on the human race as such, yet we may say (leaving aside the difficult case of young children) that only they are 'in Christ' who personally appropriate what He offers to all.

This does not, however, alter the fact that it is permissible to compare the relation of the Father to the Son with that of the Son to believers, though not to speak of the relation of the Father to believers in such a way as to neglect the Mediatorship of the Son. This is confirmed by the use of the word 'knowledge', even in the synoptic Gospels. The Father and the Son have a mutual knowledge; and, by the mediation of Christ, believers know the Father and He knows them.

Anyone who thinks this a dangerous line of thought may reflect that the phrases in which Christ's relationship to the Father is more usually expressed are similarly used also for the relationship of believers to God. The important metaphor of father and son is used to cover both cases; there is not usually any distinction in the Greek words employed. Of course, it is sometimes said that Jesus is the only-begotten Son, that we are sons by adoption, and so forth, which all points to a most important distinction; but the fact remains that the fundamental metaphor is the same for both relationships. This is partly because the choice of analogies is in the nature of the case limited, and partly because it is intended to give a very high status to the believer.

Thus the use, not indeed of κοινωνία, but of some of the associated phrases, is permissible in connexion with the Trinity, and may be held to imply that the relationships within the

Trinity are I-thou relationships. Are they something more, so as to be described as I-thou relationships merely *a fortiori*? Christ and the Father are one (Jn 10_{30}, 17_{11}); unity and indwelling are not incompatible within the Trinity. Christ also prays that the disciples may be one (Jn 17_{11}); it is the more significant that the Fourth Gospel says nothing about their being one with Christ or with the Father. Thus one at least of the expressions appropriate to relationships within the Godhead lacks Biblical warrant for its application to the relationship of believers to God.

In the last resort, of course, 'one' is a metaphor, or at least a term not altogether precise and clear when used in this connexion. The Church came to feel this lack of precision about the relation of the Father and the Son, and after a bitter struggle inserted in the Creed the term ὁμοούσιος, 'of one substance with'. This, as its derivation shows, is an 'ontological' term *par excellence*. This is an interesting parallel to those in our own day who, with a similar desire for greater precision, use stronger expressions than the Bible uses to describe the relationship of believers with God. We have from time to time pointed out the unbiblical nature of some of these terms such as 'mystical' and 'union'. Another favourite expression is the actual word 'ontological', which sounds impressive, but in fact is far from precise. But if an 'ontological' term was justified at Chalcedon, it does not follow that 'ontology' is justified in this other connexion; and the silence of the Fourth Gospel in its use of 'one' suggests that it is not. The Definition of Chalcedon says indeed that Christ is 'of one substance with us as regards His Manhood', where 'us' means men generally; but not, of course, that believers are of Christ's substance.

Nor indeed is it now clear that an ontological term is really helpful in Christology. In its day ὁμοούσιος excluded error, and was preferable to its suggested rivals. To-day we affirm it in the sense that we affirm the faith which it represented, and regard the rival views as heretical. To use metaphysical categories may have been the best way of conserving Biblical truth against hellenistic error; it is foolish to condemn the Creed for its 'Greek metaphysics', as many do. But, outside Romanist circles, many now hold 'substance' to be an outmoded category; thus William Temple in *Christus Veritas* tried hard to replace it by 'value', and the attempts of Schleiermacher, Ritschl and others to replace it are well known. Generally speaking, the attempts to replace it by axiological or psychological terms have been unsuccessful, giving the impression that they surrender something of the uniqueness of Christ's relationship to God. The quest for other categories may yet succeed; but even if ontological terms unexpectedly retain the Christological field, it by no means follows that the relation of the believer to Christ need be described in anything more than the I-thou terms of the Bible.

Indeed, what relationship can be closer than an I-thou relationship? Absorption, identity, union *sound* closer; but we avoid them, not because they are more intimate than the actual relationship which they should describe, but because they threaten its destruction. It has often been said that to describe God as supra-personal often results in a sub-personal conception; we do better to speak of personality, the highest category that we know. Similarly, we should speak of I-thou relationships, for they are the highest that we know, and indeed are simply personal relationships. The Bible presses the language of relationship far beyond its usual limits in order to describe the intimacy of the relationship between the believer and Christ; indeed many of the expressions go further than some of those used to describe the relations of the Persons of the Godhead, though in the latter sphere some few expressions like 'one' go further. We may rightly stretch language as far as it will go to describe the mysterious relationships within the Trinity; but even there we must not go so far as to 'confound the Persons' or make their relationship to each other seem less vivid and real than those personal I-thou relationships which are the most vivid of all realities to us.

COMMUNION AND THE SACRAMENTS

A somewhat similar problem arises about the sacraments. We have already treated this by a comparison of 1 Corinthians 1_9 with 10_{16} and a discussion of Romans 6_4. The New Testament does not contemplate the Christian life being lived without sacraments; but this does not mean that the sacraments and faith are to be co-ordinated. The sacraments are embodiments of the Gospel; faith is our way of receiving their benefits. But too sharp a distinction must not be drawn between these benefits and those of the other means of grace. If by Baptism a man has 'put on Christ', is 'in Christ', has become a member of the 'body of Christ', then his whole Christian life, whether at the Lord's Supper or elsewhere, is already in that close relationship to Christ which it strains the powers of language to describe. At the Lord's Supper he who is already a member of the Body of Christ receives the Body of Christ; the rich profusion of these expressions should warn us against too literal an interpretation of any one of them. The sacraments are, of course, central among the means of grace because of their divine institution; and Christ's own use of the words 'This is my body' invests this language with a peculiar significance. Certainly the bold expressions about receiving the Body are to be taken, though not with a crude literalness, yet with the utmost seriousness; but the Christ Who is received in any means of grace is the same Christ, the glorified heavenly Christ who still bears in His Body the glorious scars. He may be apprehended in various ways and degrees, as we may 'see', 'hear', 'touch' a fellow-man; but where Christ is, there He is altogether.

Just as in Christology a demand for definiteness led to the adoption of the word ὁμοούσιος, so here demands for more metaphysical terms have led to such theories as transubstantiation, where the word 'substance' is reminiscent of the translation of ὁμοούσιος. This has called forth indignant assertions that the Bread is *not* the Body of Christ. It might be argued that as most Protestants accept the use of this category of 'substance' to safeguard the truth of Christ's Divinity, so they ought to accept it to safeguard the truth that Christ is really present at His Supper. The Protestants might reply (with Gore),[1] that if we are to use these categories, transubstantiation corresponds to Monophysitism rather than to Chalcedonian orthodoxy. But many Protestants would demand what is sometimes called a more 'dynamic' doctrine, and would prefer not to use these categories at all. But this raises larger questions.

COMMUNION AND METAPHYSICS

The point has now emerged that this attempt to import ontological terms is an aspect of what is popularly known as the 'Catholic-Protestant' controversy. The use of one in the Creed has excited some suspicion among Protestants, and their use in connexion with the sacraments is often supposed to be quite

[1] Gore, pp. 281-2.

uncongenial to Protestants. Dix's view that the real eucharistic action for Cranmer lies in 'something purely mental and psychological', whether or not it is true of Cranmer (a much disputed point), is typical of a widespread view that Protestants are concerned only with the psychological effects of the sacraments, with the epistemological aspects of salvation, with imitating, following, being influenced by, Christ rather than with being incorporated into or united with Him, that they prefer moral to metaphysical change.[2]

This is very unfair to traditional Protestantism. To take but one instance, Torrance has no difficulty in supporting by quotations from Calvin the assertion that 'the substance of justification is a *real and substantial union with Christ.* Justification has ontological content.'[3] It may, however, be maintained that the charge is true of what is termed 'Liberal Protestantism'. Now it is true that the original Protestant tradition, like the 'Catholic' tradition, has been modified in the course of its history. In particular, Protestantism has been modified by Protestant scholasticism, by Pietism, and by 'Liberalism', which was itself a product of the *Aufklärung* rather than the Renaissance. Most of these were a mixture of good and evil. There was also Methodism, which stands in complex relations to these various strands. Thus the authors of *Catholicity* over-simplify when they simply divide into 'Orthodox Protestantism' and 'Liberal Protestantism'.

What then is the modern Protestant view? It is to some extent true that at various periods the forensic view of justification, the individualistic, subjective emphases from the *Aufklärung*, the psychological interest in 'feeling', and even the categories of election and regeneration, have distracted attention from such words as 'incorporation'. There is to-day a strong suspicion of any alleged change which cannot be verified in conduct. 'By their fruits ye shall know them.' Protestants are apt to ask what is the use of being 'ontologically united' with Christ through the sacraments apart from any visible results. They are tempted to join some modern analysts of language in asking what meaning, let alone truth, there can be in assertions of this kind. Some of the

[2] Dix, *The Shape of the Liturgy*, p. 671; cf. his *The Question of Anglican Orders*, pp. 20-36; *Catholicity*, esp. p. 21; (ed.) Kirk, *The Apostolic Ministry*. There is a reply in (ed.) Flew and Davies, *The Catholicity of Protestantism*. A partial agreement was reached in *Church Relations in England*. cf. *The Fulness of Christ*.

[3] T. F. Torrance in *SJT*, V.95 (his italics).

traditional Protestant language about 'imputation', 'legal fiction', and the like, easily led to the same kind of difficulty; but they wish to revise that also. Of course 'Catholics' do not deny that 'union' with Christ' normally bears ethical fruit, just as Protestants would be eager to assert that regeneration is more than ethical. But the difference remains.

Both sides admit that this must be settled by the Bible, though 'Catholics' add a reference to Tradition. In the recent revival of Biblical Theology, 'Catholics' have made good use of Paul, despite his being the most obviously 'Protestant' of the New Testament writers. Paul provides the phrase 'body of Christ', and so justifies 'incorporation'. Some Protestants used to maintain that many Pauline ideas, especially about the sacraments, were but Paul's transformation of original eschatological Christianity into a mystery-religion; and a good deal of 'Catholic' apologetics has been devoted to attacking this; it is now abandoned. The modern Biblical Protestant must take the phrase 'body of Christ' seriously. Some indeed point out that it does not occur in the synoptic Gospels, and regard incorporation as dangerously near to absorption; they disapprove a metaphor so impersonal or even possessive as that of being a limb in a body, and prefer the other conceptions of the Church which the revival of Biblical theology has also emphasized, the new Israel and the People of God.

For the most part, however, the modern Protestant is quite prepared to take the phrase 'body of Christ' seriously, and with it κοινωνία and the other similar phrases. It has been said of some such phrases, 'Put right out of your head the idea that these are only fancy ways of saying that Christians are to read what Christ said and try to carry it out . . . They mean something much more than that'.[4] Every well-instructed Protestant of this or any earlier age will say Amen to that; to deny it would involve a Pelagian view of sin and grace and a less than Abelardian view of the Work of Christ. Yet it is the fear that your opponent will deny it which impels men to try to safeguard scriptural truth by the use of unscriptural phrases. The modern Protestant has indeed much to learn by taking these scriptural categories seriously; his tradition has never entirely lost sight of them, but we have admitted that other categories have sometimes distracted attention from them;

[4] Lewis, *Beyond Personality*, p. 38; cf. J. Baillie, pp. 238-9.

the danger now, however, is that in his new enthusiasm for Biblical Theology he will accept not only these Biblical categories but also those unbiblical phrases which are often mixed with them. We may also venture to hope that, when 'Catholics' realize that Protestants are quite prepared to take the Biblical phrases seriously, they will be content to abandon the others.

Besides the use of unscriptural phrases, there is a danger of combining the scriptural phrases in new ways. Thus it is common, traditional, and indeed harmless to say that Baptism engrafts us into the Body of Christ. But it is not always remembered that this mixture of metaphors is but an inference; the Bible does not connect grafting with Baptism, and it would be an equally sound inference to say that faith engrafts us into the new Israel.

But commoner and more dangerous is the use of unscriptural phrases; we read, for instance, 'To the former [the Calvinist] . . . the determining doctrine is Election by God in His transcendent sovereignty; to the latter [the Catholic], sacramental union with Christ Incarnate in His Mystical Body. The difference is profound.'[5] But in the former phrase, if we allow 'sovereignty' as an abstract noun from 'king', only 'transcendent' is an unbiblical word; in the latter phrase 'sacramental', 'union', and 'mystical' are all unbiblical words. These words, together with 'ontological', 'metaphysical', and 'objective', as often used in these contexts, are an attempt to pin things down, a search for security rather than certitude. 'Mystical' is slightly different; it is used with other words of this type to soften the impact. Any objection to 'union', for instance, will be met by the assertion that it is a 'mystical union', and therefore presumably not to be judged by ordinary standards. It tries to conceal the plain truth that we are dealing with a metaphor, and to evade the question whether the metaphor is well-chosen.

The 'Catholic' may contend, as with ὁμοούσιος, that the Biblical language justifies the metaphysical words. The fact (he may say) that Paul strained language as far as he did shows that he would have welcomed any word which would have made his point more emphatic; he did not possess such words as 'ontological'; but, within the available vocabulary, what more could he have said than he did? The answer lies in his deliberate avoidance of certain words which he must have known, notably

[5] *Catholicity*, p. 27.

'union'; that is why we have constantly stressed their absence. He and the Johannine writer, who go furthest in this matter (apart from 2 Peter), are yet essentially Hebraic; the words we are condemning are essentially Greek. Hebraic truth may sometimes be best preserved in Greek categories; but the need for such a drastic step here is not proven.

The word 'incorporation' is in a different class, being based on the Biblical phrase 'body of Christ'; 'body' is used in the Bible in a way quite different from the Greek use. Its use for both the Eucharist and the Church may be justified by taking it to mean 'the vehicle and medium whereby I effect my purposes';[6] but it refers primarily to a physical organism, and the other uses are derivative, that is, they proceed by analogy. No one should say 'mere analogy'; they are none the worse for that. But attempts are made to take this analogy literally, or, as is said, neither literally nor figuratively but mystically;[7] and these are liable to mislead. Indeed there are sound exegetical reasons against taking too literally the idea that what happened to Christ's Body by way of death, resurrection and so on, now happens to us.[8]

When 'Catholics' take 'ontological' as their slogan, they usually ascribe to the Protestant position either the word 'eschatological' or the word 'psychological'. Neither is fair. 'Catholics' are supposed to stand for the 'ontological' presence of Christ in Church and sacraments; Protestants, for the eschatological expectation of His return in judgement; or 'Catholics' for 'eschatology as fulfilment'; Protestants, for 'eschatology as promise'.[9] There is some truth in this, but it can equally well be maintained that 'Catholics', with their conception of the Pope as the Vicar of Christ or of the bishop as the *shaliach* or representative of a presumably absent Principal, lack the sense of Christ's presence in the Church, whereas Protestants, with their stress on the Holy Spirit in the individual, notably in the doctrine of assurance, have a clear sense of God's presence. Protestants, who have taken the lead in the proclamation of 'realized eschatology', cannot be said to lack 'eschatology as fulfilment'.

The Bible holds together the ideas of Christ indwelling us and coming to judge us hereafter. κοινωνία and the associated phrases

[6] Temple, *Christus Veritas*, p. 251. [7] Nelson, pp. 67-104. [8] cf. *supra*, p. 153.

[9] cf. Nicholls, pp. 141-59, esp. 148-50, which, despite our criticism, is most illuminating and sympathetic. cf. *supra*, p. 23.

are important, but they are not everything. The Church both rejoices in His presence and awaits His return. Nicholls well observes that a solution might be found 'in the Holy Spirit as *arrhabon*, the deposit already paid on the purchased possession'.[10] The tension runs through the New Testament, though, as we have seen, some books have more of one emphasis and some of the other. They are not finally incompatible; and Christian liturgy must seek to combine them. Christ's presence and what we must call His absence must be held together as we hold both the unity of the Persons in the Godhead and their distinctness.

Just as 'Catholics' must not fasten to Protestants the word 'eschatological', so also they must not fasten to them the word 'psychological', nor for that matter, 'epistemological', 'subjective', nor (as a complete description of their interests) 'moral'. Avoiding the ambiguous and over-worked word 'existential', we may commend the word 'relational',[11] or, more simply, 'personal'. Personal relationships are the highest that we know; they are far higher than those quasi-physical relationships which such words as 'metaphysical' almost inevitably suggest to the mind. We have seen how the New Testament describes our communion with God in many rich and diverse terms which go altogether beyond the language of ordinary human influence; but these terms do not go beyond the idea of a deep relationship between persons. We Protestants may admit that we have sometimes been distracted from a proper consideration of these personal terms; may we not now appeal to all theologians to express their theology more largely in terms of personal relationships?

This does not mean the rejection of metaphysics or rational thought.[12] Descartes and his successors erred in not paying sufficient regard to human relationships; but zeal for Hebraic, Biblical, and personal categories is not the same as Kant's rejection of Pure Reason, Ritschl's theological positivism, or the rejection of metaphysics by modern linguistic philosophers. Whatever may be said of men, certainly God's Being is not exhausted or wholly constituted by His relations to us. But we cannot study the nature of God, save in so far as, whether in general or in special revelation, He discloses Himself to us; nor can we understand ourselves apart from our relationship to our

[10] Nicholls, p. 158. [11] cf. A. Raymond George in *SJT*, IV.164.
[12] *Catholicity*, pp. 23-4, errs in saying that Protestants dislike rational thought.

Creator. (Not that we should wish to embrace monistic idealism as a philosophy that stresses relationships, making them internal to the terms related; for that diminishes the difference between Creator and created.) Of course we are affected by the relationships in which we stand, whether in the sacraments or in the other means of grace; but there is no need to describe one effect as 'ontological' and another as 'psychological'. 'Spiritual things are spiritually discerned'; and we had best describe these things Biblically; the rejection of the non-Biblical terms is justified only if we take the Biblical terms seriously. This is not to reject philosophy in the broadest sense of that word; but personal relationships must be allowed to provide the data which govern speculation; here is 'faith seeking understanding' (*fides quaerens intellectum*).

COMMUNION AND THE WORK OF CHRIST

How is communion with God related to soteriology? In the first chapter we defended the discussion of the former without the latter. Conversion, important as it is, is the gateway to a whole life; and that life, though always coloured by the initial experience, is greater than it. There are most valuable discussions of the relations between 'fellowship' and the Atonement in two of Taylor's books; and we can best repay our debt to him by relating our conclusions to his.

Taylor draws a distinction between 'faith' and 'faith-union'. We cannot, he agrees, simply connect the former with justification and the latter with the later developments of the spiritual life; for faith, except when it is simple belief, always implies some kind of fellowship. He continues:

> 'None the less, the distinction we are making is useful, if only to emphasize the maturity of some of the experiences in question and, what is more important, to guard against the mistake of supposing that a highly developed, if not mystical, type of faith is needed for the appropriation of the gifts offered to men in the work of God in Christ.
>
> Like the faith by which a man is justified, faith-union with Christ, often expressed in the phrase "in Christ", is union with the Crucified and not only with Christ as the Revealer of God.'[13]

Taylor is never led by such terms as 'mystical', 'union', and 'faith-union' to the brink of absorption; nevertheless we may question his argument. That the appropriation of Christ's gifts does not

[13] Taylor, *ANTT*, p. 139; and see 100, 138-40.

require a 'mystical' type of faith is true, but we question the distinction between 'faith' and 'faith-union'. No doubt communion may be less or more rich and mature, but it is always, even in its basic form, the experience of being 'in Christ'. The 'dying and rising with Christ' which would be thought to be the highest development of 'faith-union' or 'Christ-mysticism' is connected with the initial aspect of salvation, as is shown in Romans 6 by the aorists and the reference to Baptism. The new convert, the 'babe in Christ', is entitled to all the κοινωνία language; 'faith' is not simply an initial stage to be replaced by 'faith-union'; it is the attitude of the Christian, correlative to communion with Christ. He who has faith has thereby communion. Not only faith, but communion with Christ, being in Christ, dying and rising with Christ, is the normal Christian experience.

In accordance with his view of 'faith-union', Taylor, in the careful examination of 'fellowship' which he makes in another book,[14] gives to 'fellowship' a late place, logically if not chronologically, in the scheme of salvation. He well says that this communion depends upon 'the historical foundations of Christianity, the life, death and resurrection of Christ'. To forget this 'can only lead to a misty conception of fellowship which means very little indeed or degenerates into an unhealthy type of mystical piety'. 'All thought of communion with God which ignores the Cross of Christ is theological lightmindedness.'[15] Fellowship is certainly subsequent to the Cross, but not as late in the logical scheme as Taylor maintains. Indeed, in his account of the stages which are supposed logically to precede it, he finds himself, against his will, so to speak, having to use the term 'fellowship' itself, or else 'relationship'. Thus justification is a 'relationship'; so is faith.[16] What can these relationships be but fellowship? It is not indeed easy to see whether justification is the conferment of the type of mind involved in having faith or is something appropriated by faith.[17] If צדק, the root that lies behind 'justification', meant 'to be in right relationships' as well as 'to be righteous', then it would be easy to resolve this difficulty;[18] and the connexion between justification and fellowship would be closer.

[14] Taylor, *FR*, pp. 109-43, 213-17. [15] Taylor, *FR*, pp. 140, 143.

[16] Taylor, *FR*, pp. 68-9, 58; cf. 65.

[17] Compare Taylor, *FR*, p. 66 (cf. 68-9), where God gives the righteous mind, with pp. 58-9, where God gives a new status to him who has the righteous mind.

[18] And indirectly meet the objection of Snaith, pp. 168-70.

In the actual chapter on Fellowship, Taylor uses the word, though guardedly, as a description of the apparently 'antecedent' stages. Thus he says of forgiveness or deliverance,

'Like faith, it is an anticipatory experience of communion with God; for, in forgiveness, the soul receives a warm and living sense of the nearness of God . . . Communion, however, in the full meaning of the word, is known only when the full burden of sin falls from our back and is seen no more.'[19]

Similar phrases, such as 'foretastes . . . of fellowship' and 'introduction to fellowship' are used about remission of sins, the new status (i.e. justification) and reconciliation.[20] We should ourselves say that salvation is the entry on communion with God. The communion of the mature saint is indeed richer and deeper, but is in its nature the same kind of communion with God which the sinner enjoys at the moment of his conversion.

God's offer is one and indivisible; He offers communion with Himself. In forensic categories, this is the establishment of a new status; in relation to guilt, forgiveness; in relation to estrangement, reconciliation; in relation to man's sinful nature, regeneration; but it is one and the same gift; communion with God is everything.

An account of the Work of Christ along these lines would differ only very slightly from that of Taylor. God in His love sent His Son, Jesus Christ, who by His life and death made to the Father a perfect offering of obedience and possibly also of vicarious penitence and submission to the penal consequences of human sin. God can now thus offer to the sinner a new relationship to Himself, namely that he may be in Christ and thus acceptable to God. When the sinner trustingly accepts this (which is faith), God sees him not as a sinner, but in Christ. This is no legal fiction for he is in fact in Christ, and all that Christ did counts on his behalf. There is an element of vicariousness, if not indeed even of imputation, about this, in so far as the sinner, in the first moment of salvation, though his character may undergo a remarkable transformation, often does not possess to a very marked degree the character of Christ; he is in Christ, but he is not Christlike. Yet in this *relationship* (which is the same as communion) lie both justification and regeneration, for God can require no other *status* than that a man should be in Christ, and nothing can

[19] Taylor, *FR*, p. 140. [20] Taylor, *FR*, p. 141.

refashion a man's *nature* so much as being in Christ. Thereafter, so long as he remains in Christ, he will grow towards fuller sanctification, that is, will acquire a level certain Christlikeness of character. This growth is a gift of God, but it is really imparted, so that the new character actually becomes His own. As in the solidarity of the race sin is inevitable and yet we are responsible for sin, since it is our will that is sinful, so in the solidarity of redemption (solidarity both with Christ and His Church), the sinner becomes a saint, and receives God's 'Well done', even though His new Christlike character is altogether God's gift.

It will be seen that by the use of the category of relationship and the phrase 'in Christ', many difficulties about the relation of change of status to change of nature, about the forensic and the ethical, and so forth, are transcended. The essence of this was well put by William Bright:

> Look, Father, look on His anointed face,
> And only look on us as found in Him.[21]

THE NATURE AND MEDIATION OF COMMUNION WITH GOD

The questions put at the end of our first chapter have now largely been answered. New Testament piety conforms everywhere to our type two. In the synoptic Gospels it belongs to that part of type two which is nearer to three; in the Pauline and Johannine writings, to that part which is nearer to type one. Nowhere else does the New Testament go so far towards type one; the other writings either resemble the synoptic writings or occupy a middle position. Various factors, notably the difference made by the death and resurrection of Christ, show the Pauline and Johannine development to be legitimate, but no further development towards absorption should be permitted.

If both these types, the synoptic and the Pauline, are legitimate, they perhaps correspond to different types of temperament. The contrast should not be equated with the Protestant-Catholic division. The Pauline type is perhaps to be preferred as coming after the Cross and resurrection. Both intimacy and separation must be preserved in Christian piety, and Paul perhaps provides within himself an adequate synthesis. We may thus approve

[21] *Methodist Hymnbook*, No. 759.

Heiler's desire for a synthesis of 'mystical' and 'prophetic' piety, though the word 'mystical' associates the Pauline and Johannine piety with modes of thought outside the Jewish-Christian tradition instead of seeing it as a natural development of that tradition. The New Testament doctrine of communion is not the confluence of two streams, one Jewish and one pagan. But if both types of piety are from the same tradition, the suggestion that we shall hold them together is all the more reasonable.

There remains the question of mediation. We have left out the question of mediation through Christ, though the obvious stress on this in the New Testament disposes of the idea that we should aim at an immediate knowledge of God, and condemns some later mystics. The modern question 'How can we find God?' is strange to the New Testament; it can only answer 'In Christ'. The idea that we can 'find' God in Christ, in the Bible, in history, in nature, in prayer, in the sacraments, in social service and so on (all viewed as co-ordinate) is entirely foreign to the New Testament; nor is the word 'find' common in this connexion. These half-truths would all be put in other ways.

Two matters call for special comment. First, we find a considerable stress on the traditional ecclesiastical means of grace, Baptism, the Lord's Supper, worship, and prayer. We do not find so much about preaching within the Church, but the proclamation of the Gospel to the unconverted was to them the supreme means of grace on which all else depended. We speak rightly of preaching the Word of God, for a word is a most important form of I-thou relationship. The New Testament does not indeed know the phrase 'means of grace'; and in 1 Corinthians 10_{16} the translation 'means of participation' (in relation to the Eucharist), though sometimes found, is unnecessary; the διά applied to Baptism, however, in Romans 6_4, might almost be rendered 'by means of'. But there is no doubt that all these involve participation in Christ. We may therefore call them 'means of grace', but 'means' has a different sense in the use 'means to an end'. Some indeed regard worship in just this way, as the means to a moral life. But if worship involves communion with God, then there can be no higher end to which it is the means. In order to avoid this risk of confusion, worship is better regarded as the *expression* of that communion which is the supreme end of life, a medium of communion whereby God speaks to us and we to Him.

The second matter is that though the New Testament is full of the love and service of our neighbour, it is practically only in the synoptic Gospels that we find glimpses of the idea that the service of the needy is the service of Christ Himself (cf. Ja 1_{27}). Love of our neighbour is commended in many other forms, as the fruit of the Spirit, the fulfilling of the Law, the criterion of our love for God, but it is not described as a way of knowing, meeting or participating in God. We do not read that 'to work is to pray' or that 'The service of one's neighbour is also divine service (*Gottesdienst*)'. The New Testament hardly ever echoes Jeremiah 22_{16}, 'He judged the cause of the poor and needy: then it was well. Was not this to know me? saith the Lord'. Even the κοινων-words, which are used for both 'vertical' and 'horizontal' relations, never yield an explicit statement that to have fellowship with others is to have fellowship with God. The former is rather viewed as a result of the latter; this is right in so far as it makes good works logically subsequent to our justification, but misleading if it suggests that worship is a means to service as an end. But if service is neither preliminary to worship nor the end of worship nor an accidental by-product of worship, it can be nothing else but a form of worship, (in the broadest sense of 'worship') an expression of our communion with God. In serving our neighbour out of genuine compassion for him, we do in fact have communion with God. But, apart from the Similitude of the Sheep and the Goats, the New Testament hardly says this.

This silence is perhaps not accidental. The New Testament does not tie communion with God too closely to acts of charity nor even, save in one or two passages, to the ecclesiastical means of grace, because it is the experience of a whole life. Just as it is not the experience of an esoteric few 'mystics', but the normal, typical Christian experience, so it is not the brief experience of a passing hour, a transitory ecstasy that follows a long preparation; the Christian life is in every part life 'in Christ'. We are not said to find Christ here or there or to be 'in Christ' when we do this or that, because no part of life, apart from sin, is for the Christian not 'in Christ'. It is the *whole* Christian life, lived in faith, nurtured by worship, prayer, and the sacraments, and flowing out into good works, which is the life in Christ, communion with God.

THE HEART OF THE CHRISTIAN FAITH

This relation of communion with God is linked with every part of Christianity and may fairly be called the heart of the Christian faith. Much that is often put in other terms might profitably be put in terms of communion.

Thus the inmost nature of the Godhead is the mutual indwelling and knowledge of the Persons of the Trinity. God's supreme attribute, His holy love, is a desire to communicate Himself to, and bestow fellowship with Himself upon, His creatures. Man was created in God's image, that is, with a view to having fellowship with God; and he was so constituted that, had he not sinned, he was capable of that fellowship. Sin, the transgression of God's holy law, is essentially the refusal of man to have that fellowship, the breach of fellowship from man's side. This disturbs his fellowship with other men; and so man is left lonely, estranged from God and his fellows. Christ became Man, being at once both God the Son and Man, and living a life of unbroken communion with the Father. Yet without sinning He so shared the lot of sinful man that that unbroken communion with the Father was paradoxically combined with a sense of broken communion or dereliction. The Cross, where He acts supremely as our Representative, is the climax of this paradox. After His resurrection and ascension, Christ, still Man in the heavenly places, retains His fellowship with men as our High-priest and Mediator.[22] That we might not be bereft, devoid of fellowship, He sent His Representative, the Holy Spirit. By His help, a man may trustingly accept God's offer of fellowship through Christ; and thereafter, being in Christ, who is accepted with God, he is rightly related to God, and through this relationship grows daily more like Christ.

The Christian life, which he then lives, is essentially a life of communion with God. The beliefs which are its intellectual prelude, accompaniment, and consequence (above all consequence, for 'faith precedes understanding') are themselves secondary to this communion. This 'vertical' communion with God has as its consequence a 'horizontal' relationship of communion with his fellow-Christians in the Church; and the Church proclaims to all the possibility of this communion with God. The ethical fruit, the life of good works done to all, within and without

[22] Taylor, *FR*, pp. 213-17.

the Church, is in one aspect the consequence of this communion with God, but in another aspect it is a form or expression of it. The goals which the Christian sets before him, whether the attainment of perfect love in this world or of the Beatific Vision in the next, are themselves richer forms of it; heaven indeed is so much richer that it may be described in other terms; it is being *with* Christ; it involves *seeing* God; but it is still communion with God; unto which perfect communion may He bring us all.

INDEX OF GREEK WORDS

(*This index is not exhaustive*)

INDEX OF SCRIPTURE PASSAGES

INDEX OF PROPER NAMES

www.ingramcontent.com/pod-product-compliance
Lightning Source LLC
LaVergne TN
LVHW020538100826
845148LV00010B/1519

* 9 7 8 1 6 0 6 0 8 7 3 3 6 *